The Dragon Entertains

ONE HUNDRED WELSH STARS

Also by Alan Roderick

The Folklore of Gwent

The Folklore of Glamorgan

Unknown Gwent

The Ghosts of Gwent

The Music of Fair Tongues

A Gwent Anthology

Johnny! The Story of the Happy Warrior

Travels In Gwent

The Newport Kaleidoscope

Newport Rugby Greats

Haunted Gwent

The Gwent Christmas Book

The Pubs of Newport

The Dragon Entertains

ONE HUNDRED WELSH STARS

Alan Roderick

Wales Books (Glyndŵr Publishing)

2000

ISBN 1-903529-02-6

Printed in Wales by
J & P Davison, 3 James Place, Treforest, Pontypridd
Published by Wales Books (Glyndŵr Publishing), Porth Glyndŵr,
Higher End, Saint Tathan, Vale of Glamorgan CF 6 4LW
www.walesbooks.com

INTRODUCTION

Wales is a small nation (not for nothing is it known as *Cymru Fach* or Little Wales) of some three million people which stubbornly continues to assert its own identity. It has a unique Dragon flag and a distinctive national anthem, but, so far at least, there is no Welsh citizenship, there are no Welsh passports, the seat at the United Nations is still waiting to be filled. As a country, Wales has some of the trappings of a nation state: its own language, its own football and rugby teams, and now, a National Assembly to govern its own affairs. Yet, most of the world's population has scarcely heard of Wales and even those that have often consider it to be a mere appendage of England. But if Wales as a country is little known, many of its singers, actors and musicians are household names of international fame and renown. One need only think of Richard Burton, Anthony Hopkins, Tom Jones, Bryn Terfel et al to illustrate the point.

As far as its music and theatre stars are concerned, therefore, Wales is now in a very healthy state - 'Cool Cymru Rules' but it was not always so. Opera houses and concert halls have long been conspicuous by their absence, despite Wales's unofficial title of *Gwlad y Gan*, or Land of Song. As for the theatre, historically speaking, it has never enjoyed the same status in Wales that it has in other countries and, despite numerous valiant attempts, there is still no National Welsh Theatre. Fragments of medieval Welsh language plays survive and there were Welsh actors performing in Shrewsbury and Leicester in the sixteenth century. A hundred years later actors performed in Swansea and Anglesey and the flame of Welsh theatrical life continued to flicker fitfully down the years. In the 1700s the theatrical form known as the *anterliwt* or interlude flourished. Plays were performed throughout the eighteenth century in such towns as Monmouth, Brecon, Wrexham and Aberystwyth and along the North Wales coast.

By July, 1807 a theatre had been built in Swansea and, until about the 1880s, the town would prove to be Wales's most dynamic centre of theatre. The prevailing weight of religious opinion, however, was predominantly anti-theatre. Many critics of the theatre in Wales held the profession of actress in low regard and considered the theatres to be nothing but dens of prostitutes. By the 1840s, the triumph of Methodism was so complete that theatre in Wales was almost non-existent. There was no such thing as a Welsh professional theatre: only amateur and private theatres survived. Things gradually improved, however and on October 7th, 1878 the new Theatre Royal opened its doors in St. Mary Street, Cardiff. As for Cardiff's New Theatre, it first began staging plays in December, 1906.

It was this sort of background which enabled Richard Burton to claim that, had they been born a hundred years ago, he, Stanley Baker and Hugh Griffith would all have been ministers or preachers, not actors. He went on to say that before the year 1925 or so, there were scarcely any Welsh actors worth the name. He thought that the breakthrough - when it eventually came - came in the shape of Emlyn Williams.

Nowadays, of course, things are different. The colleges are churning out Welsh actors - both English and Welsh speaking - in their hundreds. Some of them will choose to stay in Wales, particularly those who are Welsh speaking, but, as always, England, the giant neighbour to the east, holds a powerful sway. The most ambitious will, inevitably, take the road to London and its host of theatres and film and television studios. Some, if they are lucky, will make it all the way to Hollywood. Whether we like it or not, Wales as a country is just not big enough to hold all these actors, its theatrical infrastructure too weak to afford them continuing, gainful employment.

The creation of the Welsh-language television channel, S4C, has helped immeasurably, at least as far as Welsh speaking actors are concerned, but the fact remains: Wales as a country is too small to retain actors of the calibre of a Ray Milland or a Jonathan Pryce. The same is true of world class singers like Gwyneth Jones and Shirley Bassey, they have outgrown the country they grew up in and require a bigger stage on which to perform. Money too plays its part. Often artists leave not only Wales, but Great Britain behind because of the tax situation and the amount of money they are forced to pay the Exchequer.

That said, the mere fact that Wales has produced such international stars is, and continues to be, remarkable. Without these men and women there would be no *Dragon Entertains*. When the book was first conceived it was meant to be a kind of A to Z of Welsh entertainers. The aim was to create mini-biographies, word pictures, if you like, which would give all the relevant, basic, salient facts of an artist's career. But the concept became increasingly unwieldy and, somewhere along the line the A to Z idea changed into *The Dragon Entertains - One Hundred Welsh Stars*. What has not changed, though, is my utter astonishment as to just how many of those Welsh entertainers there actually are. For such a small country, Wales punches way above its weight on a world scale when it comes to entertainment (and, by entertainment, I mean entertainment in its broadest sense, not just actors and actresses but playwrights and directors, singers and musicians, composers and comedians.) One only has to look at the number of Oscar winners that Wales has provided - four in all. What other nation of comparable size can boast the same. Then there are the star names known throughout the world – the likes of Dylan Thomas, Catherine Zeta Jones, Siân Phillips and Charlotte Church.

Anyone reading through the pages of this book cannot fail to be struck by the prominent part played by the United States of America. Joseph Parry spent many years living there; Allan Jones was born there; Bob Hope, and Glenn Ford earned their living there; Dylan Thomas, Ryan Davies, Gareth Hughes, Rachel Roberts and Ray Milland died there. In our own time, Anthony Hopkins, the freshly-minted American citizen, and Catherine Zeta Jones have based their careers there. The link between Wales - the one country so small - and America - the other so huge - was, and continues to be, a strong one.

One thing *The Dragon Entertains* is not - it is not another one of those Top One Hundred lists. (Hence the alphabetical order.) It is a celebration of Welsh talent in all its vibrant variety. In a sense the book is one hundred different biographies designed to catch the essence of each person's life in the proverbial 'nutshell'. As such, it is, of course, a personal choice and one that others might, undoubtedly will, disagree with. It was an invidious task, and one that caused much heart searching, to narrow down the names to the magic figure of one hundred, there being so many to choose from and so many worthy of inclusion.

It is, however, interesting to look at the one hundred names involved and see how they break down. All figures are, of course, approximate, and only give a rough guide, the presence of six groups or bands making it more difficult to give precise figures. For example. there were seventy-eight men and twenty-two women, but this is counting Cerys Matthews of the group Catatonia as one woman and, ignoring the fact that the other members of the group are men. Eighty-four were born in Wales itself and sixteen outside. Surprisingly, of those actually born in Wales itself, the overwhelming majority - seventy- three - first saw the light of day in the South of the country, whilst only eleven can claim to be 'Gogs', i.e., come from *Gogledd Cymru* or the North of Wales (Once again, however, groups cause confusion - The Super Furry Animals, for example, appear to be roughly divided between North and South Walians.)

Roughly thirty-one were native Welsh speakers whilst the rest were not. There were forty-nine actors, seventeen singers, six groups, five composers, eight comedians, seven playwrights, three directors, four television personalities and one theatrical impresario. Of those, seventy-three took the high road to England or went further, crossing the Atlantic and settling there permanently whilst the other twenty seven were either living in Wales or had come back there to live. At the time of writing fifty were dead with, pure serendipity this, fifty still alive.

Of those who are dead, twenty-four died in England, eight in America, one in Spain, one in Portugal, one in Switzerland and fifteen in Wales. (At least five of those who are no longer with us - Richard Burton, Harry Parr Davies, Rachel Roberts, Dylan Thomas and Mai Jones died an alcohol-related death.) Of those still living, twenty-one live in England, seven in the USA, two in Switzerland, one in Spain, one in Monte Carlo and five in Wales. There were also six bands and five whose exact homes were uncertain.

For what it is worth twenty went to university; eleven attended RADA; two went to the Royal College of Music; two to the Guildhall School of Music and Drama; one to the Chelsea College of Art; one to Bangor Normal College; two to the Central School of Speech Training and Dramatic Art and one to the Royal Academy. Fifty six did not carry on with further education of any kind after leaving school. The six bands were not counted and neither was Charlotte Church who is still too young to have been to university. What all these one hundred stars had in common, however, despite their differences, was this: ambition, in some cases a burning ambition, the all-consuming desire and drive to make it to the top of their chosen profession.

Whilst the vast majority of entrants were born in Wales, I have stretched the definition of 'Welsh' to include people, both of whose parents were Welsh, but, they themselves, happened to be born and raised outside Wales, such as the great Welsh language playwright, Saunders Lewis and the TV Maigret, Rupert Davies. Similarly, I have included those who were born in Wales, but very soon left the country, as was the case with Christian Bale, Tommy Cooper and Sarah Siddons. Included also are those who were born in Wales, but have no Welsh parentage such as Timothy Dalton. Despite the recent so-called 'Granny-Gate' or 'Kiwi-Gate' fiasco which, not so long ago, stunned the world of Welsh rugby, I have also included some who have at least one Welsh parent, such as Bob Hope and Alan Rickman, and who, in the present climate, could, if they were able enough and willing enough, play football or rugby for Wales, the land of their father or mother.

Will there be a *Dragon Entertains, Volume II - More Welsh Stars?* Time alone will tell. Just in case there, is readers are invited to write to me, care of the publisher, with their own suggestions as to who should be included in the new book. Needless to say, I already have my own ideas but would be delighted to hear from interested parties. Any suggestions should fulfil the above criteria. In the meantime, long may the Dragon continue to entertain!

Alan Roderick
Newport/Casnewydd, June, 2000

LIST OF CONTENTS

THE ALARM

In the 1980s, before anyone had really heard of The Manic Street Preachers, let alone Catatonia or The Stereophonics, The Alarm were alone in flying the Welsh flag in rock circles, at least as far as guitar bands were concerned, and they are an important part of Welsh popular musical history. Their members consisted of Michael Peters (born Prestatyn on February 25th, 1959) on vocals and guitar, David Sharp (born January 28th, 1959) also on vocals and guitar, Eddie MacDonald (born November 1st, 1959) on bass and Nigel Twist (born November 1st, 1959) on drums. Of the four Mike Peters now enjoys by far the highest profile.

Speaking on BBC Radio Wales' *Celebrity Choice* Mike Peters described himself as "a singer/songwriter". As a boy he lived in Rhyl and the first record he ever bought was in 1973 - *Drive-In Saturday* by David Bowie from the *Aladdin Sane* album. At the time his sister was going out with a member of a band who got hold of a guitar for Mike. It was a funky little number decked out in the colours of the Union Jack but he had no idea how to play it. Then a friend gave him a book called *How To Play The Guitar* which featured mainly Beatles' tunes. He flicked through the pages of the book and alighted on what he considered the easiest of the lot to play - *The Ballad of John and Yoko*, it being mostly in the chord of 'C'. Having got this far, Mike then proceeded to hold down that chord, look at his guitar technique in the mirror and practise.

Now into music in a big way, in 1976 Mike and a few friends went to the Quaintways Club in Chester to see the Sex Pistols in their pre-Sid Vicious incarnation. Bowled over by what he saw and thrilled by what he heard, the naive youngster from Rhyl approached the Pistols' vocalist, Johnny Rotten, in the bar after the gig was over, intending to elicit from him the punk group's musical philosophy. But instead of answering Peters' enthusiastic questions, Rotten simply elbowed him out of the way and called to his guitarist, Steve Jones, to "get the beers in". There and then, Mike vowed to himself that, if he were ever to be in a band, he would never treat his fans the way Rotten had treated him.

He went away from the gig with mixed emotions. First there was the sheer exhilaration at being introduced to this new form of music and then there was a not inconsiderable amount of negative feeling towards the ungracious Mr. Rotten. So the young and impressionable Mike returned to Rhyl and formed his own band with his friends which they called Seventeen. They played a lot of gigs in the small seaside town but this soon palled and so they decided to try their luck in London. Initially, London promoters were reluctant to book them, reckoning that they would not bring many fans from North Wales with them. So they pretended to come from Battersea or other parts of south London, in order to fool the promoters into thinking that they would bring lots of 'punters' with them. Still they persevered with London where they slept on friends' floors and hustled their way round the English capital's pubs. At the time there was an American band newly arrived in

London called The Stray Cats which had the most amazing quiff hairdos and played the most exciting rockabilly music.

In their naivety the group decided that, if they were the best band in Wales, and the Stray Cats were the best band in America, then they should get together and play. So they phoned up the Stray Cats' manager and pretended they had seen them in a club the night before and they had agreed that Mike and his friends would be the opening band on one of their gigs. Not surprisingly, the manager knew nothing at all about any of this, but seemed to think he could live with the idea. Just as the men from Rhyl were about to board their van and head for their next gig, they received a phone call from the Stray Cats' agent. He, too, had little or no idea as to what exactly was going on, but told them to make their way to Holloway where the Stray Cats were recording *Runaway Boys* with another Welshman, Cardiffian Dave Edmunds.

The Stray Cats were amused, and not a little impressed, by the young Welshmen's cheek and, being about the same age as Mike and Co., and also being a long way from home themselves, the two groups found they had a lot in common and soon they were getting on together like the proverbial house on fire. It was 1980, and the upshot of it all was that the four young Welshmen were invited onto the Stray Cats' tour which proved to be an incredible learning experience for them. As Mike says "it wasn't really our musical skills that got us onto the tour, it was the cheek that we had really!" During the tour they appeared at the Casablanca club in Cardiff and, on December 6th, 1980 at the Marquee club in London. The boys had high hopes of this gig, hoping that the record companies would appear and give them a recording contract, but as soon as they started playing, everyone decamped en masse to the bar leaving them playing to an audience of about two people. As it happened, the hoped-for agents never showed up and neither did the record producers. Disappointed, the band packed away their instruments and headed back to the various places where they were spending the night.

Next morning they were due to meet up again to drive back to North Wales, but on his way into central London Peters was shocked to see a passenger on the Tube reading a newspaper with the banner headline "John Lennon Shot In New York". The ex-Beatle had been killed on the very same night that they had been playing the Marquee. Lennon's death was to have a profound effect on Peters. Sitting in the back of the van driving back to North Wales with the radio playing nothing but Lennon music, Mike settled down to some serious reflection. "What exactly", he thought to himself "have I really achieved with my music? What have I actually done?" And, he told himself, it was time he stopped and really started to take stock of his career to date. He there and then resolved to renounce his old material and begin writing something which had real value and real meaning. There was nothing else for it - he simply had to start again. The band now went their separate ways for a while. So, in a way, John Lennon's death, untimely as it was, proved to be the beginning of Mike Peters's new, and more succesful, musical life.

In the summer of 1981 the members of Seventeen became The Alarm and decided they would have one more go at making it in London. They found a flat in Battersea and started to try and make themselves known. They had little or no money, but what they lacked in pounds and pence, they more than made up for with their spirit and enthusiasm. It did not take long for things to look up and soon they had signed a deal with IRS records. Now their music began to be played on the radio and the musical press began to sit up and take notice. Luckily for them, their new manager was Ian Wilson who had booked U2's first ever gig at the Half Moon in Herne Hill, Dulwich. The Alarm had played a few gigs with the Irish band in 1981 and 1982 and got on really well with them. Wilson now received news from U2. They had been playing in the U.S. for over a year, were feeling really homesick and wanted a band to go out and finish the tour with them, a band they had something in common with. So they phoned Ian Wilson and asked him to send out The Alarm. At this time in 1983, Mike Peters recalls, it was very unusual for a band like The Alarm to go to America as they had had no hit records in the U.K. and no real success. They had been written about and had received a little airplay but that was it really, so they were completely unknown in America.

However, their record company was run by Miles Copeland who had been the manager of pop giants The Police and he had sent them out in a van to 'break' America. Miles and Ian somehow got the money together and the next thing they knew four incredulous "spikey-haired blokes from Rhyl" were flying on a Pan-Am jet to Los Angeles. When they got there their hairdos aroused instant, and not terribly favourable, comments from the 'natives' who had never seen anything like it. Undeterred, The Alarm played with U2 at their landmark concert in Redrocks, Denver, Colorado.

Taking time out to sight see, The Alarm came across a small town called Craig where a funfair was being held. As they walked into the nearest bar, the barman took one look at their hair and exclaimed "Boy, have you come to the wrong place" at which The Alarm just fell about laughing. When he heard their accents, however, the barman realised that they were not Americans and, swiftly changing his tune, called out "Martha, put the Beatles on!" From then on, the people in the bar could not do enough for the boys from Rhyl. Mike says "I suppose in a way The Alarm had a fantastic relationship with America from that point on". U2 were very helpful as well and made sure the Welshmen's records were played all across America.

One of the highspots of The Alarm's career was when they toured with Bob Dylan in 1987. The first concert took place in Concord in Northern California and Neil Young appeared on stage with Dylan. Dylan would swim every day and spent a lot of time talking with Mike about Wales and the poetry of Wales - especially the poems of Idris Davies. Towards the end of the tour he invited Mike up on stage to duet with him on *Knocking On Heaven's Door*. The second night Dylan asked Mike to sing with him again, but just as he was about to go on stage, Dylan's guitarist, Gene Smith, called him back,

"Hold it", he said, "he's changed the key - it's in F now". (It was in C the night before and Mike assumes that this was just Dylan's way of testing him out as, apparently, he had done this sort of thing with other musicians. Unfazed, Mike swiftly found the right key and ensured that the honour of North Wales was not disgraced.)

Mike Peters heard *Smells Like Teen Spirit* by Nirvana in the early 1990s and thought "This is the end of The Alarm ... just as with Lennon's death the record signalled the end and the beginning". The record came out in 1991 when Mike split from The Alarm. He moved back to North Wales where he turned a small chapel into a studio, spending hours in there making music which he hoped would see him through the 1990s and beyond.

His *Absolute Reality* which was a big hit for The Alarm, Mike had borrowed from Howl by the American poet Allen Ginsberg. Mike now used Ginsberg again in his first solo album which contains the song *Into The 21st Century*. He had met a young poet called Billy Lemont who played the song to Ginsberg before he died. Far from suing Peters, as he had at first feared, Ginsberg was quite enthusiastic and allowed Peters and Lemont to 'sample' his voice onto the track *Into The 21st Century*. A recent venture of Mike's has been his collaboration with the Cult's guitarist Billy Duffy on a new group called Colour Sound which they have taken out onto the road.

As for The Alarm their albums were *Declaration* (1984), *Strength* (1985), *Eye of the Hurricane* (1987), *Electric Folklore Live* (1988), *Change* (1989) and *Raw* (1991). *Change* which was produced by Mary Hopkin's ex-husband, Tony Visconti, featured members of the Welsh Symphony Orchestra and was also recorded in a Welsh-language version. Their singles lingered mainly around the lower reaches of the Top 40 but *68 Guns* did make it to Number 17 in 1983 and *Spirit of 76* got to Number 22 in January, 1986. Strangely, one of their most anthemic singles *A New South Wales* only got as high as Number 31 in November, 1989. All in all, fourteen of their singles made it into the Top 50 and their songs spent a total of fifty-five weeks in the charts.

Mike Peters has said that he never thought he would leave The Alarm. He had no plans to become a solo artist and counts himself blessed that his hobby had been his life's work. Every year he organises an event called 'The Gathering' in North Wales where he plays host to fans who come from all over the world. (Mike is the only member of The Alarm who still lives in Wales - the others live in London and America.) There are acoustic and electric sessions on separate evenings. Mike who comes across as a personable, likeable young man has a positive outlook on life. He survived a cancer scare in 1996 and has released two solo albums - *Feel Free* and *Rise Up*. He took part in the Cardiff Bay celebrations to inaugurate the new National Assembly of Wales. Backed by a Welsh Male Voice Choir he treated the audience to a rendition of one of his best known songs, *A New South Wales*.

BADFINGER

They were four boys from Swansea, hoping to make it big in the world of pop music. And, for a time, they did just that. For a brief period they succeeded in riding the wave of success, but, gradually, things began to fall apart and their high hopes ended in tragedy. But all of this was far from the minds of the four young men from Swansea as they set out on the road to fame and fortune. Originally called the Iveys, after the town's Ivey Place, they learnt their craft playing in and around Swansea and its surrounding towns and villages in the 1960s. They were Pete Ham (born April 27th, 1947, he attended Gors Primary School and Townhill Secondary School), a native of Swansea's Townhill district, a big council housing estate about a mile and a half from the centre of Swansea, who provided the vocals; Mike Gibbins on drums; Ron Griffiths (born March 12th, 1949) on bass guitar and David Jenkins on rhythm guitar. (For a time, David's brother, Alwyne, managed the group and acted as their roadie.)

The Iveys came to the attention of ex-jazz band leader Bill Collins, father of Lewis Collins (an ex-member of the 1960s Liverpool group The Mojos, and subsequently an actor who became famous for his role in *The*

The Iveys, London, July 1966. Left to right: Mike Gibbins, Ron Griffiths, Alwyne Jenkins, Peter Ham, David Jenkins. (Alwyne Jenkins/Swansea Reference Library).

Professionals). He became their manager, moved them to London and found them a job backing the singer David Garrick on his British hit *Dear Mrs. Appleby*, but they were not destined to be a backing group for long. One of their tapes found favour with Paul McCartney and they then secured a contract with the Beatles' new Apple organisation (thus becoming the first group to be signed to Apple.)

Their first single on the Apple label was the 1968 Tony Visconti produced *Maybe Tomorrow* and playing on it was a new member of the group – Tommy Evans. Unlike the others, Evans who was born on June 5th, 1947, came from Liverpool and had played in a Liverpool group called the Calderstones. (David Jenkins left the band to make way for Evans.) *Maybe Tomorrow* reached a creditable Number Sixty in the American Hot One Hundred.

The following year - 1969 - the Liverpool connection was strengthened still further when Joey Molland (born in Liverpool on June 21st, 1948) took over from Ron Griffiths with Evans switching to bass. Molland had previously done the rounds with a number of Merseyside groups including the Profiles, the Masterminds, the Merseys and Gary Walker and Rain. 1969 was also the year when the group took the decision to change its name to Badfinger. Things now began to move in the right direction. Paul McCartney took them under his wing, giving them one of his songs, *Come and Get It*, and also playing piano on the recording. *Come and Get It* got as high as Number 4 in the United Kingdom (January, 1970) and Number 7 in America (April, 1970).

In October, 1970, the group toured the States for eight weeks and, in December 1970, their new single *No Matter What* got to Number 8 in the American charts. (It reached Number 5 in Britain in February, 1971.) In August, 1971 the band played at George Harrison's concert in aid of Bangladesh at New York's Madison Square Garden.

In February, 1972 they had their last big hit *Day After Day* (produced by George Harrison) which reached Number 10 in the British charts and Number 4 in America. That same month saw Harry Nilsson's cover version of Ham and Evans's song *Without You* reach the coveted Number 1 spot in America, a feat it repeated in Great Britain in March. In April, 1972, the Pete Ham-penned *Baby Blue* climbed to fourteenth position on the American chart.

The group's last ever L.P. on the Apple label, *Ass*, was released in December, 1973 and they subsequently signed for Warner Brothers but it proved to be a step fraught with difficulties. They soon found themselves beset by problems, entangled in legal wrangles and threatened with lawsuits. As if all this were not enough, there were allegations of financial mismanagement on the part of their new business manager, Stan Polley. At one point the group's main creative force, Pete Ham, (he wrote both their hits *No Matter What* and *Day After Day*) threatened to pull out of a U.S tour but was persuaded to rejoin the group in time.

On Wednesday, April 23rd, 1975 Pete Ham was found dead hanging from a beam in his Weybridge garage. According to the *Western Mail* (Friday, April 21st, 2000) he had drunk twelve whiskeys at a nearby pub before killing himself. His last words to friends are said to have been "I know a way out of this." Gary J. Katz in his *Death By Rock And Roll* tells a different story. (significantly, the *Western Mail* does not appear to have carried any report on Ham at the actual time of his death). Katz says that, far from being in the pub on the night before his death, Ham was actually at Tom Evans's house. The two had been writing songs and discussing their seemingly ever present financial problems. Marianne Evans recalled that the Swansea songwriter was worried about Ann, his pregnant girlfriend, who was soon to give birth to the couple's first child. Ham drank with Evans before taking his leave and, according to Katz, said to the Liverpudlian with the Welsh sounding name, "I know a way out".

Again according to Katz, Ham laid the blame for their financial disasters squarely at the feet of their American business manager. The last line of his suicide note is said to have stated that Stan Polley was a soulless bastard. Gary Katz says that, two days after Ham's lifeless body was found, Polley phoned Ann Ferguson asking if there was anything he could do. He also wanted to know if Ann would confirm publicly that he, Polley, had had nothing to do with Pete Ham's untimely demise, but Ann refused point blank to go along with Polley's wishes.

Ham's tragic suicide spelt the end for Badfinger. Gibbins returned to Wales (years afterwards he would play drums on Bonnie Tyler's hit *It's A Heartache*). With Ham's death and Gibbins's departure the group effectively ceased to be Welsh in any real sense of the word. Molland formed Natural Gas and Evans Dodgers, but nothing came of either project.

With two of its main members 'reduced' to laying carpets in Los Angeles (Molland) and insulating pipes in Britain (Evans) the group re-formed in 1978. This time they featured ex-Yes man Tony Kaye on keyboards and Peter Clarke on drums. In 1981 *Hold On* was a minor US chart hit. But the problems that had caused Pete Ham to take his own life just would not go away. On Wednesday, November 23rd, 1983 came the shock news that, in almost identical circumstances to Pete Ham, Tom Evans had hung himself on a tree outside his house in New Haw, Surrey.

In April, 1995, Gibbins and Molland re-formed the group yet again but the magic had gone and the attempt was doomed to failure. Still the legal wrangles continued. In the first few months of the year 2000, Anne Ferguson, Pete Ham's ex-girlfriend, Marianne Evans, Tom Evans' widow, Mike Gibbins and the group's ex-manager, Bill Collins took their case to the High Court in London. They were seeking redress against Joey Molland whom they accused of bringing out *Day After Day* from a 1974 Badfinger live recording without their prior knowledge and were claiming compensation. The four complainants had previously won a court order assigning all pre-1975 Badfinger royalties to them and were hopeful of another success. In the event, the High Court judge found that the four, and Molland, should share the profits equally, but,unfortunately, the verdict proved to be something of a hollow victory. The costs of the court case amounted to some £100,000 but royalties on the *Day After Day* recording that Molland had issued had, so far, only brought in about £46,000.

Ironically Badfinger's biggest single success would fall to other artists – Nilsson and Mariah Carey (in 1994) both reached Number One with their versions of Ham and Evans's haunting *Without You* and a 1999 BBC Radio 2 Listeners' Poll placed the song at Number 45 in the Top One Hundred Songs of the Twentieth Century.

Despite the original Swansea line-up, the Badfinger story is shot through with Liverpool connections: two of their later members came from that city; they were closely identified with the Beatles during their Apple years and they even played the Cavern club in the mid-60s. Members of the group appeared on John Lennon's *Imagine*, Ringo Starr's *It Don't Come Easy* and George Harrison's triple album *All Things Must Pass*. The group also provided the music for the film *Magic Christian* which featured Ringo Starr. Their LPs included the 1970 *No Dice*, the 1971 *Straight Up* (produced by Todd Rundgren) and the 1974 *Badfinger*.

The Badfinger story inspired Gary Katz to write his book on how the legends of rock met their untimely ends. In his foreword he wrote that he had stumbled across the story of Badfinger, a group that had reached, as he said, the rock world's highest plateau before succumbing to, what he called, the music business's dark side. Katz also thought that the group, at the peak of their success, were more popular in America than in their native Britain. (Today, the group is said to be the subject of many American web sites.) *The Penguin Encyclopedia of Popular Music* called them a good pop group which might, perhaps, have lasted longer if a ready-made short-cut to fame had not been available to them.

Of the three surviving Ivey members, David Jenkins is now a school caretaker in Taunton, Ron Griffiths works for BT in Hemel Hempstead and Mickey Gibbins lives in Orlando, Florida. In June, 2000, Swansea Central Library organised an exhibition as a tribute to Peter Ham. Poignantly, one of the exhibits locked in a glass case was his exercise book containing the lyrics of *Without You*. His two Ivor Novello Awards were also on display, as was the jumper he wore at his first gig in London.

Badfinger were a guitar band who specialised in catchy tunes with a sound not a million miles removed from that of the Beatles. Their roots were to be found in Dylan Thomas's "ugly-lovely" town of Swansea, but with the later acquisition of two new members from Merseyside, they acquired a 'Liverpool sound' of their own and became a hybrid 'Welsh/English' group. Ironically, the tragic deaths of two of their most prominent members have ensured that the group's name will never die. Their song *Without You* will endure.

SIR STANLEY BAKER

Siân Phillips said that "going home to Stanley Baker's home was like going home with God". (She meant, of course, going back with Stanley to his Rhondda heartland.) In *Eva*, the 1962 film directed by Joseph Losey, Jeanne Moreau was not so impressed. "Bloody Welshman" are the last words she says in the film to Baker. But maybe she had a point. Baker's character in the film, novelist Teifion Jones, is a fake, forever ranting on about the chapel, the mines and singing *Sospan Fach* in his lighter moments. Now, no one could accuse Stanley Baker of having been a 'fake' in real life. He was the genuine article. He was a man who went from an impoverished childhood to being paid £120,000 a picture in his days of glory.

Born Ferndale in the Rhondda on February 28th, 1928 and brought up in abject poverty from the age of nine, Stanley worked on an early morning milk-round to help his family out. His father had lost a leg in an accident down the local pit when he was just seventeen and eked out a living doing odd jobs. Stanley attended Ferndale Secondary School from September, 1939 where, according to his wife, he was a "terror", frightening not only the other pupils but most of the teachers as well. One teacher he did not frighten, though, was Glynne Morse, who taught arts and crafts and who saw something in the rough, working class boy with his strong local accent that the other teachers did not. He would encourage Stanley to act, polish up his working class accent, write plays for him to perform and, eventually, become a lifelong friend. When Stanley moved to Birmingham to do rep and, later, was called up, Glynne continued to send him books every week and give him moral support. (Stanley would repay Glynne Morse in later life - on his retirement from school he bought him a house in England.) When Stanley left school he went to work in the Ferndale electrical factory.

He was fourteen when he first 'trod the boards' at St. Martin's Theatre, London in *The Druid's Rest*, acting as Richard Burton's understudy, then spent the next two years with the Birmingham Repertory Company before resuming his film career. Baker himself always referred to *A Sleep of Prisoners* by Christopher Fry in 1950 as his big breakthrough in the theatre.

His first film was the 1943 Ealing production *Undercover* when he was just fifteen. His fifty-five cinema films include *The Cruel Sea* (1953), playing the part of Bennett, *The Criminal* (1960), *The Guns of Navarone* (1961), *Eva* (1962), *Accident* (1967), reckoned by some to be his best performance on screen and *Robbery* (1967). "Volatile", "versatile", "a loner", these are just some of the words critics have used to describe Baker's on-screen persona. His friend Richard Burton said he "had a face like a determined fist" and described him as "the authentic dark voice of the Rhondda Valley".

Seen by many as a working class hero and with a tough guy image, Stanley was in films with Gregory Peck, Alan Ladd, Ginger Rogers, Laurence Olivier, Robert Mitchum, David Niven, Jeanne Moreau and Ryan O'Neal. He was often seen on screen as detectives/policemen, soldiers/sailors, criminal types/robbers and knights/historical warriors. In his most famous film, the

Stanley Baker

1963 *Zulu*, Baker not only co-produced but also took the leading role of Lieutenant John Chard. (Writing in 1986, Peter Stead recorded that *Zulu* had "been described as a Welsh Western" and that he had "once heard a group of football supporters at Ninian Park (Cardiff City's football ground) all agree that it was the greatest film ever".) Thirteen years later, in a July, 1999 Sky Premier Survey Welsh cinema fans voted *Zulu* Number Seven in their Top Ten. In December, 1999 *Western Mail* readers voted the Zulu warriors' final salute to their gallant foes the Greatest Film Scene of the Millennium - a title it shared jointly with the *Ben Hur* chariot race and Gene Kelly walking home in *Singin' in the Rain*. In all, Baker produced four films: *Zulu* and *The Sands of The Kalahari* with Cy Endfield, *Robbery* with Michael Deeley and *Where's Jack* by himself.

Stanley played Rochester in a 1957 TV production of *Jane Eyre*. In 1976, the year of his death, when cancer was already beginning to claim him, he gave a memorable performance as the father in the BBC production of *How Green Was My Valley* in which he played opposite Siân Phillips. Other TV productions with which he was associated in the last three years of his life were *Robinson Crusoe, Graceless Go I* and *The Changeling*. He became a director of Harlech Television (HTV) in 1968 together with Sir Geraint Evans and Richard Burton. A keen golfer and rugby fan, he was a strong supporter of the Labour party.

On Saturday, June 26th, 1976, Stanley Baker was taken ill at his Marbella, Costa del Sol home. The next day he was transferred to a public hospital in Malaga where he died on Monday, June 28th, 1976. His wife (he had married Ellen Martin in 1950 at St. George's Church, Hanover Square, London – she was then an actress and they had become engaged a week after their first meeting) was by his side. He had undergone a cancer operation the previous February. Baker was survived by his wife, three sons and one daughter. A month before his death he had been knighted in Harold Wilson's retirement honours list. In fact, at the time he died, Baker's knighthood had not yet received the Queen's accolade but moves were afoot to make the title official.

The funeral service was held on Tuesday, July 6th, 1976 at the Putney Vale Crematorium and was attended by family and friends. Sir Harold Wilson and Lady Falkender were amongst the mourners, George Thomas, Speaker of the House of Commons, and a native of the Rhondda, said prayers. Stanley Baker's ashes were to be scattered over Ferndale Mountain after a memorial service to be held in London.

The Memorial Service was held at St. Martin-in-the Fields, London on October 6th, 1976. Amongst those present were Ivor Emmanuel, Siân Phillips, Clifford Evans, Victor Spinetti, Cliff Morgan, Michael Medwin, Jimmy Tarbuck, Henry Cooper, Peter Sallis and Gordon Jackson. George Thomas gave the address, Harry Secombe sang *Cwm Rhondda*, a favourite hymn and Donald Houston spoke the words of Idris Davies's *Send Out Your Homing Pigeons, Dai*, Stanley Baker's favourite poem.

CHRISTIAN BALE

Christian Morgan Bale was born in Haverfordwest ("in a cottage on the edge of the cliffs - you had to drive through two potato fields to get there" - as he would later recall) on January 30th, 1974, the son of a pilot father and a dancer mother, but his father, who was working on a dairy farm at the time, made a habit of moving from job to job and he left there when he was two years of age. Six foot two inch Bale recalls growing up in Surrey and Berkshire and living in Bournemouth between the ages of twelve and seventeen. The youngest of four children, he has three older sisters, and made his debut at the age of nine in a Pac Man cereal commercial. He appeared in the 1986 *Anastasia: The Mystery of Anna* and played James Graham in Steven Spielberg's 1987 film, *Empire of the Sun* when he was thirteen years old. (He beat four thousand other hopefuls to the part.)

Falstaff's boy in Kenneth Branagh's 1989 version of *Henry V*, he played Jim Hawkins in the 1990 film *Treasure Island*. He was Stevie in *The Secret Agent* (1996). He was also the voice behind Thomas in the *Pocahontas* cartoon film. He has since appeared in *Portrait of a Lady* with Nicole Kidman and in *Little Women* with the likes of Susan Sarandon and Winona Ryder. Bale appeared as Chris in the 1998 film *Metroland* with Emily Watson and, in the same year, starred in *Velvet Goldmine* with Ewan McGregor, playing the part of journalist Arthur Stuart. He played Demetrius in Hollywood's 1999 version of *A Midsummer Night's Dream*, sharing the screen with Michelle Pfeiffer and Kelvin Kline.

Currently living in Los Angeles with his father and sister he starred in the lead role of the psychotic serial-killer Patrick Bateman in the highly controversial 1999 film *American Psycho*. Bale was director Mary Harron's original choice to play the role, but after superstar Leonardo Di Caprio expressed an interest, Bale was dropped. Angered by the decision, Harron then announced her own departure but, when Di Caprio withdrew from the project, both she and Bale were re-instated. Harron was quoted as saying "Christian had a real depth as an actor which was a real surprise in someone so young". On the film's release in Britain in April, 2000 *The Guardian* enthused mightily over Bale's performance. He played opposite John Hurt in the 1999 film *All The Little Animals* and took the part of Jesus in the television mini-series *Jesus and Mary*. Bale is one of the Internet's darlings with a host of web sites devoted to his doings. He secretly married Sibi Blazic in Las Vegas on January 29th, 2000.

SHIRLEY BASSEY

She could now be drawing her old age pension. Instead she is one of the most successful singers the world has ever seen. Shirley Bassey was born on January 8th, 1937 in a terraced house - 182, Bute Street, Butetown in Cardiff - the youngest of seven children (she had five sisters and one brother). Her father, Henry Bassey, a black West African seaman, was an illegal immigrant who was deported to Nigeria when Shirley Veronica, the youngest of seven children, was a mere three years old. Her mother, a white woman, born Eliza Jane Metcalfe in North Shields, then married another Nigerian seaman, Mr. Mendi. The family then moved to 132, Portmanmoor Road in the then steelworking area of Splott and Shirley began to attend Moorland Road School, Cardiff. Despite being unable to read music, Shirley would wow the rest of the class at school with her dynamic singing voice.

As a child she was a tomboy who liked nothing better than to climb trees but she was also, even then, known for her singing. A letter from a childhood sweetheart, however, complaining that she was too dirty, shocked her into leaving her tomboy days behind her and started her off on the road to becoming the diva she is today. Aged eight she was already performing in clubs in Cardiff's Butetown. After leaving school she worked for £3 a week packing enamel utensils in woodshavings at Curran's factory, but her evenings were spent singing in clubs all over Cardiff and throughout the valleys.

Her first real professional break came when she signed up for a show called *Memories of Al Jolson*. She lost her heart to another singer in the show, a young man scarcely older than herself. Their encounter led to her becoming pregnant at the age of sixteen. Her young lover urged her not to have the child, but she insisted on going through with the pregnancy and gave birth to a daughter, Sharon, at a London maternity clinic specialising in illegitimate births. Undaunted, she decided to continue her show business career entrusting her daughter to the care of one of her married sisters. Her career now began to take off and, before she was twenty, she had appeared in most of the world's top entertainment hot spots - Paris, London, Monte Carlo, New York and Las Vegas among them. But whilst she was touring Australia news broke of her illegitimate child back home in Cardiff. Uncertain as to how exactly her audience would react, she nevertheless bravely faced her Sydney fans and they gave her a rapturous reception in a demonstration of spontaneous loyalty.

By 1955 she was performing in London's Café de Paris. Her big break came when Jack Hylton, one of the top bandleaders of the time, noticed her, liked what he saw and booked her into comedian Al Read's 1955 Christmas review at the London Adelphi. The show did so well that she was kept on for Al's revue *Such is Life* which ran for a year.

Meanwhile she continued to 'enjoy' troubled relationships with the men in her life. In November, 1957 a former boyfriend, nineteen-year-old Terence Clyde 'Pepe' Davies, angered at being 'dumped' by her, pulled out a gun and held her hostage in the early hours in Room 5XK at the Cumberland Hotel, Marble Arch in London. Whilst armed police thronged the corridors outside Davies used the telephone for target practice and, thinking the police were about to storm the room, fired two shots into a wooden doorframe. Eventually he let Bassey go and the ordeal was over. Davies, who accidentally shot himself in the leg after releasing Bassey, was later sentenced to three years in gaol.

On Wednesday, June 7th, 1961 she married chain-smoking, tea-drinking film director and record producer Kenneth Hume at a registry office in Paddington, London. From London's East End, Hume was a well known gambler and not particularly liked by those who knew him. He was also a homosexual. During their married life he continued to stay in his Bayswater flat whilst Shirley lived in her house in Belgravia. In March, 1964 she began a love affair with actor Peter Finch whom she met in a West End restaurant. (Finch had already had a fling with Laurence Olivier's wife, Vivien Leigh.) The English born star of over a hundred films (he was brought up in Australia) gave Shirley the pet name of 'Cheetah' whilst she called him 'Finchy'.

Unfortunately, Finch was a heavy drinker and the affair came to an end when Shirley realised that he wanted her to sacrifice her flourishing career for his. Divorce proceedings were then instituted, both by Kenneth Hume and by Finch's wife, South African actress, Yolande Turner. Hume alleged that Samantha (Shirley's daughter who had been born on November 7th, 1963) was not his child. Instead, he claimed, her father was either Peter Finch or Shirley's Melbourne agent, Australian John McAuliffe.

Kenneth Hume and Shirley Bassey separated in November, 1962 but became reconciled five months later. However, they divorced in February, 1965 and Hume was found dead in his London flat of a drugs overdose on June 26th, 1967. The inquest recorded a verdict of accidental death. A second marriage to the 6 feet 5 inches Italian hotelier Sergio Novak, whom she met whilst he was managing a Venice hotel, took place on August 13th, 1968 at half past two in the morning in Las Vegas. He became her manager and the pair went to live in Lugano, Switzerland where they had a house built especially for them but the marriage did not last and they were divorced in 1981.

Shirley's life has not been without personal tragedy. In 1985 the dead, fully clothed body of her twenty-one-year old daughter Samantha Novak (Shirley's child by her first husband, Kenneth Hume, she barely knew her father and had taken Shirley's second husband's name) was discovered in the River Avon only half a mile from Bristol's Clifton Suspension Bridge. It seemed that she had fallen from the bridge. At the inquest it was revealed that Samantha had had problems with drink and had consulted a psychologist about her emotional difficulties. The night before her death she had been drinking heavily. When the body was found she was wearing boots with steel toe caps, a torn leather jacket and a pair of old baggy trousers with just £1-65 in their pockets. However, a detective inspector who had been investigating the death told the court there was no proof that Samantha being found in the river was anything other than a "horrible accident". The coroner agreed, saying there were no "suspicious circumstances" and the Avon and Somerset Police found no sign of any injuries. An open verdict was returned. Tragedy continued to stalk Shirley in later years. Her mother died in 1981, her eldest sister, Grace, in 1996.

Camp, kitsch, gay icon - a veteran of countless emotion packed performances, Shirley has an undeniably powerful voice which, to some listeners, can sound just a little shrill at times. Her influences include Judy Garland, Sarah Vaughan and Ella Fitzgerald. The Welsh Press have called her "a true diva", "Wales's ultimate diva", "Cardiff's Tigress from the Bay" and "a unique performer of the highest calibre".

Shirley Bassey's first hit record was *The Banana Boat Song* in February, 1957 - it reached Number Eight and stayed in the charts for ten weeks. Since then her list of hit singles has included such Bassey standards as *Kiss Me Honey Honey Kiss Me, As I Love You, Climb Every Mountain, What Now My Love, I (Who) Have Nothing,* the Beatles' *Something* and, of course, the show stopping *Big Spender.* She has also performed three James Bond themes - *Goldfinger, Diamonds Are Forever* and *Moonraker.*

In a *Wales on Sunday* 1998 telephone poll Shirley Bassey was voted the Sexiest Woman of the Twentieth Century with twenty-four per cent of the total votes cast. In August, 1998 she was placed fifteenth in a list of one hundred all time musical greats chosen by the readers of *Mojo* magazine. Awarded a CBE on February 18th, 1994, she was made a Dame in the 2000 New Year's Honours List. She also sang at the White House for President Kennedy.

Ever the perfectionist, she pulled out of the December, 1997 Royal Variety Show because she was not allowed to sing with a live orchestra. Just over a year later in January, 1998 Shirley appeared at Brentford County Court accused of slapping Hilary Levy, her personal assistant of fifteen years, in a Cape Town hotel room and calling her a "Jewish bitch", but Judge Marcus Edwards found in the diva's favour, calling Miss Levy "a less persuasive witness".

It was not the first time Miss Bassey had been before the courts. In December, 1978 the police were called to a house in London's Eaton Square after neighbours had complained about the noise. It turned out that Shirley and some friends had gone to a Fulham restaurant and then gravitated to the party in Eaton Square where she insisted on singing *Quando, Quando* even after the police had asked her to be quiet. They then arrested her and took her outside where, obviously the worse for drink, she shoved one policeman in the back, making him fall against another officer of the law. On December 21st, the Magistrates at Horseferry Road Magistrates Court bound her over to keep the peace for three months and accepted her assurances that nothing of the kind would ever happen again.

Now resident in Monte Carlo Shirley has been a professional singer since she was sixteen. In her early days she was known as a 'belter'. Famous for her glamorous, slinky, revealing dresses she performed at both the opening and closing ceremonies of the Rugby World Cup at Cardiff's Millennium Stadium in a Welsh Dragon flag dress. December, 1997 saw a new departure when she collaborated with fashionable dance musicians Propellerheads on a Top 40 hit *History Repeating* with a pronounced drum and bass backing.

On Monday, April 27th, 1998 it was reported that Shirley Bassey's appearance at an outdoor concert in the grounds of Highclere Castle in Newbury had forced a couple to cancel their dream wedding which they had planned to hold in the stately home on the same day.

The possessor of seven hundred pairs of shoes, Shirley has been known to spend as much as £10,000 a day on footwear. She has come a long way from the days when her family had no proper bathroom but had to make do with a tin tub in the kitchen. She borrowed more than one million pounds worth of diamonds from the London jewellery firm of Cartier to wear on her 1998 New Year's Eve TV concert.

There is a lighter side to La Bassey, proving that whatever Life can throw at her, she can still raise a smile. Shirley sang *Smoke Gets In Your Eyes* as a guest on one of the famed Morecambe and Wise Christmas shows. Of course, it wasn't quite as simple as that - Eric and Ernie took her shoe away and replaced it with an army boot and then, from beneath a hole in the stage, pulled at her foot, whilst she, gallantly, continued to sing.

During her time at the top Shirley says she has learnt to sing songs that her audience like and identify with. However, the lessons of her sometimes troubled private life have taught her that men cannot really now relate to her, because of her success. She is on record as saying that most men she meets appear to want her to live up to her stage image, and be some kind of wild party animal when, in reality, she is a homebody, who much prefers to stay home, watch the TV and enjoy a good meal. Men however, want to take her out to the nearest restaurant, she says, but when they get there, they are put out that everything revolves around her and they must play second fiddle. Their male self image insulted, they then decide to take their frustrations out on Shirley by insulting her, but she is too strong a woman to tolerate that sort of behaviour for long.

HUGH 'BINKIE' BEAUMONT

He never danced or sang, or uttered a line in anger on stage, but he certainly left his mark on the British theatre scene. Noel Coward, Ivor Novello and Rex Harrison were just some of his friends. Another friend, John Gielgud, called him "probably the most successful impresario of Twentieth Century British Theatre" and trusted his judgement in matters theatrical implicitly. When he died in 1973, *Who's Who in the Theatre* needed four columns to enumerate all the productions he had been associated with.

Binkie Beaumont, as he was known to all and sundry, was born Hughes Griffiths Morgan at 97, West End Lane, Hampstead, North London on Good Friday, March 27th, 1908. He was the son of Mary Frances Morgan (neé Brewer, the daughter of a wealthy Cardiff civil engineer) and Morgan Morgan, a barrister-at-law, and one-time deputy mayor of Cardiff. The family returned to Cardiff and 12, Cathedral Road, but when the child was two years old, his parents divorced, his mother having taken up with a rich timber merchant called William Sugden Beaumont, and he never saw his real father again. Indeed, he grew up believing that Beaumont was his real father, a belief encouraged by his mother. When he eventually discovered the truth years afterward he changed his name by deed poll.

William Beaumont died in 1920 and Binkie's mother took in a lodger, Major Harry Woodcock, who had come to Cardiff to manage The Playhouse (later to become the Prince of Wales Theatre - now a Wetherspoons pub). He introduced the young boy to the world of the theatre and before long Binkie was going to the Playhouse every Saturday. The day after leaving Penarth Grammar School (March 28th, 1923), Binkie began working there as a box office assistant. Within two months Woodcock had promoted him to be his assistant.

In 1925, Tallulah Bankhead, the American star, appeared at the Playhouse in a play called *The Man in the Wheelchair.* She offered the young Beaumont a place as her company manager at £10 a week and, when that came to an end, he got a job as business manager with the Barnes Theatre in London. He was eighteen years of age. Three years later, on March 27th, 1929, he received a telephone call from Harry Tennent of Moss Empires, then head of their provincial bookings department, offering him a job as his assistant. Binkie accepted and, for the next four years, carried out his duties as Tennent's right-hand man. By 1933, Tennent had become powerful enough to persuade Howard and Wyndham, one of the biggest names in British theatre, to merge with Moss Empires music hall and variety interests, with himself and Binkie as the executive heads of the new company.

In 1936, Binkie convinced Tennent that they should part company with Howard and Wyndham and set up their own firm, H.M. Tennennt Ltd. After a shaky start, the new firm prospered and became a powerful force on the London theatre scene. When Tennent died, Binkie retained the name of the firm and ensured that it went from strength to strength. During the Second World War he put on fifty-nine West End plays - only seven of them failed. 1954 saw Binkie putting on sixteen productions in the West End.

By the 1960s, however, things had begun to change and Binkie's theatrical empire no longer set the tone. Binkie had no time for the new plays like Pinter's *The Caretaker* or John Osborne's *Look Back in Anger.* The new world of Osborne and Pinter passed him by. At this point he began putting on revivals which failed to work, productions which did not excite. The star parts were, more often than not, miscast, errors of judgement began to creep in, agents no longer sent him their best new plays, little by little he was losing his touch.

In the last few years of his life, he suffered from terrible back pains which, at times, were so severe that he could not dress himself or get out of the bath without help. He began to smoke more and to drink more heavily.

On the morning of 23rd March, 1973 his housekeeper Anna found him dead in his bed in his house at 14, Lord North Street. He had died in his sleep during the night a few days short of his 65th birthday.

They held a memorial service for Binkie Beaumont at the 'actors' church', St. Paul's in Covent Garden, on April 17th, 1973. The church was packed and amongst the readers were Paul Schofield, Ralph Richardson and John Gielgud. At the end of the month his house and all its effects were sold at auction. The proceeds from the sale together with the rest of Binkie's estate amounted to close on half a million pounds. His last epitaph, to be found on the wall of the nave of St. Paul's in London, reads: "Hugh Beaumont, Theatrical Manager, 1908-1973".

Binkie Beaumont was a man who liked to collect lots of small animals carved from wood and float them in his bath. He was also a homosexual, who had a long-term relationship with John Perry, and regarded himself as a theatre manager, not as an impresario. He was a snob and could be ruthless. During his lifetime he rubbed shoulders with a host of famous actors, a veritable Who's Who of the theatrical world. From Tyrone Guthrie to George Bernard Shaw, from Vivien Leigh to Sybil Thorndike, they all knew Binkie.

Some called him a 'master fixer' with a deadly charm. Others compared him to the Borgias, finding him cold and aloof. He liked to gossip and to gamble. He smoked incessantly. He was not a 'bookish' person - he had no time for books. Nevertheless, he was responsible for getting a young Rex Harrison into the cast of *Short Story* (Robert Morley's first play) in November, 1935 and he also produced Noel Coward's *Design for Living* at the Theatre Royal, Haymarket in January, 1939.

HYWEL BENNETT

Born Garnant in the Amman Valley on April 8th, 1944, Hywel Bennett went to Henry Horton Grammar School in London, became a member of the National Youth Theatre at the age of fourteen and trained at RADA. His TV appearances include an early showing as Rynlan in *The Chase*, a 1965 Doctor Who story, Willy the Swansea delinquent in Dennis Potter's 1966 *Where the Buffalo Roam*, the part of Doctor Bickleigh in *Malice Aforethought* and the role of Tom in Dennis Potter's 1978 *Pennies from Heaven*. In his book on Dennis Potter, W. Stephen Gilbert described the part played by Hywel in *Where The Buffalo Roam* as follows: "It is Hywel Bennett's damaged-cherub looks, together with the daft pathos of cowboy language delivered in the wide-eyed accent of South Wales, that invest Willy with a glassy radiance and lift the tale into an eerie romance".

Other small screen programmes he has appeared in are: *Tinker, Tailor, Soldier, Spy*. He has guest starred in *The Sweeney* (he played Steven Castle in *Sweet Smell of Succession*, Episode 35 of *The Sweeney*, November 8th, 1978). and appeared in *Artemis 81* in the early 1980s. His recent TV appearances include Dennis Potter's last work for the medium and the detective drama *Harper and Iles* in which he played Chief Constable Desmond Iles.

One of his best-loved TV roles was his portrayal of the sardonic intellectual layabout Shelley on Thames Television in the 1970s. He played the part of the unemployed (unemployable?) ex-university student with a PHD in Geography and a somewhat cynical, idiosyncratic outlook on life in seventy-one half-hour episodes between 1979 and 1992. He also appeared in the seventh series of *Casualty*, episode seventeen, playing a drunk driver.

Hywel was born into a Welsh-speaking family but forgot the language when the family moved to London. When he appeared in the Welsh thriller *Night of the Hunter*, which was filmed in English first and then Welsh, Hywel needed to pick his mother's brains for help in playing the Welsh language scenes. In the theatre he has played parts as diverse as Toad in *Toad of Toad Hall*, Marlowe in *She Stoops to Conquer*, Prince Hal in *Henry IV (Parts I and II)* and Andrei in Chekhov's *The Three Sisters*. He was made an honorary fellow of the Welsh College of Music and Drama in July, 1997. He read Bram Stoker's *Dracula* in eight episodes on Radio 2 in December, 1997. His films include *The Family Way, Percy, Loot* and *Virgin Soldiers*.

The 'baby-faced' star was once married to the 1960s starlet, Cathy McGowan, co-hostess of the definitive sixties pop show, *Ready Steady Go*, famous to a generation for its weekly incantation "The Weekend Starts Here". His performance in an episode of the BBC detective series *Dirty Work* set in Cardiff, certainly caught Caroline Boucher's eye. Writing in *The Observer* on March 12th, 2000, she had nothing but good to say about Bennett's role, firmly believing that he had stolen the show. Rhodri Owen in the *Western Mail*, Saturday, March 18th, 2000 was not so impressed, however. "Sadly," he wrote, "all credibility finally snapped under the weight of Hywel Bennett's over-the-top 'look-you' hoodlum as he held a funeral for his late lamented fish".

MAX BOYCE

Welsh-speaking Maxwell Boyce was born in Glyn Neath in 1943. His father died just a month before he was born after a mining accident at the Onllwyn Colliery not far from Banwen. Also called Maxwell but known to everyone as Leonard, he had been married for just three years to Max's mother, Mary Elizabeth. After the death of her husband she took Max and went to live with her sister and her family. He regards himself as not just a comedian but a raconteur and anyone who has listened to his long, involved and convoluted tales of mirth and merriment will know what he means. After leaving school at the age of fifteen without any qualifications he found work down his local pit. Wishing to become a mining engineer he spent five years as an apprentice electrician with the National Coal Board before being given a place at the Treforest School of Mines. In his spare time he learnt to play the guitar and appeared regularly every Friday night at the Valley Folk Club in Pontardawe. He also found himself writing songs about subjects he had first hand knowledge of and decided to turn professional in 1973, giving up his job as a maintenance electrician. (In the late 1960s he was given three-and-a-half minutes to show what he could do on the BBC's *Opportunity Knocks* but success eluded him.) He started playing the working men's and rugby clubs with his brand of music and humour. (Latterly, he has made his mark as a story teller and raconteur rather than a mere joke teller).

He first made an impact on a national basis when *Max Boyce in Concert* was first shown on television in 1977. Since his breakthrough as a singer and poet-cum-comedian, Boyce has made many more TV appearances, including BBC Wales's The St. David's Special *How Green Was My Father* with Ryan Davies, and the 1985 *Boyce Goes West* which featured Max riding a steer at the Rodeo. Apart from Britain he has taken his stage act to such places as New Zealand, Hong Kong, Kathmandu, California and Abu Dhabi, and his albums have sold by the million all over the world.

His first LP *Live at Treorchy* had an inauspicious beginning. Only one hundred of the two hundred and fifty tickets needed to fill the club and give the record that precious 'live' atmosphere had been sold. It looked as if his first disc was going to be a wash-out. However, and in the nick of time, Max had the brainwave of giving the rest of the tickets away free. His friends raced through the streets of Treorchy giving away the tickets to anyone who would have them. The ploy worked. Max got his sell-out atmosphere and the record succeeded beyond his wildest dreams. It hit the shops in 1975, got to Number 21 in the L. P. Charts and remained in the Top 40 list for a total of thirty-two weeks.

His emphasis on Wales and his stage props - the giant leek and Welsh rugby scarf led to some regarding him as the worst kind of 'professional Welshman', (*The Independent on Sunday* called him a "professional Taff" in October, 1999) but his songs such as *The Pontypool Front Row* and *Hymns and Arias* (the latter being sung as a kind of unofficial Welsh national anthem at international rugby matches) struck a chord with a public used to the success of the 1970s 'Golden Era' Welsh rugby teams. Incidentally, the same song was sung by the Glamorgan cricket team as they celebrated their title-clinching defeat of Somerset at Taunton in September, 1997.

His follow-up L.P. to *Live at Treorchy, We All Had Doctors' Papers* did even better reaching the coveted Number One spot. He guested on the Parkinson and Wogan chat shows and played the London Palladium and the Royal Albert Hall to packed houses. Unfortunately for Max, however, his fortunes had now become inextricably linked with those of the Welsh Rugby Team and, when the National Fifteen went into decline during the 1980s, his star began to wane with them. But he kept on going and, latterly, he has experienced something of a comeback. He appeared on TV's test of wit and quick-fire repartee *Have I Got News For You*, and did not disgrace himself. He also toured South Africa, for six weeks at seventeen different venues, playing to crowds of over nine thousand in Johannesburg.

His December 21st, 1998 Christmas special *An Evening With Max Boyce* filmed in front of a celebrity audience attracted BBC Wales's biggest audience of the year - 574,000 viewers. At Wembley Stadium on Sunday, April 11th, 1999 he performed his new version of *Hymns and Arias* in front of a capacity crowd - a fitting prelude to what would prove to be a stunning Welsh victory over England. He appeared in the October, 1999 Rugby World Cup opening ceremony. Max was also one of the guests at the Cardiff Bay Voices of a Nation concert to mark the National Assembly of Wales's official opening. In the 2000 New Year's Honours List he was awarded an MBE. Max and his wife Jean have two daughters.

RICHARD BURTON

It was the voice that made him. Described by one of his biographers (Peter Stead) as being of "wonderful precision, clarity and firmness" and the voice "of a preacher and a believer", it was a beautiful instrument, distinctive and, once heard, never forgotten.

The owner of this wonderful voice was born Richard Walter Jenkins on November 10th, 1925 in a semi-detached house called Danybont in the village of Pontrhydyfen near Port Talbot. (The house had been rented to his family by a woman called Elizabeth Clement.) He was the twelfth of thirteen children. His mother, aged forty-two at the time of his birth, would die when he was two years old. His father, a miner, was prone to long drinking binges. On the death of his mother, the young Richard went to live with his sister, Cis, and her husband, and stayed with them for the next fifteen years. He attended Eastern Infants' School and, at the age of eleven, was accepted into Port Talbot Secondary School after passing a scholarship.

The young Richard Jenkins grew up a rugby-loving, beer-drinking, independent-minded, literature-liking womaniser. Once he reached the fifth form at school, he chose to leave and take a job in the local Co-operative shop as a haberdasher's assistant but, his old primary school teacher, Meredith Jones, managed to get him back into his former grammar school eighteen months after he had left it. Philip Burton was the schoolmaster who ran the Air Training Corps at the school. Not long after Richard's return to full-time education, he took the wayward pupil under his wing and, on March 1st, 1943, Richard Walter Jenkins became part of Philip Burton's household at 6, Connaught Street, Port Talbot where he lived with his landlady Mrs. Smith. Burton coached the young boy so well that he passed seven subjects in his School Certificate exams. Together, they read verse and rehearsed Shakespeare and psalms in the quiet of Mrs. Smith's living room.

Philip Burton was now virtually a surrogate father to his young protégé, Richard lived under his roof, ate his food and was generally looked after by him. He used his contacts to get Richard into Exeter College, Oxford for some six months before he was called up into the RAF. At this point it seems to have been decided that it would be best if Burton adopted Richard. He became his legal guardian, his name was changed by deed poll and Richard Burton was 'born'.

(It may be appropriate here to say a word or two about Philip Henry Burton without whom there may very well have been no Richard Burton, actor of world renown. Although inevitably overshadowed by the man he helped to make famous, Philip Burton was not without some entertaining talents of his own. He was born in Mountain Ash on November 30th, 1904, the son of Emma Burton and Henry Burton, a coal miner and will always be

Richard Burton as Jimmy Porter in Look Back in Anger

remembered for the part he played in furthering Richard Burton's acting career. As we have heard he became the young Richard Jenkins's mentor, teacher and legal guardian giving him his own surname, the name by which he was to become world famous. The two men became so entwined that, when told of his father's death in 1957, Richard's first reaction was to ask "which one"?

Philip Burton attended his local university college where he read history and maths. He then moved to Port Talbot to teach and, in his spare time, wrote plays (unsuccessfully) for the West End theatres. Then he met Richard Jenkins and both men's lives were changed forever, but Philip seems always to have had an element of the Svengali about him. Before he became involved with Richard he had helped launch the career of Owen Jones, another Port Talbot boy. Jones won a scholarship to RADA and appeared on stage at the Old Vic playing Laertes to Olivier's Hamlet.

During the war Philip Burton wrote radio plays for the BBC. His *San Demetrio* told how a badly damaged tanker was able to reach port safely using a school atlas. The programme was broadcast no less than three times on the Home Service and a number of times on the Overseas Service. It was even made into a film, the first time that a radio play had ever been turned into a cinema film. Other programmes Burton was involved with included *Pride of Britain* which celebrated the second anniversary of the successful evacuation of Dunkirk. After the War he began carving out a new career for himself. He first worked in Cardiff as a producer for the BBC. He produced *The Battle for Coal* and then, in 1948, he produced a series which had as its aim the improving of relations within the coal industry. In the 1950s Burton headed for America. He landed first in New York where he founded the American Music and Dramatic Academy and later moved to Key West in Florida where he set about writing books and publishing his memoirs. He never married.

Philip Burton once said of Richard: "He came into my life in 1943 and out of it in 1984" (the year Richard died). Even so, their relationship was not without its dramas. After Richard became divorced from his first wife Sybil, Philip did not speak to him for three years. (In the end he accepted Elizabeth Taylor and became as fond of her and of Richard's other two wives as he had been of Sybil.) Eventually he became reconciled with Richard Burton when the actor asked him to help with rehearsals for a performance of *Hamlet* in Toronto. In 1960, Philip was called in to take over from Moss Hart after the latter had collapsed during the pre-Broadway tour of *Camelot* featuring Richard Burton as King Arthur. Philip took over as director and, according to *The Times* obituarist, made a great difference to the organisation of the production.

He died on January 28th, 1995, in a Florida hospital aged ninety. The previous week he had become seriously ill and was moved to hospital from the nursing home he had been living in since suffering a stroke in 1993.

A Memorial Service was held for Philip Burton on St. Valentine's Day, February 14th, 1995 at the church he had regularly attended – St. Paul's

Church, Key West, Florida. Sally Burton, Richard Burton's last wife, was amongst the mourners. Regarded by many as one of the greatest Shakespeare scholars in the world, Burton had expressed a wish for his ashes to be scattered in three places: Mountain Ash, where he was born; New York, where he first set eyes on the United States and Stratford on Avon, because of his great love and regard for Shakespeare. In the event his ashes were buried alongside his parents in Mountain Ash cemetery.)

Richard Burton's first stage success was in 1943 when Emlyn Williams cast him, in his first professional appearance, as Glan in *Druid's Rest*, first in Liverpool at the Royal Court, and then in London in January, 1944. (The first words Burton spoke in the play were in Welsh - his audition for the play had been at the Sandringham Hotel in Cardiff, following a newspaper advertisement in the *Western Mail*.) That same year, April, 1944, he went up to Exeter College, Oxford University. After serving in the RAF, which he left in 1948, he returned to acting in *Castle Anna* at the Lyric Theatre in Hammersmith.

He then went on to appear in three Christopher Fry plays: *The Lady's Not For Burning* (1949), *Boy With A Cart* (1950) and *A Phoenix Too Frequent* (also 1950). The London cast of *The Lady's Not For Burning* transferred to New York and Burton made his Broadway debut in November, 1950. In 1951, he played Prince Hal. In 1953, he was Hamlet, Coriolanus and Othello and people were now beginning to sit up, take notice and label him the new Olivier but, after the 1956 production of *Othello*, in which he played alternately the parts of Othello and Iago, Burton virtually bade farewell to the English stage. (In the original January 1954 Third Programme performance of Dylan Thomas's *Under Milk Wood*, he had read the Narrator and First Voice, a role the author himself had been set to perform before his untimely death - Thomas died two months before the broadcast went out over the radio.)

In 1960 he took the part of King Arthur in the Lerner and Loewe musical *Camelot* and, in 1964, he played Hamlet in New York. The Broadway *Hamlet* was a huge box-office success with Burton's 136 consecutive performances helping to bring in gross takings (including the record and film versions of the play) of some six million dollars. He moved house to the village of Céligny in Switzerland in 1967 to avoid the punitive British tax system.

His passionate, stormy relationship with Elizabeth Taylor first began on the set of *Cleopatra* in 1963 although the couple had actually first met eight years before. At the time *Cleopatra* was being filmed Taylor was still married to singer Eddie Fisher. Taylor and Burton divorced on June 26th, 1974 - married in Montreal, their marriage had lasted a little over ten years. In 1975, the couple remarried in Botswana, but, at Christmas of that year, Burton met Suzy Hunt (then married to James Hunt, the racing driver, but on the point of divorcing him) and told Taylor he wanted to divorce her to marry Suzy. He married Susan Hunt in Virginia in August, 1976 and divorced her on February 28th, 1983. It was then the turn of Sally Hay, a former BBC continuity girl, whom he married in Las Vegas in July, 1983.

Towards the end of his life he suffered from severe back pain and, at one stage, withering pain in both arms. He died, aged 58, in a Geneva hospital from a cerebral haemorrhage on Sunday, August, 5th, 1984. He had complained of a headache at his Céligny home and was taken to hospital in the morning. He died at three in the afternoon with his wife Sally Hay at his bedside. On Thursday, August 9th, he was buried in Céligny. At the funeral, his daughter, Kate, read the Dylan Thomas poem *Do Not Go Gentle Into That Good Night.* Burton's brother, Graham Jenkins, read in both English and Welsh from First Corinthians, Chapter 13 and Welsh language hymns were sung.

There were memorial services in New York, Los Angeles, London and, last but not least, Pontrhydyfen where it had all started. The Pontrhydyfen service was held in the village's Bethel chapel. Sir Geraint Evans and Stuart Burrows were present. Brooke Williams, Burton's godson and Emlyn Williams's son gave a reading as did his daughter, Kate, and his brother, Graham. Elizabeth Taylor was to have attended but did not. She later visited Burton's family in Wales. (She went to his grave in Switzerland on Sunday, August 12th but was forced to leave without seeing it because of the great numbers of photographers and tourists.)

On film Richard Burton played Trotsky, Tito, Wagner and Mark Anthony. The roll call of his fifty five cinema films includes: *The Last Days of Dolwyn, The Robe, Alexander the Great, Look Back in Anger, Cleopatra, Becket, The Spy Who Came in from the Cold, Who's Afraid of Virginia Woolf, Dr. Faustus, Where Eagles Dare, Anne of the Thousand Days, Under Milk Wood* and *The Wild Geese.* His last film was the Mike Radford directed *1984* in 1984. He was nominated a record seven times for an Academy Award (once as Best Supporting Actor in the 1952 film *My Cousin Rachel* and six times for Best Actor - *The Robe* (1953); *Becket* (1964); *The Spy Who Came In From The Cold* (1965); *Who's Afraid of Virginia Woolf?* (1966); *Anne of the Thousand Days* (1969) and *Equus* (1977)) but the prize always eluded him. Nor was he ever knighted and he had to make do with a CBE awarded in 1970.

Burton's first marriage was to Sybil Williams. Described in Alexander Walker's book on Rachel Roberts as "a tenaciously academic actress", she was born in Wales. Her father died when she was at a young age and her two sisters raised her and gave her a good education. She moved to England to stay with one of her sisters and went to a London acting school. She was an extra (playing the part of a Welsh peasant lady) paid by the day in the Emlyn Williams directed film *The Last Days of Dolwyn.* It was on the set of this film that she first met Burton whom she married in February, 1949.

Said to have not taken her own acting career very seriously, at Stratford, in the early 1950s, she, and Rachel Roberts, filled some relatively minor Shakespearian parts. In the first performance of *Under Milk Wood,* she played Miss Myfanwy Price, Second Woman and Second Neighbour.

According to Eddie Fisher's autobiography *Been There Done That* published in October 1999, Fisher approached Sybil when the Elizabeth Taylor/Richard Burton affair started to become serious, but she calmly replied that she intended to do nothing as Burton always returned to her. Nevertheless, she gatecrashed the shooting of *Cleopatra* and filming had to be stopped, costing the producers a cool $100,000. Then, in March, 1963, Burton met Sybil in the foyer of the Savoy Hotel and asked for a separation. Despite all the advice of family and friends he wanted to be with Elizabeth Taylor. Sybil flew to New York where she granted Burton his separation. (At first, she did not want a divorce but, when the divorce eventually came through in December, 1963, she received a generous settlement from Burton). She invested in a small theatre just off Broadway and opened a nightclub called Arthur's, which she organised so well that it rapidly became one of New York's most successful nightspots. In 1965, she wed Jordan Christopher, the leader of The Wild Ones, a rock group that had played in Arthur's. Eleven years her junior, he would later become a Hollywood actor.

Married five times, including two marriages to Elizabeth Taylor, Richard Burton also enjoyed innumerable affairs - Susan Strasberg and Claire Bloom being just two of his 'flings'. Claire Bloom even wrote that Burton was her first, her "greatest love", the only man to whom she had fervently and completely given all of herself. Joan Collins was less impressed. She played opposite Burton in *Seawife*, and conceded that his voice was amazing and his eyes piercingly green, but found his face with its lined features to be rather coarse, pockmarked and pitted as it was.

John Gielgud was kinder. He recognised Burton's immense generosity, but thought that he would have been just as happy drinking with his mates in a pub, talking and telling tales as he would have been on the stage thrilling an audience. He described the man from Pontrhydyfen as a "strange mixture of naivety and sophistication". "He came out of nowhere", said Gielgud and, indeed, Burton never went to Drama School nor did he spend much time learning his trade with one of the long established provincial repertory companies.

No less a personage than Marlene Dietrich was enamoured of Burton. In her autobiography, she praised him to the skies, calling him not just a great actor, but a heart-throb, a man who fairly exuded charisma, in short, the kind of man of whom young girls and young women dreamt at night. The great German actress proceeded to lament the fact that she happened to meet the Welshman when he had given his heart to another woman and insisted that she would have flown to London just to watch Burton make his stage comeback, she rated him so highly as an actor. She also praised him for never having stooped so low as to endorse commercial products in advertisements.

A raconteur and a conversationalist, a great reader, a great drinker (by the end of his life he was drinking too much) and a gifted mimic, Burton had literary pretensions and went to Oxford for summer courses. He was friends with Rex Harrison, Marlon Brando, Robert Kennedy and the Duke and Duchess of Windsor, Prince Rainier and Princess Grace, Marshal Tito and the French Rothschilds. Nevertheless, despite his high profile friends and his rise to fame Richard Burton never forgot his Welsh roots. A native Welsh speaker, he always insisted on having St. David's Day off and called his house in Switzerland *Le Pays de Galles* (French for Wales).

JOHN CALE

The Western Mail has called him "Wales's most gifted musician" and "The Godfather of Rock" dubbing his 1998 album *Dance Music* "breathtaking". *Wales on Sunday* called him a "cult rock star". For *The South Wales Argus* he was

John Cale

"a child prodigy who became a frazzled genius". (At one stage in his career he thought nothing of beheading chickens live on stage.) His autobiography *What's Welsh for Zen?* was published in 1999.

Born March 9th, 1942 in the village of Garnant, not far from Ammanford in West Wales, John Cale's father, William, was a coal miner whilst his mother, Margaret, taught in a primary school. Both his parents were Welsh-speaking and Cale himself, their only son, has said "I spoke Welsh. I learnt English in school".

As a boy his talents lay in the world of classical music - he took piano lessons when aged about seven - and started playing the organ in the local church. He then went to Ammanford for organ lessons and to play in a larger church. His mother encouraged him to devote himself to music. At the age of ten he was sitting about four music exams a year and spending all his evenings practising. By the time he was thirteen he was playing viola with the Welsh National Youth Orchestra. (He took up the instrument at Amman Valley Grammar School allegedly because it was the only instrument the school had left.)

Cale studied viola and keyboards at Goldsmiths' College in London. He graduated from the University of London and then won a Leonard Bernstein scholarship to study at the famous Tanglewood Music College in Massachusetts. Here he came under the influence of John Cage who was well known for his compositions without either melody or harmony. Next Cale moved to New York where for a time he slept on friends' sofas, before selling his air ticket back to Wales to find an apartment in New York, and make his way in the Big Apple. Cale soon became involved in the avant-garde music scene of the time. He was one of the pianists who performed Eric Satie's eighteen hours and forty minutes long *Vexations* at the Pocket Theatre. He then became a member of La Monte Young's Theatre of Eternal Music and formed a group called the Dream Syndicate with which he played for about eighteen months. (During his time with La Monte Young, Cale learnt how to amplify his viola so as to achieve the powerful drone effect which would have such an influence on the Velvet Underground's future sound.)

Then came the meeting with Lou Reed and the formation of the legendary Velvet Underground. (The group's name was derived from a trashy sadomasochist novel they found lying in the street.) For a year they rehearsed together at Cale's apartment in Ludlow Street. By 1965 the leader of the then Pop Art Scene, Andy Warhol, had become aware of their existence and invited them to his Factory, the centre of the New York Underground scene. Much against the wishes of Cale and Reed, Warhol recommended that the group adopt German-born Nico as their female lead singer. Warhol became the group's first manager and, in May, 1966, produced their first L.P. *Velvet Underground and Nico* a seminal recording in the history of rock music, although at the time of its release the majority of record buyers resolutely refused to recognise its significance and it sold comparatively few copies. In the event Warhol was proved to be right - Nico's amazing voice gave the band that extra edge. Cale, too, made a significant contribution to the group's musical ethos until he was fired from the band following personality differences with Lou Reed, leaving Velvet Underground in 1968. (The two would not speak to each other for years although, in time, they eventually patched up their differences.) Since the group split up Cale has achieved cult status and released a continuous series of some twenty-five solo albums including *Paris 1919* (described by *The Virgin Encyclopedia of Seventies Music* as 'haunting', it is regarded by many as his finest work), *Fear, Music For A New Society, Walking On Locusts* and *Words For The Dying* (released in 1989 it featured Cale's settings of some of Dylan Thomas's poems).

As well as viola and piano he also plays guitar and performs his own idiosyncratic, not to say unique live rendition of the old Elvis Presley standard *Heartbreak Hotel* and a rock version of Chuck Berry's *Memphis Tennessee.* Lou Reed paid him the compliment of saying "I always enjoyed playing music with John ... music runs out of him like water down a mountain". Cale himself said "The thing I grew most from was being on stage and performing".

He has also collaborated on albums with Lou Reed, Brian Eno and Bob Neuwirth. He produced Iggy Pop and The Stooges, Squeeze, The Happy Mondays, punk poet Patti Smith's 1975 album *Horses* and, in 1990, collaborated with Lou Reed on the critically acclaimed *Songs For Drella* which paid homage to their recently deceased ex-mentor Andy Warhol. The Velvet

Underground reformed in 1993 but it did not take long for the old animosities between Cale and Reed to resurface and the Welshman was soon back to a solo career, singing and performing in his own inimitable, idiosyncratic manner. He has written the music for many films as well as ballets (one of his ballets was devoted to the life and times of Nico who died at the age of forty-nine, ravaged by alcohol and heroin) and orchestral pieces.

Although anxious to leave Wales as soon as he could in his early years (as a boy in Garnant he was fascinated with the idea of New York and listened avidly to The Voice of America and Radio Moscow), he has kept his Welsh heritage alive - he called his daughter Eden Myfanwy and wrote the soundtrack for the Welsh film *House of America*. John Cale's attitude to his homeland also appears to have mellowed as he grows older. He has made several trips home (he headlined the 1998 Hay Festival) and collaborated with a number of home grown Welsh bands on a film called *Beautiful Mistake* which was shown at the Aberystwyth Film Festival in April, 2000. The bands involved included Super Furry Animals, The Manic Street Preachers, Gorky's Zygotic Mynci and Catatonia as well as the Welsh-language hip-hop band Tystion. Now resident in New York City, Cale has spent most of his adult life in America so much so that he has been dubbed "The Welsh New Yorker". "The bard of the black piano", as *The Western Mail* called him, has come a long way from the days in Garnant when a childhood friend, speaking on *The Slate* programme about Cale, recalled him being so frightened of returning home late that he collapsed when he saw his mother coming to look for him.

SIR LEWIS CASSON

Sir John Gielgud called him "a fighter" but others were not so charitable. The comedian and wit Kenneth Williams thought him "a stupid man" and "a fool" and rejoiced in his diaries on Saturday, May 17th, 1969 that "that ghastly old man Lewis Casson is dead". Kenneth Williams's opinion notwithstanding, Lewis Casson was on stage from 1904 to 1967, appearing in plays by Ibsen, Vanbrugh and Shakespeare. In the early 1920s he appeared with his wife Sybil Thorndyke in a series of *Grand Guignol* theatre pieces in London. (For two years he appeared at the Little Theatre with wife Sybil and brother-in-law Russell Thorndyke in such *Grand Guignol* classics as *The Kill, Fear* and *The Hound of Death.*) He also directed and produced, so much so that his acting sometimes suffered and he was often referred to simply as "Sybil Thorndike's husband". He directed not only his wife but also Ivor Novello, Laurence Olivier, (in his role as Henry V) Gertrude Lawrence and Douglas Fairbanks. He played Griffith in Shakespeare's *Henry VIII* and was in Shaw's *St. Joan*.

For the last ten years of his life he could not see to read and became increasingly deaf. He was also finding it difficult to walk. Nevertheless, with his 92nd birthday only a few months away, he appeared in Bristol and Southsea, with Sybil and ex-pop star Adam Faith, playing the Judge in *Night Must Fall*.

On Tuesday, May 13th, 1969, he was taken to London's Nuffield Hospital and his family told that he was seriously ill. He died there on May 16th, 1969. He was 93 years of age. A Memorial Service was held at Westminster Abbey on Tuesday, June 3rd, 1969. Lewis's son, John, read his father's favourite poem, *Margaritae Sorori* by W.E. Henley and John Gielgud read one of Prospero's speeches from *The Tempest*, the one beginning "Our revels now are ended".

Noted for his socialist and pacifist views (he actively supported the 1926 General Strike), Lewis Casson was born in Birkenhead in 1875, one of seven children. His father was Major Thomas Casson, J.P. of Ffestiniog and Porthmadog. Lewis attended Ruthin Grammar School and then the Central Technical College in South Kensington. He started out as a teacher, became apprenticed to an organ building firm in London and began to take an interest in the theatre, doing amateur dramatics in his spare time and then turned professional in 1903.

His first professional job was playing a minor role in a play called *The Duke of Killiecrankie*. He was then asked by Harley Granville Barker to become a member of the Vedrenne Barker company which acted at the Court Theatre in London's Sloane Square. In 1907 Lewis joined Miss Horniman's company which was just starting up in Manchester. He became the leading director for Miss Horniman at her Manchester Gaiety Theatre, and it was here that he met Sybil Thorndike, who was to be his wife for over sixty years.

He married Sybil Thorndike at Aylesford Church, Kent in December, 1908. It was Lewis who was able to restrain Sybil's enthusiasms on stage and stop them from getting out of hand. Stories about the couple abound, they were supposed to learn passages of Greek verse over the breakfast table, Gielgud recalled that Sybil once said to Lewis: "Oh, Lewis, if only we could be the first actors to play on the moon".

In the First World War he joined the Army Service Corps as a camp cook and then drove lorries. He became a captain in the Royal Engineers in 1916. Wounded, he was awarded the MC.

In 1930, Lewis and Sybil, along with Godfrey Tearle, Dame May Whitty, her husband Ben Webster and others founded Equity, the British Actors' Union. (Lewis was President of the Union from 1940 to 1945). In 1940, he and Sybil toured the mining villages of Wales with their production of *Macbeth*. He was knighted in 1945.

Lewis Casson played the Earl of Kent in *King Lear* at the Old Vic in 1940. He also directed the play together with Harley Granville-Barker. He played Antigonus in *The Winter's Tale* at the Phoenix Theatre in 1951. He was Friar Lawrence in the 1952 Old Vic production of *Romeo and Juliet* with Claire Bloom and Alan Badel playing the two principals. Still acting when he was 90, in his long stage career he also played Petruchio, Shylock, Owen Glendower, Benedick, Henry V, Macbeth and Socrates. His films include: *The Merchant of Venice* (1927), *Midshipman Easy* (1935), *South Riding* (1938), *The Winslow Boy* (1948) and *Shake Hands with the Devil* (1959).

CATATONIA

Wales on Sunday calls her 'The Queen of Pop'. Andrew Smith in *The Sunday Times* labelled her "Pop's new Princess of Wales" (and why not - she has been known to wear a tiara on stage). Clearly intrigued, if not smitten, by the Welsh singer, Smith went on to compare her to sixties star Marianne Faithfull and Jefferson Airplane's loud-voiced singer, Grace Slick. With a voice variously described as "gravelly", "unique", "rasping", "throaty", "breathy" and "superb", she has what is known as a "feisty", "bolshy " personality, (she was once referred to as "a cross between Nancy Sinatra and Tank Girl"), and is famed for her ability to sink copious amounts of alcohol. We are, of course, talking about Cerys Matthews. Most newspaper articles devoted to Catatonia are, in reality about Cerys. Very little, if anything at all is said about the 'blokes' who make up the rest of the band and contribute to the overall sound. Similarly, Cerys appears to hog all the photographs. Very rarely do the men get a look in. Just for the record, then, here goes. The 'blokes' are Owen Powell, Mark Roberts and Paul Jones all of whom come from Cardiff and Aled Richards, a 'Scarlet' from Llanelli. Cerys herself comes from Pembrokeshire. For the time being, at least, the rest of the band appear to be happy with this arrangement and content to see Cerys pick up the Sexiest Women awards while they languish in the background. (Still, Deborah Harry and Blondie seem to have had the same scenario going for a long time and it doesn't appear to have done them any permanent harm.)

So, for Catatonia, read Cerys Matthews? Born April 11th, 1969 in Canton, Cardiff, she was brought up in Morriston, Swansea. She was one of four children - she had two brothers and one sister. Her mother Pauline's family came from Devon whilst her father's family hailed from Pembrokeshire. Each of their children had an English name and a Welsh name and, in the beginning, Cerys went by the name of Elizabeth. Her father was a consultant at Swansea's Morriston Hospital. Cerys/Elizabeth attended Cwmbwrla Welsh medium Primary School in Swansea and Brynymor Junior School. She then went to a private school - St. Michael's School in Llanelli where she took three sciences at 'A' level. At St. Michael's the first instrument she learned to play was the violin. Hers was, apparently, an average talent, but she was good enough to play in the school orchestra and sporty enough to make the school hockey team. She never really had any formal musical training - she would later buy a book which taught her how to play the blues - and never joined a stage school.

Aged nineteen she spent a period of three years working for Pembrokeshire County Council during the summer, collecting debris from the county's villages and beaches. At one stage she attempted to follow in the family tradition and trained to become a psychiatric nurse, when all she really wanted to do was to become another Bob Dylan, but felt unable to let her family in on the secret. Then, realising that nursing was not for her, she gave it up and, at the age of twenty-two, decided to move to Cardiff. It was there that she met Mark Roberts and Catatonia came into being.

Mark Roberts, who had been lead singer and guitarist with the Welsh language band *Y Cyrff* for ten years, heard her singing in the street one day, liked what he heard and convinced the other members of the group that she should join them as their new frontwoman. They changed their name to Catatonia and recorded their first demo disc at Cardiff's Grass Roots Studios. At first, the group wrote only in Welsh, but Grass Roots Studio manager, Paul Durrant, advised them to start writing some songs in English. (Subsequently Cerys worked in the video department at the studio for about nine months.)

Catatonia played their first gig at *The Yellow Kangaroo* pub in Cardiff. Then they took to the stage at Clwb Ifor Bach, Cardiff's Welsh language club, where they were signed up by Crai Records, a Welsh record label. Here they released *Tinkerbell* which the *New Musical Express* pronounced Single of the Week, an almost unheard of accolade for a Welsh language recording, yet, despite such praise, it failed to make a dent in the charts. Both their first two E.P.s with Crai were, unusually for a Welsh record label, well received by the music papers. In 1994, Catatonia appeared a few times on S4C's *Dim Tafod* show but the line-up at that time included Dafydd (now with The Super Furry Animals) on drums and their current guitarist Owen was then with the Crumblowers.

In 1995 they signed to Blanco y Negro, a Warners label (they were the first bilingual band to be signed by a prestigious record label) and released their first album *Way Beyond Blue* including *You've Got A Lot To Answer For* which featured on the soundtrack of the Swansea-based film *Twin Town*.

By 1996 they had done two national tours but their big break came with the release of *International Velvet*, their second album which was full of catchy tunes and sing along choruses. (The title track *International Velvet* with its "Every day when I wake up, I thank the Lord I'm Welsh" refrain has already become another Welsh national anthem.) The album reached Number One in the charts on May 16th, 1998, stayed there for a week and went platinum. It sold 700,000 copies and was voted the 1998 Album of the Year by *The Melody Maker's* music writers. Andrew Smith in *The Sunday Times* dubbed it "something of a triumph".

I Am The Mob was the first single from *International Velvet* to hit the charts but it only got to Number 40 before sinking back into obscurity. In so doing it followed the lead set by the band's previous two singles *Lost Cat Sweet Catatonia* and *You've Got A Lot To Answer For* which also only just made the Top Forty. In January, 1998 *Mulder and Scully* hit the Top Ten. (The video for the single was filmed in T.J.'s Club in Newport.) Later, in May, 1998 the band flew to New York to promote the single, their first to be released in the U.S. *Road Rage* was a Top Ten hit in 1998 - it reached Number 5 and *The Melody Maker* writers voted it the Second Best Single of the Year.

In April, 1998, their third album *Equally Cursed And Blessed* sold one hundred thousand copies in a week and went straight into the charts at Number One. (The HMV store in Cardiff made a point of opening specially to meet the demand for the new album.) Harpist Elinor Bennett, wife of former Plaid Cymru President Dafydd Wigley, featured on one of the tracks *Bulimic Beat.* One of the tracks from the album, *Dead From The Waist Down* went in at Number 7 in April, 1999 but subsequently slipped.

In May, 1998 *B Magazine* chose Cerys as one of its Most Successful Women. In September, 1998 the readers of *Melody Maker* magazine voted her 'sexiest lass' (unsurprisingly, the other, male, members of Catatonia did not get a look in).

When Catatonia backed The Manic Street Preachers at the Cardiff International Arena in January, 1999 Cerys wowed the crowd of six thousand people by lying flat on her back and playing the recorder. Now, according to the dictionary definition, Catatonia means "a form of schizophrenia characterised by stupor, with outbreaks of excitement". The "outbreaks of excitement" line seems to belong particularly to Cerys. Finding herself in a rather inebriated state during a TV debate on Welsh devolution at four o'clock in the morning she joined in the argument, but only to ask in Welsh "Who's Sian Lloyd sleeping with now?" and was promptly frozen out by the other participants in the discussion. The miffed weather forecaster, who had not been present, and was herself a staunch devolutionist, at first thought of slapping a writ on Cerys (something along the lines of defamation of character) only to think better of it when she was told that the youth vote was vital if the Yes Campaign was to win. She did, however, go as far as sending a solicitor's letter to the BBC, and S4C apologised for what had happened. Cerys herself told the newspapers: "What it was, there were all these media darlings air-kissing and telling each other how much they loved each other at the party which was on devolution night. And I just questioned their nightly habits. I haven't said anything slanderous."

On May 20th, 3000 it was reported that Cerys along with other members of the band would be adjudicating the best bands in the rock group competition at the Llanelli National Eisteddfod in August, 2000.

CHARLOTTE CHURCH

The rise and rise of Charlotte Church began when, aged eleven, she appeared on Jonathan Ross's *Big, Big Talent Show.* She was supposed to introduce her aunt, Caroline Cooper, a cabaret singer, as the new talent but it would prove her own passport to fame, not Aunt Caroline's. Charlotte sang only four lines of *Pie Jesu* but it was enough to bring her to the attention of agent Jonathan Shalit. He signed her up and got her a five-album deal with Sony in April, 1998 said to be worth at least £100,000.

Her first album *Voice of an Angel* was released in November, 1998. A mixture of Celtic and religious music including some Welsh songs it was recorded with the Welsh National Orchestra and Chorus at the BBC Wales studios in Cardiff in August, 1998 and reached Number One in the British Classical Charts and Number Ten in the Pop Charts. That same year she earned a spot in *The Guinness Book of Records* when she became the youngest ever solo singer to secure an album in the Top Twenty and be Number One in the classical album charts. In March, 1999 the record went straight into the US album charts at Number 28, thus making her the youngest solo singer to hit the US Top Thirty and eclipsing the previous record held by Stevie Wonder. It went on to sell more than a quarter of a million copies in the

Charlotte Church

States and, within its first week of release, had reached the coveted Number One spot in the US Classical album charts. Meanwhile, back in Britain, *Voice of an Angel* had gone double platinum and sales were heading towards the 700,000 mark.

1999 was a full year for Charlotte. *Ascent of an Angel*, a BBC Wales Documentary recording the singer's hectic schedule was seen throughout Great Britain on March 28th, 1999. She sang at the closing ceremony of the Rugby World Cup at Cardiff's Millennium Stadium. Her second album *Charlotte Church* was released in November, 1999 and, by December, had chalked up sales of 500,000 copies in Britain alone. (It went platinum before it was even released.) It revealed a more mature approach and its seventeen tracks featured *Just Wave Hello* - the accompanying song to the Ford Cars TV advertisement - as well as some Welsh songs and opera standards. She sang at the Pope's Vatican City concert in December, 1999, serenaded the Prince of Wales at his fiftieth birthday party and also became the first singer in the world to appear live at the London Millennium Dome when she sang *Just Wave Hello* on December 21st, 1999. (The song was released as a single in December, 1999.) In 1999 she outsold even such established stars as Elton John, Robbie Williams and The Corrs in America, yet at the beginning of the year she was still able to feed the ducks at Roath Park Lake in her home city of Cardiff. With the showing of the Ford TV advert she was seen throughout the world.

TV shows she has appeared on include *Live and Kicking*, *Blue Peter*, *The Des O'Connor Show*, *Good Morning with Richard and Judy* and Gay Byrne's *The Late Late Show in Ireland*. In America she has been seen on *The Jay Leno Show*, *The Today Show*, *The David Letterman Show*, *USA Today* and *The Rosie O'Donnell Show*. In July, 1999 US news giant CBS came to Cardiff to film a ten-minute documentary about her life.

Among those she has met are the British Prime Minister, Tony Blair, Joan Collins, Barry Manilow, Shirley Bassey, Caprice, Gloria Gaynor, George Michael, Geri Halliwell, Mel B and Robbie Williams but the famous person she has most enjoyed meeting is Pope John Paul II. (Charlotte herself is a Catholic.)

Encouraged by such runaway success, Charlotte's mother, Maria, gave up her job as a Cardiff City Council housing officer to accompany her daughter all around the world. With a small entourage which included Richard Leyshon, a former Cardiff City colleague of her mother's, as her personal tutor, Ms. Church travelled the world, taking in Paris, Milan, Düsseldorf, Cologne and Berlin, Hamburg, Dublin and Rome. (When not touring she attends Howells Girls School, Llandaff.)

But it has not all been plain sailing. In 1997 Church tasted rejection when she failed to make the cast of the West End musical *Les Misérables* – she was turned down after the audition judged her voice to be not "good enough".

Young Charlotte is a member of the Rhiwbina Youth Drama Group and has acted in a few school plays but that can scarcely have prepared her for the role she played in the Christmas 1999 production of ITV's *Heartbeat*. She took the part of Katie Kendall, a singer who was unable to sing at the village carol concert, because her parents were going through a bitter divorce. Eventually, of course, Katie relented and regaled the entire village with her rendition of *Ave Maria*. Not surprisingly, perhaps, considering the corniness of the plot, the newspapers had a field day. Westgate in *The Western Mail* for one was not particularly impressed. "Somehow one wishes that Ms. Church would either stick to her singing career or, if she is desperate to act, wait until there is a part that is not so nauseatingly clichéd." *The Observer's* television critic, Kathryn Flett, damned with less than faint praise, casting aspersions on Charlotte's acting ability, and implying that the plot had had to be written especially to fit her in.

The pint-sized diva's image took a further knock (through no fault of her own, it must be said) when, in January, 2000 it was revealed that her manager, Jonathan Shalit had been sacked by her mother. To add insult to injury, Mr. Shalit, who was under contract to manage the star until 2002, first heard the bad news by fax from Charlotte's solicitors. Shalit who had guided her fortunes and brought her to fame, also had the likes of Leo Sayer, Larry Adler and cruise ship star Jane McDonald on his books. He showed no hard feelings towards Charlotte herself calling her "the new Barbara Streisand" and reserving his disdain for her mother who, it was later announced, had taken over as her daughter's manager.

Only time will tell whether child prodigy Charlotte Church is here to stay. There are many examples of child stars who failed to make the grade into adult stardom. Yet others, if not quite continuing to capture the glory of their childhood years, managed to earn a good living as adult entertainers. Whatever becomes of Charlotte when she reaches maturity, no one can deny that, so far, she has packed more into her short life than most of us will ever dream of, let alone experience. After all, anyone who has her own dedicated website, visited on a regular basis by many devoted young admirers, especially from America, must be doing something right.

On the same day that Charlotte celebrated her 14th birthday - Monday, February 21st, 2000 - it was announced that Jonathan Shalit was counter-suing his former protégée for a sum of five million pounds. This followed Charlotte's parents issuing a suit for compensation against Mr. Shalit. There was, after all, plenty of money to play with and for - in March, 2000, Charlotte was placed forty-second in the *Sunday Times* list of the sixty richest people in Great Britain with a personal fortune of £10 million.

Yet by any standards Charlotte Church is a phenomenon. (*The Big Issue* exulted that she had "exploded into the music business like a soprano supernova".) Her records sell by the million, she rubs shoulders with the politically rich and powerful and the glitterati of the world of pop music. She is invited to turn on the Christmas Lights in Cardiff and Covent Garden and jets everywhere around the world. But she is still a fourteen-year-old schoolgirl, with schoolgirl likes and dislikes. She was, for instance, distraught when she had to give up her pet iguana, Iggy, as she was away from home so much, but a fellow pupil from Cardiff's Howells Girls School gave it a good home.

In January, 2000 it was reported that the young singer had rocketed into the Top Ten of Britain's highest rock and pop earners. At Number Ten Charlotte was mixing it with the likes of the Beatles, Rolling Stones, Spice Girls and Robbie Williams.

Soprano star Charlotte Church was born in St. David's Hospital, Cardiff. She comes from a musical background. Her mother Maria says Charlotte listened to the radio from the age of three and started singing the songs she heard. At the age of eight she was singing along to her cabaret singer Aunt Caroline's backing tapes. Her grandfather played the piano and saxophone for a group called The Solid Six - nicknamed Duff, he also played saxophone on a sixties record made by the Newport group, The Interns. Maria, who became pregnant with Charlotte at the age of nineteen had ambitions to become a classical guitarist. An only child, Charlotte started out singing publicly at St. Mary's Roman Catholic church in Canton, Cardiff.

Whilst her personal fortune is said to be some ten million pounds it is being kept in a trust fund for her until she becomes eighteen. At present Charlotte earns £50-00 a month in pocket money. Her own musical likes include Placido Domingo, Lesley Garrett, Maria Callas and Kiri Te Kanawa. In a lighter vein she enjoys the music of The Corrs, Catatonia, Robbie Williams and The Manic Street Preachers.

On Saturday, May 6th, 2000, at the Royal Albert Hall at the holding of the first ever Brit Classical Awards, Charlotte was presented with the Best British Artist Award. She sang two songs at the ceremony – *La Pastorella* and the Welsh hymn tune beloved of rugby supporters, *Cwm Rhondda*. After receiving the Award, Charlotte, never lacking in self confidence, told anyone who would listen that it was not her intention to compete with the likes of teenage pop sensation Britney Spears. Sporting a new look hairdo and trendily dressed, the Cardiff songbird preferred to look upon herself as a future Barbra Streisand or Whitney Houston.

On Monday, June 5th, 2000, Charlotte launched the first-ever official Welsh Top Forty Hit Parade on BBC Radio Wales. She also told the July edition of *Q magazine* that she still harboured hopes of an acting career and was particularly anxious to break into films, but not at any price. She had, it transpired, turned down the chance to play the part of a teenager under the influence of drugs in a Hollywood film. The role had been found for her by her new American agency, the prestigious Los Angeles based William Morris organisation.

PETULA CLARK

Petula Clark's Welsh grandmother would not speak English to her. Her Welsh mother, a soprano, was a "natural singer" and Petula herself would sing anywhere and, in fact, started singing in Wales, in chapel. In an hour long special, *Our Pet*, broadcast on BBC Radio Wales on September 26th, 1999 she

Petula Clark (Petula Clark Fan Club)

stated that "I was a real little Welsh kid, I used to run around the mountains, sliding down the tips. My childhood is about Wales. The things that are important to me happened in Wales."

Petula was born in West Newell, Epsom, Surrey on November 15th, 1932. Her mother, Doris Phillips, was raised as one of three sisters in the little village of Abercanaid, near Merthyr Tydfil. Her father, William Phillips, was a miner. Born in a small cottage in David's Square, Abercanaid, Doris, like her other two sisters, became a nurse and found a job working at Longrove mental hospital, near Epsom where she met a male nurse called Leslie Norman Clark. Coming from the area around Chichester, Leslie had himself harboured theatrical ambitions, but these had been thwarted by his parents. The couple fell in love and married early in 1932.

According to Petula's unofficial biographer, Andrea Kon, Doris and Leslie's first child was registered as just Sally Clark, but the reference books insist on referring to her by three given names: Petula Sally Olwen Clark. (Her father is said to have arrived at the rather unusual Petula by combining the names of two of his old girlfriends: Pet and Ula.)

Like her father before her, she harboured theatrical ambitions. The first play she ever saw was when he took her to see Flora Robson playing Mary Tudor. On their way back home in the bus Pet was very silent and, when Leslie asked her "What are you thinking about", she said "I want to be an actress". Even as a young girl Pet could cleverly mimic the likes of Vera Lynn, Carmen Miranda and Sophie Tucker and, as a small child, she would mount the table in Abercanaid's local pub *The Colliers Arms* and entertain the customers.

She began singing at the age of six and, although "basically a very shy little girl", she made her debut at the age of nine in a Forces' request programme called *It's All Yours* singing *Mighty Like A Rose*. When war was declared Pet and her younger sister Barbara were evacuated to their grandparent's house in Abercanaid, but the house proving to be too small, they were moved to their aunt and uncle's house in neighbouring Pontlottyn. Pet acclimatised so well to her new surroundings that she was soon speaking fluent Welsh, but after about six months she returned to London.

During the war years Petula Clark appeared in over three hundred troop concerts and was often heard on the BBC. The constant entertaining affected her education, so much so that about the only time she spent in real full-time education was at Moor Lane Elementary School and a girls' private day school. Her father Leslie was determined that she should enjoy the showbiz success that had been denied him and pushed her career whenever and wherever he could, but he proved to be a dominating, showbiz parent who would interfere and argue with Pet's producers and directors.

Her first commercial record release was *Put Your Shoes On, Lucy* in 1949. Other hits included *The Little Shoemaker*. (Her first British Top Ten hit, it reached Number 7 and stayed in the Hit Parade for a total of nine weeks.) Soon after she began starring in films, sharing her first kiss with Alec Guinness in *The Card* and dancing with Fred Astaire in *Finian's Rainbow* (1968). She was put under contract to the Rank Organisation and, between 1945 and 1958, made approximately twenty-five films not all of which were critically acclaimed. Ephraim Katz for one was dismissive of her film appearances saying they were "mostly in syrupy roles in films of little consequence".

"Syrupy" or not her films included *Medal for the General* (her first in 1944) and *Strawberry Roan* (1944), *I Know Where I'm Going* (1945), *London Town* (starring the acclaimed English comedian Sid Field, whose daughter Pet played, the much hyped 1947 film was a commercial and critical disaster), *Vice Versa* (1947 with Anthony Newley), *Here Come The Huggetts* (1948), *Vote for Huggett* and *The Huggetts Abroad* (1949), *Dance Hall* (1950, *The*

Card (1952), *The Happiness of Three Women* (1954), the 1969 *Goodbye Mr. Chips* (with Peter O'Toole) and *Never Never Land* (1980).

As she moved into adolescence, Pet encountered growing personal problems. Whereas she, naturally, wanted to develop and enjoy being the young woman she was fast becoming, the Great British public still saw her as 'Little Pet' and expected her to stay their little girl and not grow up. Her father, too, was determined that she should maintain her little girl image for as long as possible. When she finally did break from her father (in the business sense), when she was about twenty-five years old, she was devastated to learn that, of all the money she had earned, very little remained. She set about organising her own financial affairs and beginning singing the type of songs she wanted to sing, not the childish tunes others had wanted her to perform. (As a sideline, Petula kept busy working for BBC radio on the long running series *A Life of Bliss* with George Cole.) Her accompanist at this time, as he had been for many years, was Joe 'Mr. Piano' Henderson and the two, almost inevitably perhaps, formed a romantic attachment which, at one stage, looked as if it would lead to marriage, but Joe eventually broke the relationship off.

Resuming her singing career, she branched out into Europe and went over to the Paris Olympia to perform for one night. The next day she met Claude Wolff, the young PR man, who would become her husband and manager. At the time she did not speak a word of French, did not even like France and found it extremely hard going when she first began to work in the country. But her love for Claude pulled her through and she did so well, that, in 1961, she won the French Girl Singer of the Year Award. On June 8th, 1961 Petula married Claude at the town hall in Bourg-la-Reine, Paris (coincidentally, on the same day Shirley Bassey married Kenneth Hume). Petula and Claude would eventually have two daughters and a son.

The hits now began to flow: *Sailor, Ya-Ya* (sung in French), *Romeo* and *Don't Sleep In The Subway* which reached Number 2 in the States. The 1965 Tony Hatch composition *Downtown* was recorded in five different languages and reached Number One in the United States staying in the U.S. hit parade for the grand total of fifteen weeks. *Who Am I* was in the American charts for six weeks. *I Know A Place* got to Number 2 in America and another Tony Hatch/Jackie Trent composition, *My Love* attained the coveted Number One spot in the American charts. *This Is My Song*, the words and music for which were written by Charlie Chaplin, went straight to Number One in Great Britain, all over Europe and in the States.

So much chart success in the States led to her touring the country and she played L.A. to an audience including such entertainment luminaries as Fred Astaire, Lucille Ball (in whose *I Love Lucy* show Pet would later appear), Sammy Davis Junior and Frank Sinatra. They gave her a rapturous reception. She went on to play Ceasar's Palace in Las Vegas and the Copa Cabana nightclub in New York, besides appearing in *The Dean Martin Show* and with Andy Williams on television. She also sang with Jack Jones. She had now not only conquered her own country and France, but also the big one - America. Her French language proficiency also meant that she could tour successfully in Montreal and Quebec as well as the rest of Canada.

Petula is the first ever woman to be featured twice on *This Is Your Life* and she it was who launched the BBC's first ever colour transmission service on November 15th, 1969 at exactly one second after midnight when BBC1 broadcast her Royal Albert Hall concert (the first time she had given a live concert in her own country, since she first appeared at the same venue in 1944, when she was twelve years old) under the title *Just Pet.*

In 1981 she made her West End debut as Maria, Baroness von Trapp in *The Sound of Music* at the Apollo Theatre and took the theatre audiences by storm. Then, in 1989, she proved that she was much more than just a pretty face and a good singer, when her self-penned musical, set in the American Civil War, opened in London. Writing in his book *Our Theatres In The Eighties*, theatre critic Sheridan Morley had this to say: *Someone Like You* is a new and first musical by Petula Clark, for which she has written all the music ... it tackles such issues as slavery, feminism and racial intolerance with a cool intelligence ... this is a highly energised and superbly played musical". In 1993, she appeared on Broadway in Willy Russell's *Blood Brothers*. In 1995 she played Norma Desmond in the musical production of *Sunset Boulevard.* Described by Honor Blackman as "such a little thing" she toured the USA in a new production of *Sunset Boulevard* in September, 1999.

Incredibly, Petula Clark has now been a star for nearly sixty years and her marriage is still going strong. She herself is now nearly sixty-eight, old enough to be drawing her state pension. Not that there is any need of that, of course. Pet, who has been having hit records since 1949, was said by Alan Franks in *The Times* on Saturday, January, 17th, 1998, to have sold more records than either David Bowie, Paul McCartney or the Rolling Stones. Franks went on to write that the different facets of Pet's personality -the child/woman and the woman/child - had succeeded in thoroughly intriguing both the Americans and the French. Indeed, both nations found her really quite sexy. With her Grammy Awards and South Bank specials devoted to her, Pet Clark continues to re-invent herself for each succeeding generation and has even, like those other women with Welsh connections, Shirley Bassey and Dorothy Squires, been transformed into a gay icon. The child-star image - that she tried so hard and so long to shake off - is finally gone.

TOMMY COOPER

Thomas Frederick Cooper was born in a terraced house at Number 19, Llwyn On Street, Caerphilly, on March 9th, 1922. He moved with his family to Exeter (his mother Gertie's hometown) when he was one year old and was brought up and educated there. (His poultry farmer father came from Caerphilly.) He became interested in magic at the age of nine when an aunt presented him with some conjuring tricks. At the age of seventeen he was working as an apprentice shipwright at a shipyard in Hythe, Kent and it was there, in the works canteen, that he performed his first magic show.

When the Second World War broke out he joined the Horse Guards, for which his physique - he stood six feet three inches tall and weighed fifteen stones - amply suited him. He stayed with the guards for some seven years, four of them in the Middle East where he earned his Sergeant's stripes. It was during his time in Egypt that he acquired his trademark Red Fez. He was performing his act in Cairo, wearing a Pith Helmet which, until then, had been his favoured form of headgear, when he noticed that all the waiters were wearing fezzes. He decided to take one himself and wore it on stage ever afterwards.

It was whilst serving in Egypt that he met his wife, Gwendoline (Gwen) Henty whom he himself always called 'Dove'. A skilled pianist she had been sent out to North Africa by the Combined Services organisation to entertain the British soldiers billeted there. The couple met whilst appearing in the same show in Alexandria on Christmas Eve, 1946 and, within two weeks, Tommy had asked her to marry him. Two months after their first meeting in Alexandria they were married in a chapel in Nicosia on the island of Cyprus. Gwen then gave up her own career to support and look after Tommy and, later, their two children, Thomas and Vicky.

In his entertaining and informative biography of the lunatic magician, Jeremy Novick wrote that the couple enjoyed "one of those 'partnership' marriages where both parties know exactly what their role is and both get on with it. Gwen's role was sorting out the finances, keeping the house, cooking the food, making Tommy as many raspberry sponges as he could eat. Tommy's role was being Tommy Cooper".

After leaving the army Tommy was auditioned by Scotsman Miff Ferrie (a one-time trombone player with a group named The Jackdaws) who advised him to drop the rather poor comedy impressions he had been peddling at the time and switch to comedy and magic. Tommy took Ferrie's advice and the latter promptly booked him for his November, 1947 floor show at The Windermere. Cooper had found his niche. His bungled conjuring tricks that never quite came off, his "Just like that" catchphrase and his inspired line in crazy repartee (nobody else could have got away with the jokes that he did - one particularly hilarious anecdote about bringing down the Walls of Jericho seemed to go on forever) ensured that he blew the house down. In reality, he was, of course, a first class magician and belonged to the Magic Circle's Inner Six but he soon discovered that making people laugh was where his true talents lay. And, with Cooper, making people laugh did not seem to be all that difficult. Indeed, he merely had to walk on stage, say nothing and just stand there and the audience would be besides themselves with laughter.

On Christmas Eve, 1947, Tommy made his TV debut in Leslie Henson's *Christmas Party*. He then had eighteen weeks at The Windermere before appearing at other well known West End night clubs. He also began touring the music halls and, at times, was doing as many as fifty-two shows a week. He made his first London Palladium appearance in July, 1952. He then undertook a headlining tour of the Moss Empire Theatres circuit before touring with the revue *Peep Show* in Spring, 1953. Tommy co-starred at the Prince of Wales Theatre with Benny Hill (for seventeen months) and Shirley Bassey (for ten months). The Variety Club named him ITV Personality of the Year in 1969.

Tommy Cooper worked in America appearing in Las Vegas and he also made a few appearances on *The Ed Sullivan Show*. Tom to his friends, he starred in a few British films towards the end of the 1950s and the beginning of the 1960s, including *And The Same To You* in 1960, *The Cool Mikado* in 1963 and he also appeared in Eric Sykes's 1967 comic film *The Plank*. Tom could often exasperate his family and his friends, of whom Sykes was one, with his total disregard for punctuality and cavalier attitude towards rehearsals. Nevertheless, as far as his act was concerned, he was a total perfectionist, everything had to be just so and he would spend hours honing the nuances of his performance before going on stage. He would chain smoke cigars and, according to rumours surfacing after his death, was rather too fond of the bottle for his own good. Not the slightest bit interested in politics, he loved expensive clothes and joke shops - his house was full of childish joke props - rubber bouncy eggs, soap that turned your face black and the like. Amongst his comic heroes he counted Max Miller, Stan Laurel, Jacques Tati and also Arthur Askey. A former heavyweight boxer and an army champ during his time with the Horse Guards, Tommy's friends included the Hollywood actor Cary Grant.

Jeremy Novick's biography is sprinkled throughout with examples of Tommy's infectious humour including the famous, or should that be infamous, 'tea bag' routine. After paying off his taxi driver, Tommy would stoop his huge frame, press something into the driver's pocket and, with a cheery farewell, exhort him to have a drink on him later. Pleased as punch, and expecting at least a five pound tip, the driver would then reach into his pocket and find - a tea bag.

On the night of Sunday, April 15th, 1984, Tommy Cooper collapsed on stage during a live performance of the ITV show *Live From Her Majesty's*. Used to Tommy's lunatic sense of humour, the audience roared with laughter, imagining it was just another of the much loved comic's hilarious gags. But it was deadly serious, Tommy, a heavy smoker, who had only recently stopped smoking, had already had problems with his heart. He was taken to Westminster Hospital in London, but, unfortunately, died soon after.

On Tuesday, April 17th, 1984, *The Times's* Alan Hamilton went into overdrive, memorably describing Tommy Cooper, on page three of the paper, as having a face which resembled nothing so much as a statue from Easter Island, a map of Norway in all its craggy glory and the Eiger mountain's north face all rolled into one. Further on the 'Thunderer's' obituarist recalled Tom's shambling gait as he ambled on stage and exhorted his bemused audience to "watch! watch!". Then, when he was sure they were really watching, he would produce from out of nowhere an oversize pocket watch.

Tommy's Memorial Service took place on Thursday, June 19th, 1984 at the London church of St. Martin-in-the-Fields. The church was crowded to capacity with Tommy's family, his wife Gwen, his two children and his brother Dave, showbiz celebrities such as Roy Hudd, Leslie Crowther, Cardew Robinson, Danny La Rue, Russ Abbott, Jill Gascoine and many of his fans. The TV magician Paul Daniels gave the eulogy and Tommy's son, Thomas, read the lesson. Three months later, *The Times* reported that Tommy had left £326,686 in his will.

After Tommy's death, a woman called Mary Kay, an ex-stage manager for Thames TV, published a book called *For The Love Of Tommy* in which she claimed to have had a seventeen-year-long affair with the Caerphilly comic. Gwen stoutly denied the claims but Tommy's name was being dragged through the mud and, as always, some of the mud stuck. Worse was to come as, what the newspapers called 'The Curse of Tommy Cooper' appeared to strike home. First, his son Thomas died, aged thirty-two, on August 16th, 1988. He had been having marital problems, his wife had left him, taking their three children with her, and then it all became too much for him and the drink that he had been consuming in large quantities did the rest. Then, Tommy Cooper's younger brother, David, died after putting on Tommy's stage gear and impersonating the great comedian in one of his stage routines. He had impersonated his brother for a TV documentary but never lived to see himself on the small screen. Finally, in a tragic re-run of Tommy's own final performance, a Cooper fan and amateur magician called Gordon Williams, died on stage of a heart attack whilst doing his magic act in April, 1997. One of life's bizarre coincidences? Or something more sinister? Happily, nothing more appears to have been heard of the so-called 'Cooper's curse' since.

The 'Cooper Curse' even affected Gwen in a 'mild' way. On Friday, September 21st, 1984, she was brought before Acton magistrates in West London and charged on two counts: driving after drinking too much, and driving whilst under the influence of drink or drugs. The charges arose from a collision between her Mercedes and an Austin Allegro parked outside her house in Barrowgate road, Chiswick. It was alleged that she had twice hit the Austin and then backed her Mercedes into a tree. Her own car was a write-off and the Allegro suffered serious damage. She denied the charges and also revealed how the last few months without Tommy had been dreadful, and her sense of loss was not getting any easier. The hearing was adjourned to Tuesday, November 20th, 1984 when Gwen admitted that she had driven without the requisite due care and attention and was fined one hundred pounds for careless driving. The charges concerning drink driving were dropped.

Defending Gwen, Mr. Lawrence Kershen said that, on the day in question, auctioneers had arrived at her house to remove Tommy Cooper's stage props, many of which she had helped to build. That, coupled with a general feeling of grief and loss, had led to the accident. (As it happened, Tommy's props fetched £7,500 at an auction sale in Christie's, south Kensington. Poignantly, Tommy's son, Thomas, kept the fez his father had been wearing the night he died on stage.)

In 1993 a plaque bearing the unmistakable red fez was placed on the small terraced house where Tommy was born at No. 19 Llwyn-On Street, a quiet side street some distance from the town centre and not far from the Valleys Railway line. At the time of Tommy's birth his family were renting a small room from the woman to whom the house belonged, Maud Shattock. (She was still living there in the 1970s.) Tommy was said to have been "a sickly baby" and was taken to Exeter for the sake of his health. He returned to the town of his birth to play the renowned Double Diamond Club in the 1970s. In April, 1998, his was one of the faces featured on a series of stamps showcasing British comedians - Tommy's face adorned the 20p issue.

On TV he could be seen in the early fifties clowning in *It's Magic*. He then filled the small screen with such programmes as *Cooper* or *Life with Tommy*, *Cooper's Capers* and, in the sixties, *Cooperama*, *Life With Cooper* and the seventies shows *Tommy Cooper, Cooper, Cooper - Just Like That* and, in 1980, *Cooper's Half Hour*. His comic single *Don't Jump Off The Roof Dad* reached Number 40 in June 1961 and stayed in the Charts for two weeks, re-entering for a further week in July. His catchphrase "Just like that" will probably live forever.

TIMOTHY DALTON

Born in Colwyn Bay on March 21st, 1946, where his father was stationed during the war, Dalton is the oldest of five children. He regards himself as a mixture of English, Irish and Italian - according to one website his mother comes from the Bronx district of New York. Timothy's father, a Manchester advertising executive, moved the family to Manchester in the late 1940s but Timothy was raised in a prosperous area of Belper in the county of Derbyshire. At school he did well in sports and sciences and also took part in amateur dramatics with the Belper Dramatic Group and The Belper Players. He became a member of the National Youth Theatre between 1964 and 1966. (It may have helped that both of his grandfathers had music hall connections.) He then studied at RADA (The Royal Academy of Dramatic Art) but left before two years were up to join the Birmingham Repertory Company where he found himself playing the leading role in many of the company's productions. In the 1970s he joined both the Royal Shakespeare Company and The Prospect Theatre taking centre stage in such plays as *Romeo and Juliet*, *King Lear*, *Henry V*, *Love's Labours Lost* and *Henry IV, Parts I and II*. He has several times appeared on stage with Vanessa Redgrave (with whom he had a ten-year-long affair). In the 1980s he achieved critical acclaim for his stage performances as Hotspur in *Henry IV, Parts I* and *II* and also his role as the boastful Irish bar-keeper in *A Touch of the Poet*, a veteran of the Duke of Wellington's army and too fond of the drink for his own good.

A green-eyed six-footer, Timothy Dalton made his film debut in the 1968 film *The Lion in Winter* as King Phillip of France. He played James Bond in *The Living Daylights* (1987) after having previously turned the job down twice. (He appeared in two Bond films in all - the other being *Licence to Kill* which made less money than any other Bond film - only £50 million. Desmond Llewelyn - 'Q' to Dalton's Bond - said of his performance as 007, "Timothy made Bond into a real person and on film it didn't work.") On the big screen he has been seen as Prince Rupert in *Cromwell*, Heathcliff in *Wuthering Heights*, and also in *The Voyeur, Mary Queen of Scots, Permission to Kill, Agatha* and *Channel Solitaire*. His other films include *Flash Gordon* (1980), *Mistral's Daughter* (1984), *Hawks* (1987), *The Racketeer* (1991) and *The Beautician and the Beast* (1997).

He made the mini-series *Sins* together with Joan Collins playing the part of her brother. He made *Sextette* with Mae West in 1978, a film which, as he told Joan Collins, nearly finished his career and took him years to live down. Described by some as "taciturn", "serious-looking" and "gloomy", Joan Collins found him well endowed with sex appeal and "very good-looking".

His TV ventures include *The Three Princes, Five Finger Exercise, Candida, Centennial* and *The Flame is Love*. In a 1979 episode of *Charlie's Angels*, the character he portrayed, Damien Roth, was, rather prophetically, said to resemble James Bond, a full eight years before Dalton first took on the role of 007. He kept busy throughout the 1990s appearing in various films and in 1994, played Rhett Butler in the eight-hour-long mini-series *Scarlett* based on the bestselling *Gone With The Wind*. His interests include fishing, particularly in the Pacific, attending antique fairs and auctions, reading and jazz. He jealously guards his private life and, apart from the fact that his Ukrainian actress-cum-model girlfriend Oksana Grigorieva bore him a son, Alexander, on August 7th, 1997, little is known of his personal life. Incidentally, Oksana is twenty-six years younger than Dalton.

GWEN FRANGCON DAVIES

Born London, January 25th, 1891, of Welsh parents, her father was a baritone from Bethesda (born December 11th, 1855, died London April 13th, 1918). She herself began as a soprano, appearing in Boughton's *Immortal Hour*, before switching to acting. (Unkind critics have suggested that her father added the 'Frangcon' - taken from a Welsh beauty spot - to add colour to his run-of-the-mill surname. Indeed, *The Times* was later to remark that her surname was too long to fit on theatrical posters and advised she shorten it - advice she ignored, with no ill effects to her theatrical career, as it turned out).

She made her stage debut as a fairy in *Midsummer Night's Dream* in April, 1911. A member of the Birmingham Repertory company in 1921, she was Juliet to John Gielgud's Romeo in 1924 and subsequently appeared with him in *The Importance of Being Earnest* (1940) and *Macbeth* (1942). In the 1930s she was Elizabeth Browning in *The Barretts of Wimpole Street*. She enjoyed her

first great London triumph as Eve and the Newly Born in G.B. Shaw's *Back to Methuselah*. She played Miss Mason in Emlyn Williams's play *He Was Born Gay* on May 26th, 1937 at the Queen's Theatre in London.

In 1942 she went to South Africa with the South African actress Marda Vanne, her lifelong companion, and they established the country's first classical theatre company of any importance. Returning to Britain in 1947 she played Ranevskaya in *The Cherry Orchard* at the Hammersmith Lyric Theatre in 1954. She appeared as the Queen Mother in the first performance of Jean Anouilh's *Becket* by the RSC at the Aldwych Theatre on July 11th, 1961. In 1965 she was Beatrice in *Much Ado About Nothing*. A founder member of the Royal

Gwen Ffrangcon Davies (Angus McBean)

Court and of the RSC she enjoyed great success for her interpretation of the role of Mary Tyrone in Eugene O'Neill's *Long Day's Journey Into Night*, a role which won her *The Evening Standard* Award for Best Actress. She made her Broadway debut when she was in her seventies as Mrs. Candour in *The School for Scandal*. Her film credits include Countess D'Urfe in *The Devil Rides Out*, Gran in *The Burning* (both 1968) and Hilda in *Leo the Last* (1970).

In a way it was, perhaps, her misfortune to be 'competing' for the 'best' roles against such actresses as Peggy Ashcroft, Sybil Thorndike and Edith Evans but this did not stop her appearing on stage when she was in her eighties, or being made a Dame of the British Empire in 1991. Her last stage appearance was in 1970 as Madame Voynilsky in a Royal Court production of *Uncle Vanya*. Her last ever appearance, came in a Sherlock Holmes story shown on TV just after Christmas, 1991. In her time Gwen Frangcon Davies brought the parts of Cleopatra, Lady Macbeth, Eliza Dolittle, Mary Queen of Scots and Florence Nightingale to life. She herself died on January 27th,

1992, aged 101, at the seventeenth century cottage near Halstead, Essex where she had lived since 1934. According to her agent, there had been no signs of any illness.

HARRY PARR DAVIES

It is the stuff of which legends are made. A seventeen-year-old youth from Wales bursts into the dressing room of one of the foremost songstresses of her age at the Winter Gardens, Blackpool, demanding to be allowed to play one of his songs. Then, far from throwing the intruder out, the singer listens patiently, likes what she hears and appoints the young Welshman there and then to be not only her piano accompanist but also her song writer-in-chief. If we saw it on TV nowadays we would scarcely believe it, dismissing it as too 'corny' for words, but it really happened. The name of the singer? - the pride of Lancashire, 'Our Gracie', Gracie Fields. The name of the young man? - Harry Parr Davies, from Neath. (Accounts differ as to how exactly Davies introduced himself to the Lancashire songbird. One biographer, Joan Moules, says he was "nervous" and "mumbled" whilst another, David Bret, accuses him of storming into Fields's dressing room without so much as a by-your-leave, not even bothering to knock and says that Gracie was "taken aback" by the young Welshman's arrogance.

Whatever the truth of the matter she was undoubtedly impressed by the musical ability of the boy from Neath (the song he played was called *I Hate You*) and the very next night the young Parr Davies found himself unexpectedly in the limelight. He had taken his place with the other musicians down in the orchestra pit when the audience, anxious to see what the talented new pianist looked like, complained loudly, wanting to know where the newcomer was. At this point, Gracie Fields is supposed to have said to the theatre manager, "I'll give the lad a break. I'll bring him up on the stage. Nobody that looks like him could be a rival to me". So Harry Parr Davies was brought up onto the stage but, by now, he was so utterly consumed by stage fright that he found himself unable to play a single note. Needless to say, before Gracie had finished her first song, Harry was back with the other musicians in the orchestra pit. He soon overcame his fears, however, and, from then on, regularly accompanied Gracie Fields on stage as well as writing some of her best known numbers including: *Sing As We Go, Wish Me Luck As You Wave Me Goodbye, The Sweetest Song In The World, An English Garden, Smile When You Say Goodbye, My Love for You* and *Pedro the Fisherman*.

Harry toured the world with Gracie including South Africa where she closed her show with Parr Davies's theme from *The Show Must Go On* and Canada where *The Toronto Star* paid the Welsh pianist/composer the compliment of calling him "an accomplished musician", having no doubts that he could easily fill a concert hall by himself. The touring show also visited New York and Hollywood. Apparently, Gracie would often change key right in the "middle of the trickiest arrangement", just to keep her pianist on his toes but she never fazed Harry - he always managed to follow her. (He never used sheet music - because being so short sighted he could hardly read it.)

He accompanied the singer for nine years and, according to one biographer (Joan Moules) "became like one of the family" but, in 1943, he was conscripted into the Army and made to play in the Irish Guards Orchestra. Sadly, the relationship with Gracie Fields ended in acrimony. Harry announced that he had no wish to do any more war work. He had seen more than enough of military uniforms, he said, during his time with the Irish Guards, to last him for more than one lifetime. Gracie, however, did not see things this way, to her such an attitude smacked of cowardice and was not what she required in her accompanists and song writers.

Joan Moules, who wrote a 1997 biography of Gracie Fields said that Harry Parr Davies was "grumpy and temperamental but extraordinarily talented, both as a composer and a pianist". David Bret in a 1995 biography of Gracie called him "this temperamental individual - who had an utter lack of subtlety and manners when, according to Gracie, he was feeling 'that road out', which seemed to be most of the time". (When the singer first saw Parr Davies he was wearing thick-lensed glasses and sporting a "pasty, spotty complexion". He was said to have suffered from constipation - hence the grumpiness.) In her own autobiography, Gracie Fields called Harry "as Welsh as they come" and referred to his "pronounced Welsh accent".

"A long, lanky lad", Gracie Fields's own description of him, Harry Parr Davies was born in Briton Ferry on May 24th, 1914 and brought up in Arthur Street, Neath. He attended Neath Intermediate School and studied music privately with Sir Walford Davies. Harry Parr Davies was something of a child prodigy. At the age of five he had written a song for Princess Mary's wedding. Aged six he learnt to play the piano. By the age of thirteen he had composed some thirty songs and two operettas (one of them entitled *The Curfew*). Aged seventeen, he had had six songs published. Then came the meeting with Gracie Fields and he never looked back.

He composed a number of very successful West End shows including: *Black Velvet* and *Haw Haw* (1939), *Come Out To Play and Top of the World* (1940), *Gangway* (1941), *Big Top, Full Swing* and *Best Bib and Tucker* (1942). *The Lisbon Story, Pedro the Fisherman* and *The Knight Was Bold* (1943). *Jenny Jones* (1944), *Fine Feathers* (1945), *The Shephard Show* (1946), *Her Excellency* (1949), *Dear Miss Phoebe* and *Blue For A Boy* (1950), *The Glorious Days* (1953).

He also wrote the film music for *Sing As We Go* (1934), *The Show Goes On* (1937), *It's In the Air* (1938), *We're Going To Be Rich* (1938), *Shipyard Sally* (1939), *Sailors Three* (1940), *We'll Meet Again* (1942), *Suspected Person* (1942), *Bell-Bottom George* (1943), *It Happened One Sunday* (1943), *Valley of Dreams* (1946) and *Maytime in Mayfair* (1946).

The Lisbon Story (for which he wrote the music, Harold Purcell wrote the lyrics) was performed at the Hippodrome Theatre. In 1950, Parr Davies adapted J.M. Barrie's (of Peter Pan fame) *Quality Street*, renamed it *Dear Miss*

Phoebe, set it to music with words by Christopher Hassall (one of Ivor Novello's main collaborators) and put it on at the Phoenix. Some weeks later His Majesty's Theatre was the scene of another Parr Davies musical offering *Blue for a Boy* which featured the rather large, not to mention obese, comedian Fred Emney dressed as a baby. Despite, or perhaps because of, its main attraction the show racked up a creditable more than six hundred performances. Three years later Anna Neagle starred in Harry's last ever musical *The Glorious Days* which was more or less a compilation of his old song-hits.

On Friday, October 14th, 1955 the Welsh composer was found dead in his mews flat at Harriet Walk, Chelsea where he lived alone. The inquest held at Hammersmith on Monday, October 31st, recorded a verdict that death was due to stomach haemorrhage caused by acute alcoholic gastritis. A Dr. Patrick Warren said that Harry Parr Davies had been his patient since 1951 when he had been diagnosed as suffering from an acute gastritic attack and a peptic ulcer. Dr. Warren concluded by saying that the composer should not have been drinking alcohol. No death ever comes at the right time, but on this occasion it was even more of a cruel blow than usual as, for Harry Parr Davies, further success had seemed to be just around the corner. He had been to Hollywood to meet Charlie Chaplin and his wife Paulette Goddard and there had been talk of his working together with the great comedian. Now, sadly, his death had put an end to all that.

In all, Harry Parr Davies wrote about thirty revues and some six or seven hundred songs. He is inextricably linked with Gracie Fields but others he wrote for include Betty Driver, Evelyn Laye, Flanagan and Allen, Hutch, Tommy Trinder and Bebe Daniels and Ben Lyon. For that other famous Lancastrian, George Formby, he penned the hits *Noughts and Crosses* and *It's In The Air*. Parr Davies's song *In My Little Snapshot Album* was originally written for Gracie Fields, but she turned it down, saying "Better give that one to Formby, love. It's a bit too rude for me!" It duly appeared in the ukulele strummer's 1938 film *I See Ice*.

Formby and Harry got on well together. Formby's biographer, David Bret, called the Welshman "the perfect foil for George's decidedly off-beat sense of fun". During the filming of the 1938 *It's In The Air* George and Harry could often be found together, more often than not in the local pub just across the way from the studio. Harry was also the only one who could look Beryl, George's formidable and not very well-liked wife, straight in the eye, call her "a miserable bleeder" and live to tell the tale. Beryl, for her part, referred to the composer as "a grumpy nancy boy".

Whilst on leave from the Irish Guards Orchestra Parr Davies was given ten days to write the music for George Formby's 1943 film *Bell-Bottom George*. Harry was not to realise it at the time but three of the songs he wrote for the film - *Swim Little Fish*, *If I Had A Girl Like You* and *Bell-Bottom George* would later be classified by the Dance Music Policy Committee (the wartime body which searched out potential collaborators with the enemy and vetted artists' songs, music and even comedy routines) as "enemy-friendly". The allegations were, of course, preposterous, the songs were totally unpolitical and it can only be assumed that someone who held a grudge against Formby had lodged a complaint with the Dance Music Policy Committee. Nevertheless, in the prevailing paranoid atmosphere of the time, the allegations hung over George's head like a dark cloud until common sense prevailed and, in February, 1944, he was allowed to continue performing the three songs. Even then, the whole business left a legacy of bitterness behind it and Formby would never forget it.

One of Harry Parr Davies's songs, *Smile When You Say Goodbye*, earned him advance royalties of One Thousand Pounds. Today his best known songs, the cheerful, up-beat anthems *Sing As We Go* and *Wish Me Luck As You Wave Me Goodbye* still live on and, along with his other music, continue to bring in royalties. As for the man who wrote them he is buried in Oystermouth churchyard in Swansea.

RUPERT DAVIES

Rupert Davies will forever be known for his portrayal of the French police detective, Commissioner Maigret, on BBC TV in the early 1960s. A great favourite of the policeman's creator, Georges Simenon, Davies starred in fifty-one episodes of the programme, covering four series, between 1960 and 1963. The opening sequences of the programme where Davies strikes a match against a wall to light his trademark pipe, Ron Grainer's evocative instrumental music playing in the background all the while, have gone down in television history. Life after Maigret was never the same again for Davies but he did appear in other roles, even if the great French detective cast a long shadow and threatened to typecast the actor forever.

Davies appeared in BBC TV's 1955 sci-fi thriller *Quatermass II* and in *The White Falcon*, BBC TV's 1956 version of the Henry VIII/Anne Boleyn story. He was the voice of puppet Joe 90's stepfather in the 1968 TV series. In the early seventies he appeared as Count Rostov in BBC 2's production of *War and Peace*. In *Arthur of the Britons*, HTV's 1972 series, he played the eponymous hero's Saxon foe, Cerdig.

Rupert Davies was born in Liverpool in 1916. His father, a bank manager, hailed from Cross Hands and his mother came from Cardiganshire. Both his parents were Welsh speaking but they did not pass on the language to their son. Indeed, Davies was on record as saying that they used the language as a secret code whenever they did not want him to understand something.

He had always wanted to act but started out in the Merchant Navy and, in 1938, joined the Fleet Air Arm. During the war he was fished out of the sea by a German tanker after his plane had crashed and spent five years as a German prisoner of war. Set free in May, 1945, he immediately started to act and worked with the Company of Four at the Lyric Theatre, Hammersmith, the Citizen's Theatre of Glasgow, Birmingham Rep and the

Old Vic. Minor parts were the order of his day at the Vic - he played Host of the Garter in *The Merry Wives of Windsor*, Soldier Williams in *Henry V* and Snout in Tyrone Guthrie's 1951 production of *Midsummer Night's Dream*.

Maigret changed all that. In 1963 Davies was named TV actor of the Year. Amongst his films were *The Spy Who Came In From The Cold*, *Sea Fury*, *Violent Moment*, *Life In Emergency Ward 10*, *Sapphire*, *Bobbikins* and *Devil's Bait*.

According to Kenneth Griffith, Rupert Davies was popularly known as 'Pud' within the acting profession. He died of cancer in Guy's Hospital, London on Monday, November 22nd, 1976, aged fifty-nine.

RYAN DAVIES

Pianist, harpist, singer, actor, comedian, writer, mime, mimic, clown, writer of songs and music - Ryan Davies was all of these. He was also part of the most talented entertainment duo ever to come out of Wales - and his partnership with Ronnie Williams drew inevitable comparisons with Morecambe and Wise.

He was born Thomas Ryan Davies on January 22nd, 1937 at 'Mountain View', Glanaman, Carmarthenshire, his grandmother's home (Rachel Roberts, his grandmother, and his mother, Nans Davies, were also born there). His father was William Thomas Davies who at the time was running a children's home in Nantgaredig and, because of his parent's occupation, Ryan's family moved house frequently to Llangadog, Llandovery, Felinfoel and Llanfyllin.

When Ryan was ten the family moved to Llanfyllin where his parents kept an old people's home. Both parents were deeply immersed in Welsh language culture and the young Ryan competed in *eisteddfodau*, singing and reciting besides attending school at *Ysgol Uwchradd*, Llanfyllin. It was at school that he acted in Welsh and English plays and it was there that he met his future wife, Irene Williams, when they were both aged fourteen.

After leaving school Ryan did two years' national service in the RAF where his piano playing skills came in handy before embarking on a two year teacher training course at the Bangor Normal College in September 1957. At Bangor he acted in Welsh versions of Molière's plays and played the part of Thomas Mendip in *The Lady's Not For Burning* by Christopher Fry. The evenings he spent entertaining in *Noson Lawen* or 'merry evenings'. After leaving Bangor, Ryan did a one-year course at the Central School of Speech and Drama, and wasted no time immersing himself in the Welsh language life of the capital. He was then offered a teaching post at St. John's School, Shirley in Croydon where he taught elementary school children music and drama from 1960 until 1966. Whilst at Croydon he performed many times in plays at the National Eisteddfod and also began to appear in Welsh language programmes for the BBC and TWW. He married Irene in Llanrhaeadr-ym-Mochnant in April, 1961. In 1966, he decided to abandon teaching and make his way as a professional entertainer-cum-actor buoyed up by the prospect of a BBC Wales contract. He moved to St. Fagans with Irene and made his first

Ryan Davies

professional appearance on stage at the Aberavon National Eisteddfod in *Pros Kairon* by Huw Lloyd Edwards. In September, 1968, he took a leading role in *Y Drwmwr*, the first Welsh TV drama to be broadcast with sub-titles.

He was asked to do *Ryan a Ronnie* in Welsh for TV. Myfanwy Talog also appeared in this programme as did Margaret Williams, Bryn Williams and Derek Boote. On January 29th, 1971 the press announced that Ryan was to play Second Voice to Richard Burton's First Voice in the film of *Under Milk Wood*. Whilst filming *Under Milk Wood* there was a St. David's Day *Ryan a Ronnie* special and then Bill Cotton Junior asked BBC Wales to do a programme for the Network from the BBC theatre in London. There was a favourable review in *Stage and Television Today* on July 1st, 1971. After the BBC1 series Ryan and Ronnie were invited to do a summer season at the Central Pier in Blackpool called *The Good Old Days*. Then it was back to Wales to do another series of *Ryan a Ronnie* in Welsh and continuing to write their own material, Ronnie providing most of the dialogue and Ryan thinking up the funny ideas and situations.

In January, 1973, the duo appeared in *Cinderella* at the Swansea Grand. The following year they were back at the Grand again in *Dick Whittington*. On May 4th, 1974, the press announced that Ryan and Ronnie were splitting up. At the time they were doing a week at the Double Diamond club in Caerphilly and it was reported that Ronnie was giving up for medical reasons. Ryan then decided to go it alone, his first solo pantomime performance coming in *Mother Goose* in January, 1975.

On November 9th, 1976, Ryan opened as Willie Clarke in the Neil Simon comedy *The Sunshine Boys* at Cardiff's New Theatre. (Playing opposite him in the part of Al Lewis was Bill Owen, 'Compo' of *Last of the Summer Wine* fame). He also acted in two Welsh plays, *Welsh Not* and *Merthyr Riots*. In 1976 he appeared in *Jack and the Beanstalk* at the Swansea Grand Theatre. The following year he was in *Babes in the Wood* at the same theatre.

Ryan now appeared in the variety programme *Ryan* based on his all-round talents showing off as the Cossack-hatted Russian stealing the show from the Welsh Male Voice Choir. He appeared in HTV's tribute programme to Saunders Lewis, *A Necessary Figure* and was also heard on the radio in Gwyn Thomas's *The Breakers*. Ryan appeared in *Poems and Pints* on BBC2 and played a variety of roles in BBC Wales' *How Green Was My Father* including the American tourist. Max Boyce also appeared in this programme as the 'spirit of the valleys'.

Ryan died on Friday, April 22, 1977 in Buffalo, New York State. Together with his family, he had been visiting Brian Jones, an old friend who had been best man at his wedding, for a holiday after working in the Swansea pantomimes. The weather had changed and the previous firm snow had turned to a humid heat which led to Ryan, a life-long sufferer from asthma, suffering a bad asthma attack. The day before he was due to fly back to Wales Brian Jones decided to hold a barbecue in his garden. Ryan had helped with the preparations and only then did he realise how bad his asthma really was.

The doctor was called but before he could arrive, Ryan had lost consciousness. He was given mouth to mouth resuscitation and taken to the New York State West Cenotaph hospital where he died soon afterwards, the strain on his heart following a further two heart attacks having proved too much. Ryan's widow decided that the funeral should be a private, family service and he was buried in the Hen Bethel cemetery. His friends rallied round and a memorial concert was organised at the Grand Theatre in Swansea.

Ryan was largely self taught on the harp. His LP *Live at the Rank* was released by his own recording company. Apart from his partnership with Ronnie Williams, he will undoubtedly be remembered for his portrayal of the feckless Twm Twm, the archetypal South-Walian with his pigeons, his darts and his pints of beer in *Fo a Fe*, where he was contrasted with the North Walian ways of his son-in-law's father. His catchphrase, *"nefar in Iwrop, gw boi"* (never in Europe, good boy) will live for a long time in Welsh language popular culture.

WINDSOR DAVIES

His catchphrase is "Lovely boy" and he was born in Canning Town, London on August 28th, 1930 the son of Welsh-speaking parents. When he was ten the family returned to Wales and Windsor was brought up in Nantymoel in the Ogmore valley. In his time he has been a miner, a factory worker and a teacher in south London before taking the plunge and becoming a professional actor. He made more than five hundred appearances in the West End show *Run for Your Wife* and in *Roll On Four O'Clock* at the Lyric Theatre, Hammersmith. It is as a TV actor, however, that Windsor Davies has enjoyed his greatest successes. On the small screen he has been the booming, stentorian voice of Battery Sergeant-Major Williams in *It Ain't Half Hot Mum* (the big comedy hit of 1974 which ran from 1973 to 1981), Oliver Smallbridge in *Never The Twain* alongside Donald Sinden, and he has also been seen in such shows as *Doctor Who*, *A Little Bit of Wisdom*, *Billy Liar*, *Sam*, *The Heavy Mob*, *Coronation Street*, *Sporting Chance*, *Old Scores* and *Sean's Show*. Film appearances have included *Not Now, Comrade* and *Carry On England*. He also provided the voice for Sgt-Major Zero in Gerry Anderson's puppet show *Terrahawks*. Other TV credits include the part of Henry the Chauffeur in *Matt's Milllion*, the 1997 TV series. In February, 1998 he played David Lloyd George in Channel 4's *Mosley* and, in the same month, he played Pugh, the eccentric former coroner for the Welsh Marches, in the first episode of the BBC six-part drama series *Mortimer's Law*.

As a spin-off from *It Ain't Half Hot Mum* Windsor enjoyed some unexpected chart success in 1975 with *Whispering Grass* which got to Number One and *Paper Doll* which reached Number Forty-One, both of them sung in combination with Don Estelle.

On stage he played Wallace Morton in the English Stage Company's production of Gwyn Thomas's *The Keep* when it opened at London's Royal

Court Theatre on November 22nd, 1961. Windsor took a leading role as Mog Jones in *Grand Slam*, the much loved 1978 film broadcast on March 17th by BBC Wales. In 1997 he appeared in *Oh Doctor Beeching* and played the loser Charlie in the National Theatre production of Peter Gill's play *Cardiff East.* (He was also heard on radio in this play.)

MAUDIE EDWARDS

Maudie Edwards was known as a "dialectician" - she would sing a song containing choruses in Irish, Lancashire and Jewish accents and dialects. Dialects came easy to Maudie. She was in panto in Glasgow for five successive seasons and was even billed as "Glasgow's own comedienne". (In Lancashire, she was frequently billed as "Lancashire's own *comedienne*".) She often appeared in *Welsh Rarebit* and spoke Welsh until she was three or four years old, both of her parents being Welsh-speaking. She was born Maud Elizabeth Edwards on October 16th, 1906 in Neath. She made her first appearance on stage, aged four, with her six-year-old sister, May. Their father, Ned, who was himself a semi-professional entertainer, christened his two daughters the "Two Little Queenies" and they performed in workingmen's halls and theatres all over South Wales. When Maudie was just seven years old her father died, but she and May continued to work the music halls of Great Britain with their mother acting as their chaperone and manager.

On May's death at the age of twenty-one, Maudie continued her career alone. Between the wars, she appeared in revues, played the principal boy in pantomimes and toured in the United States, Canada and Australia. During the war she featured in *Workers' Playtime* and travelled abroad to entertain the troops. Besides being a stand-up comedienne, Maudie possessed a good singing voice. (It was her voice which was heard in the 1945 Gainsborough Studios film musical, *I'll Be Your Sweetheart*, although Margaret Lockwood played the part of music hall star Edie Storey. Maudie herself played a supporting role.) In the 1940s she became a well known entertainer, topping the bill in such radio programmes as *Palace of Varieties*, *Music Halls* and, the top showcase for Welsh talent, *Welsh Rarebit*. She appeared in films like *Pink String and Sealing Wax* and *Only Two Can Play*, playing Mrs. Davies, Peter Sellers's Swansea landlady. She played in the West End theatres as a straight actress, at one time part-owning a Swansea theatre herself, and was seen on TV.

Vivacious and versatile she played Elsie Lappin, the corner shop owner, in the first ever episode of *Coronation Street*. In fact, Maudie spoke the first words ever to be heard on the long-running show. At the height of her fame, Maudie was driven everywhere by a chauffeur in a Rolls Royce inscribed with her initials. Once when she opened a store in Cardiff, her adoring public was so anxious to get to grips with her, they rushed towards her, only to fall right through the store's massive plate-glass window. Maudie Edwards died in London on March 24th, 1991. She was married twice - to Ralph Morgan, a marriage that was dissolved - and (in 1956) to Colonel Bill Foulkes.

Best known as "a supporting and character actress", Maudie played in films like *The Flying Doctor* (1936), *My Learned Friend, The Shipbuilders* (both 1943), *I'll Be Your Sweetheart, Murder In Reverse, Pink String and Sealing Wax* (all 1945) and *Walking on Air* (1946). She was also seen in *School for Randle* in 1949 and in the 1952 film *Girdle of Gold. Take a Powder* (1953), *The Key Man* (1957) and *The Ugly Duckling* (1959) were other showcases for her talent. She was "the prying landlady" in the 1962 Peter Sellers vehicle *Only Two Can Play* and joined other Welsh actors in the 1972 film version of *Under Milk Wood* in which she played Mrs. Utah Watkins.

MEREDITH EDWARDS

Welsh-speaking Gwilym Meredith Edwards was born in 1917 in Rhosllanerchrugog, near Wrexham, the son of a collier. Educated at Ruabon Grammar School, he acted with the Band of Hope and the local chapel. He began his working life as a laboratory assistant in Flint where he met Daisy Clark (whom he was to marry in 1942). In 1938, he joined the first Welsh

Meredith Edwards (S4C)

National Theatre Company which disbanded on the outbreak of war. During the war he was a conscientious objector and worked as a fireman in Chester, Liverpool and London. He also belonged to the Non-Combatant Corps.

He played opposite Donald Houston as one of the two Welsh miners who visited London to see Wales play England at Twickenham in *A Run For Your Money* made by Ealing Studios. He also featured as Taff Hughes, the Welsh police sergeant who was forever organising the station's impromptu choir in *The Blue Lamp*. He had a bit part, again as a policeman, in T*iger Bay.*

He was Griffiths the Hearse in the 1952 *Girdle of Gold.* and Yeoman Wells in *The Cruel Sea.* Other films out of the forty or so British films he has been involved with include: *The Lavender Hill Mob, The Trials of Oscar Wilde, Doctor in Love,* and *Only Two Can Play.*

Meredith played the Rev. Eli Jenkins in the 1957 live TV production of *Under Milk Wood.* He appeared as Inspector 'Taff' Evans in the ITV Children's Detective series *Sexton Blake* (1967 - 1971). (He seems to have played a plethora of policemen!) Other TV credits include: *Z Cars, Softly,*

Softly, Coronation Street, Hawkmoor and *Off to Philadelphia in the Morning.* He once played Lloyd George on the radio, and Uncle Lloyd in the BBC Wales television series *The Life and Times of Lloyd George.*

On stage he played Owain Glyndŵr in *Henry IV* at the Old Vic. His last performance was in Chekov's *Three Sisters* for Theatr Clwyd. In a radio interview with Patrick Hannan (BBC Radio Wales, June 11th, 1997) Edwards described himself as "a character actor" and said that he "did not want to be a star". He spoke of acting as "a job like any other job, I suppose". A Plaid Cymru supporter (he campaigned for Gwynfor Evans in Merioneth in 1945 and once stood as a candidate for the party himself) he lived in Cilcain, near Mold. He died in Ysbty Glan Clwyd hospital on Monday, February 8th, 1999. (He had been operated on two weeks before, but complications had set in.) The funeral took place on Friday, February 12th and he was buried in Cilcain cemetery.

A campaigner for CND, Amnesty International and disabled people, Meredith habitually turned down parts glorifying war. In the 1958 film *Dunkirk* he wanted to do his death scene in Welsh. Amazed, the director, Les Norman, asked why. Meredith replied that a dying man would revert to the language of his childhood. After his death, his son described him "as a kind of Welsh renaissance man". Fellow Welsh actor John Ogwen said "We have lost our patriarch".

İVOR EMMANUEL

Ivor Emmanuel was born in Margam but his mother hailed from Pontrhydyfen, and it was there he went to live with his grandfather when he was about six years old and there he grew up. From a very early age his mother had made him sing and his grandfather also encouraged him in his musical ambitions. His mother and his father, his little sister and one grandparent were killed when a Second World War German bomb exploded on the village in 1941 and the orphaned boy was brought up by his Auntie Flossie. He first started to take singing seriously about the age of fourteen, taking lessons in Port Talbot with Madame Miriam Joseph James and beginning to sing with the village operatic society and, eventually, the Port Talbot Operatic Society.

Those who remember him in his prime say Ivor was constantly singing, could harmonise on anything, that he had a terrific range and was capable of hitting the highest notes. Always in tune, he always knew his words, the mark of a true professional.

In the late 1940s Ivor was a frequent visitor to London. One day he visited Covent Garden and could hear the choir inside rehearsing. Desperate for a job in the music industry he asked himself how he could 'infiltrate' the chorus. At the time he was quite friendly with Richard Burton who was then appearing in *The Lady's Not For Burning.* He stayed overnight with Burton and asked his fellow countryman if he could get him into anything, anything at all, he would sweep the stage if necessary. Three weeks went by, and Ivor was back at home working in Port Talbot steelworks, when a telegram arrived from Burton, instructing him to be at Drury Lane at twelve o'clock the next morning to audition for the chorus of *Oklahoma*.

At the audition Ivor sang *Some Enchanted Evening* trying hard to sound as American as possible. It worked. He got the job and spent a year with the show. Subsequently he auditioned for the D'Oyley Carte Opera Company where he also spent a year and then returned to the Royal Theatre, Drury Lane for the smash musical, *South Pacific.* Amongst the cast were Larry Hagman (later JR in Dallas) who, like Ivor, had a relatively small part to play and figured mainly in the chorus while Hagman's mother, Mary Martin, took centre stage. After this, Ivor was in *The King And I* at the same theatre before getting a part in *Damn Yankees* at the Coliseum Theatre.

A meeting with Rhydwen Williams in Liverpool led to Ivor being offered a spot in a Welsh-language programme for Granada TV called *Dewch i Mewn* (or Come In in English). He became a regular performer in this show and this, in its turn, led to his becoming front man for TWW's (Television Wales and the West - the company first broadcast in 1958) flagship Welsh-language programme *Gwlad y Gan/Land of Song* which was broadcast nationwide on a Sunday evening once a month.

Introduced by Siân Phillips, *Land of Song* was the first Welsh language programme to be seen on the entire ITV network and it was Ivor Emmanuel who made it tick. Completely 'live', it started in 1958 and continued till 1965. The programme led on to summer seasons in Blackpool with the likes of Morecambe and Wise and Shirley Bassey. Cabaret appearances and pantomime also followed plus a TWW programme where Ivor visited various towns in Wales and the West Country to talk, and sing, with local people.

Land of Song notwithstanding, Ivor will probably always be associated with the Stanley Baker and Cy Endfield produced *Zulu* in which film he played Private Owen. As the Zulu armies begin their terrifying advance, Emmanuel turns to Baker and says: "They've got a very good bass section, mind, but no top tenor, that's for sure". For the film Ivor wrote the English lyrics which the South Wales Borderers sing to the tune of *Men of Harlech.*

In 1963 Ivor found himself entertaining the cruise passengers on the old *Queen Mary* along with Max Jaffa. He came ashore in Spain, liked what he saw and decided to buy some property on the southern coast. In 1982, he made the move permanent and has lived in Spain ever since, still prepared to burst into song at the drop of a sombrero, but he is still remembered with affection by the inhabitants of his home village. Signs leading to Pontrhydyfen proudly proclaim: "Pontrhydyfen: Home of Richard Burton and Ivor Emmanuel".

Life since Ivor's move to Spain has not been without its ups and downs. In 1991 he lost a considerable amount of money - over £220,000 - when the Bank of Credit and Commerce collapsed, taking most of Ivor's fortune with it. His Thai/American wife, Melanie, had to find work in an old people's home and friends and family helped the Emmanuels weather the storm. They also received a certain amount of compensation for their financial losses. Ivor resisted the temption to return to 'show business', reckoning he had been too long away from his former trade. Undaunted by the buffeting he had received Ivor settled down to a life of tranquil anonymity in his mountain-top village. So anonymous in fact that some people began to mourn his premature 'demise'. In October, 1998 BBC Radio 2's Desmond Carrington spoke of him as "as the late Ivor Emmanuel" and tourists even appeared on Ivor's doorstep asking to see his grave! It is now many years since Ivor lived in Wales - he left his homeland in 1949 but one of the things he does miss about Wales is speaking the Welsh language.

CLIFFORD EVANS

Clifford Evans died in hospital in Shrewsbury on Sunday, June 9th, 1985, at the age of seventy-three. He was married to Hermione Hannen, the daughter of actor Nicholas Hannen, whom he met at RADA. They were to marry in 1940 and she would pre-decease him. In 1989 Evans sold his home in London and returned to Wales. His new home was a converted farmhouse in the Powys countryside.

He was born at Senghenydd, near Caerphilly on February 17th, 1912 but attended grammar school in Llanelli where he appeared in school plays. He first performed in public at Llanelli's Haggers Theatre, playing in Shaw's *You Never Can Tell* and made many other appearances at the theatre in his teenage years. In February, 1929, he embarked on a course of training at RADA where the likes of Robert Donat, Helen Hayes and Claude Rains were to be found teaching. In 1930, he made his London stage debut in *The Witch*.

In 1933 Clifford Evans made his West End debut in *Gallows Glorious* and followed this up a year later playing opposite Sybil Thorndike for three months in John Van Druten's *The Distaff Side*. (He also made his Broadway debut in this play.) A Welsh-speaking Welshman he appeared in a Welsh-language version of *Jedermann* at the National Eisteddfod in the early 1930s and remained a devoted reader of Welsh literature to the end of his days. In 1937 he gave an acclaimed performance on Broadway as Laertes to Lesley Howard's Hamlet and also played the part of Oswald in Ibsen's *Ghosts*. Eloquent - and an admired speaker of verse - he appeared on stage with Charles Laughton and Sybil Thorndike. He played the parts of Cassius, Don Juan, Ferdinand from *The Tempest* and Comus in Milton's play of the same name. He acted in Britain, Canada and the USA. Later in life he strove valiantly to establish a Welsh National Theatre but with no success.

He also directed and produced. After the war he directed *Don Giovanni* at the Cambridge Theatre and productions at the Swansea Grand Theatre in 1950. The company he directed at Swansea contained a number of actors destined to become household names - Richard Burton, Kenneth Williams and Rachel Roberts among them. Williams, for one, did not get on with Evans calling him a "drip" and a "boor" and nicknaming him "Church of England" in his diaries, but he would later revise his opinion, claiming that "with all his faults as a producer, he is theatre", and that Evans had been responsible for much that had been made possible in his career. Williams was part of *The Land of My Fathers*, the pageant play which Evans co-wrote and staged in Cardiff in May, 1951 as a Welsh contribution to the Festival of Britain.

On TV - a medium he disliked intensely - he played the policeman Stryker of the Yard, but his best remembered role will probably be as Caswell Bligh, "the ruggedly individual tycoon" in *The Power Game*, an ATV programme shown on the nation's screens in the 1960s. He also appeared in two episodes of *The Avengers* in the 1960s.

Evans's films included his first, *Ourselves Alone* from 1936, *Love on the Dole* (1941), *The Foreman Went to France* (1942), *Passport to Treason* (1956) and the 1970 picture, *One Brief Summer*. In the Welsh-based *Proud Valley*, he played Seth, the bloody-minded coal miner. He was also the choir conductor in the 1953 film *Valley of Song*. His was the original story behind the 1949 film *A Run For Your Money*. Between 1943 and 1946 Evans served his country as an army private.

EVAN EYNON EVANS

Evan Eynon Evans was born in Nelson in 1904. For many years he earned his living as a bus-driver and had his home in Caerphilly. He was amongst those founding the Tonyfelin Dramatic Society and wrote an annual three-act comedy for them. Evans's plays include *Affairs of Bryngolau* (1936), *Cold Coal* (1939), *Kith and Kin* (1946), *Half a Loaf* (1950) and *Bless This House* (1954). Evans's best known play is *Wishing Well* (1946). This established his reputation as a professional playwright, being produced in the West End and later filmed as *The Happiness of Three Women* with himself taking the part of Amos the postman, and acting alongside Donald Houston.

His comedies such as *The Prodigal Tenor* (1957), *The Bachelor Brothers* (1960) and *Jubilee Concert* (1961) were given an airing on BBC Wales TV and he was also a prolific writer for radio, where his creation Tommy Trouble enjoyed great popular success on the *Welsh Rarebit* programme in the late forties and early fifties. (He wrote the Tommy Trouble scripts for eleven years and even played Trouble's pal, high-voiced Willie, for a while.) Some of Evans' plays for radio in the thirties and forties came in for strong criticism. He was accused of turning the Welsh into caricatures with his use of Welsh turns of phrase and tones of voice, but as John Davies pointed out, the *Manchester Guardian* (as it then was) welcomed his *Winning Ways* play for its use of Welsh accents which were not only intelligible to English listeners but also pleasant to their ear. Others were not so sure, a House of Commons meeting in April, 1943 attacked the way Evans' characters spoke on the radio, but the playwright defended himself stoutly. John Davies in his book *Broadcasting and the BBC in Wales*, quotes Evans as saying: that he did not use "Look You or Indeed to Goodness, but I do use Sit You Down and Come You In. Why should we deny our peculiarities of speech?".

Evans was in BBC TV's 1957 production of *The Peaceful Inn*. He played the "old hard drinking seaman" father in the 1959 BBC Armchair Theatre production of Alun Owen's play, *No Trams to Lime Street*. He appeared opposite Rachel Thomas in the 1959/1960 production of *How Green Was My Valley* as the father in the Morgan family. On the big screen his films included *Undercover* (1943), *Private's Progress* (1963), *Battle of the River Plate* (1956), *The Sheriff of Fractured Jaw* (1958), *Tiger Bay* (1959), *I'm All Right, Jack* (1959), *Two-Way Stretch* (1960) and *Only Two Can Play* (1962).

He died suddenly on Thursday, January 12th, 1989 at the Glynbargoed Nursing Home in Trelewis, not far from his Nelson birthplace, after having lived in Caerphilly for many years. Survived by his son Keith, his wife Lydia having predeceased him, his funeral service took place on Wednesday, January 18th at the Tonyfelin Chapel in Caerphilly and he was cremated that same afternoon at the Thornhill Crematorium.

In all, Eynon Evans wrote a number of stage plays, six plays for television and fifteen radio plays. He was over forty when he gave up his bus driver's cab for the uncertain prospects of the theatre, and was still appearing in amateur dramatics in his mid-seventies. In his *Western Mail* tribute Mario Basini described how Eynon started out writing. At the time he was with an amateur company working out of a Nelson chapel. They were looking for a play to perform and so Eynon began writing out the lines from a play he had seen performed at Cardiff's Empire Theatre. When he could not remember the exact words of the play he put in his own and was amazed to find that his lines were getting more laughs than the original had. From then on he never looked back.

SIR GERAINT EVANS

Geraint Llewellyn Evans was born on February 16th, 1922 in the village of Cilfynydd, near Pontypridd. The son of Williams John Evans, a miner, his mother, Charlotte May Evans (neé Thomas), died when he was only a baby. Besides working down the pit, his father was a choirmaster and his son began to sing when he was very young. He was only four years old when he won his first gold medal. He left school at the age of fourteen and started working as a messenger boy/window dresser in Mr. Theophilus's outfitter's shop in Pontypridd. As a teenager he could be heard singing on the local radio programme, *Welsh Rarebit*.

When war broke out he joined the RAF where he trained as a radar operator and started to sing professionally. The war over, he sang and produced with the British Forces Network in Hamburg. He studied there and in Geneva. He also attended London's Guildhall School of Music. He successfully auditioned for the Covent Garden Opera Company and joined them in 1947. He made his debut for the company in the very minor role of the Nightwatchman in *The Meistersinger*. (He actually rehearsed the part in the gents toilet of all places, space being at such a premium in the Garden at that time.) The Garden's management then decided to take a chance and

Geraint Evans as Claggart *(David H. Fishman)*

offered their young talent the part of Figaro which he proceeded to make gloriously his own. He first sang it in January, 1949 and would go on to sing it more than five hundred times over a period of almost thirty years to great national, and international, acclaim.

Also famed for his role of the old reprobate Falstaff, Evans's singing took him all over the world. He sang in Vienna with the Vienna State Opera, in Salzburg, Berlin, Paris, and at La Scala, Milan. He appeared at the Metropolitan Opera, New York, the San Francisco Opera, the Lyric Opera, Chicago, the Mexico City Opera and The Teatro Colon in Buenos Aires. Famous throughout the world he put Wales and Britain 'on the map' as far as opera was concerned. A firm believer in the power of acting as well as singing, Geraint Evans even practised ballet to improve his agility around the stage. The first President of the newly independent Welsh College of Music and Drama he was a director and co-founder of HTV Wales. A Founder Member of the Gorsedd of Bards he was the Principal Baritone at the Royal Opera House Covent Garden from 1948 to 1992. His farewell performance at Covent Garden took place in front of the Prince and Princess of Wales in June, 1984 when he gave a gala rendition of *L'Elisir d'Amour*, singing the part of Dr. Dulcamara in the Donizetti opera.

He was awarded the CBE in 1959, knighted in 1969 and retired from opera singing in 1984. Living at Aberaeron on the West Wales coast in a house which had been converted from a former pub he spent his time "doing-it-yourself" and sailing. He became a part-time coastguard in 1987.

With his "powerful voice" and "twinkling eyes" his other major roles included Figaro and Balstrode in Britten's *Peter Grimes*. Geraint Evans was renowned for the humanity he put into his roles - there were more than seventy of them, including Beckmesser, the town clerk in *die Meistersinger,* Don Pasquale (he first performed this role from Donizetti's opera in Buenos Aires), Wozzeck (in Alban Berg's opera), Leporello (Don Giovanni's servant) and Papageno (one of his favourite roles from *The Magic Flute*). He sang in Benjamin Britten works: *Billy Budd* and Bottom in *A Midsummer Night's Dream*. He was instrumental in furthering the careers of other Welsh operatic talent - Gwyneth Jones, Margaret Price and Stuart Burrows among them.

A baritone, he died on Saturday, September 19th, 1992 at Bronglais Hospital, Aberystwyth. He had been admitted to the hospital more than a week before after suffering a heart attack in his Aberaeron home. Brenda, his wife (née Brenda Davies), whom he had married in 1948, and his two sons, Huw and Alun, were at his bedside when he died. When they heard the news of his death Jeremy Isaacs, the then General Director of the Royal Opera House, called him "one of the greatest artists and greatest personalities to sing at Covent Garden" and the Labour M.P. Gerald Kaufman said "he was a wonderful singer".

Geraint Evans was born into a Welsh speaking household in Cilfynydd at a time when the mine still dominated the lives of those living in the village. He grew up in the terraced house he was born in, 55 William

Street and, after the early death of his mother, was brought up by his mother's parents who both hailed from Cardiganshire. When he was ten he went to live with his father and his new stepmother in Hopkinstown in the Rhondda, but eventually moved back to his grandparents in Cilfynydd. The move to Hopkinstown took its toll. It affected his schooling and he failed the crucial Scholarship Examination which meant, the way things worked at the tine, that he would have to leave school at fourteen and find work.

He started singing with local societies and having singing lessons in Cardiff and his musical talents would prove to be the key which opened the door to a wider world. Signed on by Covent Garden for a year at £12 a week, he married schoolteacher Brenda Davies, the sister of Welsh rugby outside half Glyn Davies, on Easter Saturday, 1948 in a Welsh language chapel service in Cilfynydd. Like Evans, Brenda came from Cilfynydd, indeed, he and she were both born in the same street. In his entertaining and informative biography *Sir Geraint Evans, A Knight at the Opera*, the singer recalled how he was once slapped by Joan Sutherland - he had inadvertently come a little too close to his fellow artist, and told of the only time he was booed on stage.

"The only time I've ever been booed on stage was after playing the brutal Claggart in ... Billy Budd before an audience of Chicago schoolchildren ... They identified totally with Billy, one or two of them shouting remarks like "That's got the bastard" when he laid me out with the fatal blow."

Then there was the time when he was besieged by autograph hunters in Buenos Aires signing his name for about two hours until he was rescued by the Director of the Opera House. In a Chicago all-night movie theatre, Evans and his companion, fellow singer Marilyn Horne, gasped in disbelief when what appeared to be a ten-foot-long pole with a boxing glove stuck on the end, passed in front of them and nudged a customer, who had fallen asleep, awake.

The famed (or should that be notorious?) conductor Sir Thomas Beecham was equally as abrupt as the Chicago boxing glove. Auditioning at London's Wigmore Hall for a role with the Glyndebourne Festival in 1950, Evans was perturbed to hear that Beecham would be coming to listen to him too. Sure enough the cantankerous conductor arrived and promptly began to enliven the proceedings, enquiring in a loud voice whether Evans was singing the Messiah in his native Welsh (when in fact he was trying to sing Harlequin in German). Beecham also took exception to Evans's nationality, complaining that if this glut of Welshmen continued, they would have to remove Glyndebourne from Sussex and take it down to Cardiff.

Beecham may have scoffed at Geraint Evans's Celtic roots but the baritone's knowledge of Welsh came in handy when he was singing in Warsaw. The Poles had bugged his hotel room, but Evans and his wife Brenda effortlessly got round that by speaking to each other in their native Welsh and no doubt giving their Communist eavesdroppers a headache into the bargain! If Beecham had not been impressed with Geraint Evans's singing talents, Herbert von Karajan undoubtedly was, recording him singing in *die Meistersinger* in Dresden in East Germany, and asking the man from Cilfynydd to sign up for the Vienna State Opera. All through his career Evans thought long and hard about how best to tackle his differing roles and this dedicated approach paid off. He would immerse himself totally in his roles, a process which required not a little acting ability. When he was singing Figaro in Milan's La Scala in 1960, he played the part so well that he became a source of puzzlement to the opera house's stagehands. They had no quarrel with his Italian (with his natural dark looks, he could even be taken for an Italian). What baffled them was his outlandish surname which was unlike any other Italian name they had ever heard of. They were about to give up in bewilderment when one of them came up with the solution - Evans must come from Sicily!

GLENN FORD

HTV Wales's *The Welsh in Hollywood* broadcast on September 18th, 1999 claimed Glenn Ford's parents hailed from Tonypandy in the Rhondda. They were certainly Welsh enough to give their son the 'daddy' of all Welsh Christian names. But Gwyllyn Samuel Newton Ford was born far from Wales in Quebec, Canada on May 1st, 1916, the son of a railway executive. The family moved to Santa Monica, California when he was seven and the young Gwyllyn attended Santa Monica High School. He had a variety of jobs after leaving school: he was a jobs salesman, a bus driver, a telephone repair man and a paint-shop worker. For a time he even worked as Will Rogers's stable-boy. He acted with the Wilshire Theatre in Los Angeles and made his stage

debut in *The Children's Hour* in 1935 as Glenn Ford, the 'Gwyllyn' having been lost somewhere along the way.

Some critics have spoken of his "stoic style" and of his dependability and efficiency. Others have taken a different view. Richard Schickel, one of Marlon Brando's biographers, called him "a sort of second string William Holden but without Holden's incisiveness or capacity for dangerous anger". He claimed that Brando despised Ford. Brando himself, who appeared with Glenn in the 1956 *Teahouse of the August Moon* was scarcely

Glenn Ford (The Glenn Ford Library and Archives) more charitable. In his own autobiography, published in 1994 he accused Ford of "scene stealing to Olympian heights" and of being "a miser about food", refusing to share a box of cookies he kept hidden in his room during filming. Brando found them and ate some. Glenn assumed Japanese children had eaten them and posted guards on the door, but Brando ate them anyway, even crushing some on the floor. Ford exploded but he never did find out who ate his cookies.

Ford could be unpopular with directors too. Frank Capra, who directed him in the 1961 film *Pocketful of Miracles* said that Glenn Ford had made him "lick his boots" and that the constant arguments with the actor had made him lose his appetite for film making. David Swift, who co-wrote and directed the 1962 *Love is a Ball* thought that the Welsh Quebecker's approach to acting was that of "a twelve year-old temperamental child. Were he mine I would have spanked him physically".

Nevertheless, Glenn was charming enough to wed Eleanor Powell - she of the dancing feet who once danced with Fred Astaire. The Powell marriage lasted from 1943 to 1959, that to actress Kathryn Hays from 1966 to 1968. His fourth, and present marriage, to actress Cynthia Hayward has lasted from 1977.

Quoted as saying "I've never played anyone but myself on screen", Ford's best known films (he appeared in some 95 cinema films and 13-odd TV movies) include: *Gilda* (1946, with Rita Hayworth), *A Stolen Life* (1946, with Bette Davis), *The Big Heat* (1953, with Gloria Grahame), *Human Desire* (1954, also with Gloria Grahame), *Blackboard Jungle* (1956), *The Teahouse of the August Moon* (1957), *3.10 to Yuma* (1957), *Don't Go Near The Water* (1961), *The Four Horsemen of the Apocalypse* (1976) and *The Battle of the Midway* (1978). His first appearance on screen was in the 1939 cinema film *Heaven with a Barbed Wire Fence*.

In the Second World War Glenn fought with both the French Foreign Legion and the U.S. Marines. From 1971 to 1972 he starred in the TV series *Cade's County*. He took the part of Superman's human stepfather in the 1978 Superman film. He was also in the 1993 *Finnegan's Wake*.

PETER GREENAWAY

Film maker, painter, opera librettist, opera director and installation artist - Peter Greenaway is all of these. Born in Newport in April, 1942, his mother came from nearby Croesyceiliog. He was still very young when he and his family moved to London. (Nevertheless, one of his earliest memories is being taken, aged five, to the Odeon cinema in Newport by his widowed grandmother.) He was educated at Walthamstow College of Art. On leaving he worked for the British Film Institute.

This controversial film maker first came to public notice in 1983 with his film *The Draughtsman's Contract* after previously being confined to the art-house circuit. (In the British Film Institute's Top One Hundred British Films of the Twentieth Century it was voted Number Eighty-Eight.) *Belly of an Architect* followed in 1987. 1990 saw the release of *The Cook, the Thief, his Wife and her Lover* which proved to be his most successful film as far as box-office takings were concerned. He directed John Gielgud in the 1990 TV film of *Dante's Inferno*. 1991 saw the release of another of his films *Prospero's Books*. In 1993 he brought out *The Baby of Macon* which proved to be less than universally popular with the critics and public alike, but this same year saw him winning the second Welsh International Film Fellowship. His television work includes *4 American Composers*, a four part series he directed for Channel 4 in 1984.

Peter Greenaway (Cinzia Camela)

He often describes himself as "a painter in cinema" and has wanted to be a painter since he was eleven years old. He regards most conventional cinema as simply "illustrated text". None of his films has cost more than three million pounds to make, but his work deeply offends a lot of people. Actress Helen Mirren, who starred in *The Cook, The Thief etc.,* has said that many people have to leave before the end of a Peter Greenaway film. His latest project is *Eight and a Half Women* inspired by Fellini's 1963 film *Eight and a Half*. He has said "I wish to celebrate the world". When it was previewed at the May, 1999 Cannes Film Festival *Eight and a Half Women* received a rough ride from critics and filmgoers alike. Philip French of *The Observer* was just one critic who was far from impressed, and, at its Cannes showing, the audience booed and hissed the film. *The South Wales Argus* called it "a classic Greenaway tale of sex, death and cinema". (Later French was to modify his criticism somewhat, calling Greenaway one of Btitain's best filmmakers but he still found the actual film itself disappointing, even embarrassing) Greenaway, who now lives in Amsterdam, has himself said "Vituperative antagonism is not unfamiliar. If one of my films gets cheered, I wonder what's gone wrong". Married, he has two daughters.

HUGH GRIFFITH

He may have won an Oscar for his part as the Arab sheik in *Ben Hur* (he did not acually attend the Oscar ceremony himself, and only learnt he had won when his sister rang him from North Wales to tell him the good news, having heard it on the radio) but, for Welsh viewers at least, Hugh Emrys Griffith will always be associated with his part in the TV play *Grand Slam*. The larger-than-life, bushy-eyebrowed, Welsh-speaking actor was born in Marian Glas, Anglesey on May 30th, 1912, the son of William and Mary Griffiths, and was educated at Llangefni Grammar School. He began working as a bank clerk, serving in various North Wales branches for some eight years before the lure of the stage proved too strong. He won a scholarship to RADA and there, in 1939, he won the Bancroft Gold Medal. After leaving RADA two of his first professional parts were in Irish plays and another in Jack Jones's *Rhondda Roundabout* before war intervened and he spent the next six years with the army in India. In 1946 he joined the Shakespeare Company and played his favourite role of King Lear at Swansea in October, 1949.

Among Hugh's stage roles were Mephistopheles in *Dr. Faustus*, the Cardinal in *The White Devil*, John of Gaunt in *Richard II* and Caliban in *The Tempest*. He also played the part of the General in Anouilh's *The Waltz of the Toreador* for one year at the Arts and Criterion Theatre in London's West End in 1956; took part in *Look Homeward Angel* in New York in 1957 and was Falstaff at Stratford in 1964.

Hugh Griffith made his film debut in 1940 in *Neutral Port*. His other films include *The Last Days of Dolwyn*, *Kind Hearts and Coronets*, *A Run For Your Money*, where he played the boozing harpist, *Lucky Jim*, *Laughter in Paradise*, *The Titfield Thunderbolt*, the 1955 sci-fi thriller *Quatermass II*, *Ben Hur*, (William Wyler's 1959 film for which he won an Academy Award for Best Supporting Actor, for his role as the outgoing Sheikh Ilderim) and *Tom Jones* (where he stole the show as the carousing, hard-drinking Squire Western, being nominated for an Oscar). In the 1962 *Mutiny on the Bounty*, he played Smith, one of the mutinous crewmen who followed Marlon Brando's/Fletcher Christian's lead, and overthrew the disciplinarian Captain Bligh.

He appeared in the comedy series *The Walrus and the Carpenter* broadcast on BBC1 in 1965. He was amongst the cast of *Clochemerle*, BBC2's 1972 stab at a French farce. *Grand Slam* - where a party of Welshmen embark on a rugby trip to Paris - was Griffith's last screen role. At the time of his death (he died in his London home on Wednesday, May 14th, 1980, at the age of 67) he was involved in another BBC Wales project, a play built around his childhood experiences in Anglesey. Hugh Griffith was married to Adelgunde Dechend - the couple wed in 1947 and had no children - and, in 1965, was awarded the Hon. D. Litt. from the University of Wales.

Known for his mordant, brilliant wit (once when asked by an American journalist if he was a Method actor, he replied, no, but I am a Methodist), Griffith was remembered with affection by his fellow actors. Meredith Edwards recalled the day, just after the end of the war, when he and

Hugh were walking the streets of Cardiff. They were just about to pass Plaid Cymru's offices when Hugh enquired if Meredith were a member? On hearing the negative reply, Hugh insisted there and then that Meredith enter with him and join the party that very day. Donald Houston remembered the time when Griffith was making a big name for himself at Stratford. Richard Burton was there as well and some of their fellow actors were not at all pleased that the Welsh seemed to be stealing the show. Once he became aware of his fellow professionals' antipathy, Griffith roused their anger even more by speaking nothing but Welsh to Burton. (However, when Griffith took Burton along to a Plaid Cymru meeting during the filming of *The Last Days of Dolwyn*, Burton was, apparently, too shy to address the meeting in Welsh. And, recalling the days in Stratford when he shared a house with both Burton and Griffith, the harpist Ossian Ellis recalls that Burton was reluctant to speak Welsh, but when he met him several years later in America, the Welsh was "spilling out of him".)

Hugh Griffith played the part of Captain Cat in the original 1954 radio broadcast of *Under Milk Wood*. With his bulging eyes, bushy brows and roaring voice he could steal the show from anyone and frequently did. In a Tribute to him broadcast on the Welsh-language channel S4C, Charlton Heston called his performance in *Ben Hur* extraordinary and said that "his Welshness made him special". In the same programme director John Hefin called him an instinctive actor, a magnetic actor. In his later years Hugh Griffith was regarded as having something of a drink problem - something which, as Sir Peter Hall recalled "softened his mental and physical muscles". It also led to many actors being reluctant to work with the man from Anglesey. Nevertheless, he remains one of the finest actors ever to emerge from the land of Wales and one of the country's few Oscar winners.

KENNETH GRIFFITH

Kenneth Griffith was born at Rhos Cottage, Church Park, Tenby on October 21st, 1921 and attended the town's Greenhill Grammar School. He was brought up by his paternal grandparents Emily and Ernest Griffiths, his parents, Harold and Margaret, (born Margaret Davies) having left Tenby, and each other, when he was about six months old. At the age of five Kenneth attended Tenby Council School. Christened Kenneth Griffiths, on leaving school he dropped the final 's' from his surname on the advice of his headmaster, J.T. Griffith. Whilst at Tenby Grammar School he was encouraged by his teacher, Evelyn Ward, to take up acting. After leaving school his mother got him a job working as an assistant in a Cambridge ironmonger's shop. This did not last long and he was soon to be found with the Cambridge Festival Theatre, his first part being Cinna, the poet in *Julius Caesar.*

He then played Danny in Emlyn Williams's *Night Must Fall* in summer season at Tenby before moving to London to look for work. Eventually he landed a small part in Thomas Dekker's *The Shoemaker's*

Holiday. He then became understudy to David Tree in *Little Ladyship*, got various parts in rep and was given a small part in *The Corn is Green* by Emlyn Williams. He then played Gormy in *Boys in Brown* at the Gate Theatre.

His attempt to join the RAF as a pilot having been rejected, he was recruited into CEMA. (The forerunner of the Arts Council.) He tried again to join the RAF but the decision was deferred and, in the meantime, he introduced *Macbeth* to CEMA audiences. Returning to London he had a part in an anti-Nazi play *Till The Day I Die* by Clifford Odets. Eventually, he was allowed to join the RAF and met Joan Stock (his first wife) at a cadets' ball in Stratford upon Avon. He passed out of training as a pilot and continued his air training in Canada where he became very unwell. Having lost a lot of weight he was sent back to Britain to convalesce and then discharged from the RAF.

Somewhat recovered he toured Britain as Heathcliff in *Wuthering Heights*. In 1952, Tyrone Guthrie asked him to join the Old Vic company in the Waterloo Road and he made his return to the stage, after four years of playing in films, by taking the part of The Chorus in *Doctor Faustus* and Oberon in *A Midsummer Night's Dream*. Griffith then played Darius the Persian king in *Tamburlaine*. Both productions were directed by Guthrie and were then taken to South Africa where Kenneth met his second wife, Doria Noar. Back in England, he left Joan and began to live with Doria. Offered a small part in the Boulting Brothers' *Private's Progress*, he spent a year out of acting, working in the postal history business. He was then asked to play Raskolnikov in the BBC TV live production of Dostoyevsky's *Crime and Punishment*.

Films followed: *The Naked Truth, I'm All Right Jack*, then TV: *The Pier* where he was a leader of a gang of Brighton Teddy Boys and also a BBC Wales drama - a Saunders Lewis play about assassinating Hitler. He appeared in *The Babysitter*, a 1965 BBC 1 Wednesday thriller and was amongst the cast of *Clochemerle*, BBC2's 1972 stab at a French farce.

Kenneth Griffith started his film career in 1941 in *The Farmer's Wife*. He appeared in two Peter Sellers films - Ieuan Jenkins in *Only Two Can Play* and Dai, the informer in *I'm All Right Jack* and also featured in another Peter Sellers vehicle, *Heavens Above*. He was often cast as smarmy, untrustworthy types or the 'stage Welshman' in his film career. Amongst the many films he has appeared in are *Love on the Dole* (1941), *Fame is the Spur* (1947), *Blue Scar* (1949), *Lucky Jim* (1957), *Tiger Bay* (1959), *Carlton-Browne of the FO* (1959), *Expresso Bongo* (1959), *The Lion in Winter* (1968), *The Wild Geese* (1978) and *The Sea Wolves* (1980). Recently he has been seen to good effect in cameo roles in the hit movie *Four Weddings and a Funeral* (where he was billed as 'Mad Old Man', an irascible wedding guest) and also in *The Englishman Who Went Up A Hill and Came Down a Mountain*.

After seeing him expound his views on the Boer War on the *Tonight* programme, the BBC commissioned him to do a film on the siege and relief of Ladysmith (called *The Widow's Soldiers*, 1972). He has since made documentary films on the life of Irishman Roger Casement, Afrikaner runner Zola Budd, Nehru and Napoleon, Cecil Rhodes, Boer War veterans and the rubbish collectors of Pretoria. Other films Kenneth Griffith himself has been responsible for include *Hang Up Your Brightest Colours* (1973) in praise of the Irish Republican, Michael Collins; *The Most Valuable Englishman Ever,* a 'biopic' of Tom Paine, the eighteenth century political campaigner and author of *The Rights of Man,* and *The Sun's Bright Child* dealing with the man thought by many to be England's greatest actor, Edmund Kean. He has also been involved with *Curious Journey* which takes as its subject the travels of the Magi and *Bus to Bosworth* (1975) which follows the route taken by Henry Tudor from his first landing in Wales to his arrival at Bosworth and the battle with Richard III. The 1977 film *A Touch of Churchill - A Touch of Hitler* took as its theme the life of Cecil Rhodes.

Black as Hell, Thick as Grass is Griffith's treatment of the Anglo-Zulu wars; *The Man on the Rock* his interpretation of Napoleon's last days on St. Helena; *Clive of India* tells the story of the conquest of India by the British; *Heart of Darkness* shown on the BBC 2 *Timewatch* slot in October, 1992 takes as its subject the story of Roger Casement at first feted by the British government for his humanitarian work in the Congo, but then vilified by them (and later executed) for his espousal of Irish republican causes.

Unlike many other actors, Kenneth Griffith prefers TV and the cinema to the theatre. He has, nevertheless, played such classic roles as Shylock, Hamlet, Oberon and Iago, although he turned down the chance to become a founder member of the British National Theatre.

A maverick personality, he has devoted a large part of his life to supporting relatively unfashionable causes such as the Afrikaners of South Africa, the Untouchables of India, the Israelis and Irish Republicans. He is the recipient of a BAFTA Cymru Lifetime Achievement Award. Married three times: to Joan Stock and, subsequently, the actresses Doria Noar and Carole Hagar, Griffith has five children. He also enjoyed extra-marital relationships with a number of women, including Madeleine Bell (whom he met whilst watching an American Gospel show called *Black Nativity* in which she was appearing) before she achieved fame as the lead singer with the sixties pop group Blue Mink.

IOAN GRUFFUDD

His mother and father both taught Welsh (his father is currently headmaster at Llanharry Comprehensive School). Born in Cardiff's St. David's Hospital, he lived for a year in Penarth but was brought up in Llwydcoed, Aberdare, but the family returned to Cardiff when he was nine. He attended Ysgol Glantaf and Ysgol Melyn Griffydd, Whitchurch. He starred in *Pobol y Cwm* as Gareth Wyn, the son of Reg Harris, for more than six years. Aged eighteen, he went to RADA. After RADA he came back to Cardiff to appear in BBC Wales's *A Relative Stranger.* His other TV credits include *Poldark, Double Exposure* and *A Mind To Kill.*

Ioan Gruffudd in a scene from Solomon a Gaenor *(S4C)*

In the cinema he has portrayed one of Oscar Wilde's lovers, John Gray, in the film, *Wilde*. His best known role on the big screen to date was as the Welsh hero from Barmouth, Harold Lowe, who single-handedly organised the rescue of survivors from the ill-fated ship, *Titanic*. Aged twenty-eight at the time and a ship's officer, Lowe returned to the scene of the disaster with lifeboats searching for survivors. In the 1998 film, *Titanic*, Ioan, as Lowe, rescues the heroine of the movie, Kate Winslet, from a watery grave. (Strangely enough, at the time of his audition for *Titanic*, Ioan was earning expenses money only in his role in *The Decameron* at London's Gate Theatre.

He continued his nautical prowess as Horatio Hornblower in the £40 million ITV series of the same name which went out in the autumn of 1998. Also in 1998, he took the lead role in *Solomon and Gaenor*, a film shot in two languages - Welsh and English. (The film was nominated as Best Foreign Language Film in the 2000 Oscars but lost out to a Spanish film.) In April, 1999, he starred as Pip in the BBC2 adaptation of Charles Dickens's *Great Expectations*. Meanwhile, he continues to dub cartoons into Welsh for S4C. He appeared as the British lieutenant John Feeley in the November 1999 Screen One TV production about the Bosnian War originally called *Peacekeepers* but screened as *Warriors*. At present he shares a house in Kilburn, north-west London with his fellow Welsh actor Matthew Rhys. Ioan took part in Channel 4's new drama series *Love in the Twenty-First Century* and attracted some notoriety for his role in the fifth episode broadcast in August, 1999 and entitled *Masturbation*. Going to the other extreme, he was chosen to be the voice of Jesus in the S4C/BBC Wales animated film *Gwr y Gwyrthiau* (*The Miracle Maker*) which had its premiere at the Welsh International Film Festival in November, 1999.

In the last year of the Twentieth Century, growing demand for his services saw him modelling clothes for River Island and advertising American Express credit cards. He played the part of sailor Freddie Bywater in the film *Another Life* shot in the autumn of 1999 and had a leading role in the film *102 Dalmatians* alongside Gérard Depardieu and Glenn Close, playing the naive young owner of a dog home. On Thursday, April 6th, 2000 he was given the Best Single Drama Award, from the Broadcasting Press Guild at the Theatre Royal in Drury Lane, for his part in the BBC drama *Warriors*.

LYN HARDING

In his day he was quite possibly Wales's premier actor, as well known to theatregoers as Anthony Hopkins or Richard Burton are today. He was a star of stage, screen and radio with a career which occupied two and a half pages of *Who's Who in the Theatre*. He toured the United States, India, Burma and Japan and shared the stage with the likes of John Gielgud, Ralph Richardson and Anthony Quayle.

Yet today, barely fifty years after his death, the name of David Llewellyn Harding is scarcely known in the land of his birth, his only memorial to be found in a Gwent country pub, a short distance from where he was born.

The bronze plaque on the wall of the *Church House* pub in the village of St. Brides near Newport bears his likeness and states simply:

> DAVID LLEWELLYN (LYN)
> HARDING, THE FAMOUS ACTOR
> BORN ON OCTOBER 12th 1867
> AT ST BRIDES, WENTLOOG
> BEGAN HIS EDUCATION IN
> THIS HUMBLE VILLAGE SCHOOL

But just who was David Llewellyn or Lyn Harding - the forgotten man of Wales? He was born into a strict Welsh Congregationalist family in the village of St Brides on the Monmouthshire Moors, the son of one of Lord Tredegar's tenant farmers. He grew up Welsh speaking and a sturdy six footer, helping out on the family farm. At the age of 16, he left the moors and became apprenticed to Robert Little, Draper, of "Scotland House", Commercial Street in Newport.

Lyn Harding

It was while living in Newport that David first acquired a taste for the theatre. After seeing *It's Never Too Late To Mend* at the Old Victoria Hall (later the Lyceum Theatre, one of old Newport's most famous lanmdmarks) he found himself bitten by the acting bug. He read every book on the theatre he could find.

Lyn's parents were far from pleased at their son's new interest. They had always wanted him to be a preacher, certainly not an actor. His father's shocked reaction on seeing Lyn first perform was a despairing "I have been in hell this night". Nevertheless, despite his parent's opposition, Lyn continued to act. Still in Drapery, he moved to Cardiff where he made his first stage appearance at a chapel. He gave Shakespeare readings, reciting at parties and banquets and acted as an amateur in farces and plays. At one such performance a local printer, finding Llewellyn to be a bit of a mouthful, altered his name to Lyn. Far from being offended, David/Lyn took this as a happy omen, as indeed it turned out to be.

Then came the train journey which was to change his life. Travelling to Bristol on a Sunday he was delighted to find that his fellow passengers were a professional touring company. Luckily for Lyn, one of their number was ill and Lyn was persuaded to take over his role. On August 28th, 1890, he appeared on stage in *The Grip of Iron* at the Theatre Royal in Bristol, playing the part of Monsieur Guerin, an old man strangled in bed. He was paid only fifteen shillings a week but it was to be the start of a glittering career.

After gaining useful experience touring the provinces, Lyn made his

London debut at the Shakespeare Theatre, Clapham, on July 19th, 1897. Then came one of those lulls which seem to occur in every actor's life and he returned to farming for a while, combining working the land around St Brides with appearing in Shakespearian revivals at Manchester.

Soon, however, he was back to his first love, the stage. Bushy-browed and physically big, he specialised in playing villains. The sinister hypnotist, Svengali, the evil Professor Moriarty, Dr. Roylott from Conan Doyle's *The Speckled Band* and Bill Sikes from *Oliver Twist* were just some of the roles he played. He is said to have "played Bill Sikes with such brutal force as to terrify those who saw it". Other leading roles he played were those of Sir Walter Raleigh, Julius Caesar, Sir Francis Drake and Captain Hook. He played in musical plays, melodrama and in Shakespeare. He returned to the land of his birth and played in *Trilby* at Cardiff's New Theatre in December, 1906. One of his own favourite roles was Macbeth a part he played for some seven and a half months in New York in 1928, a record at that time. He also appeared in New York in the same year in *The Patriot* which, however, only ran for ten days, despite also starring John Gielgud.

Lyn Harding always preferred the stage but he starred in more than a dozen films, appearing in both silent films and "talkies". Leslie Halliwell, author of *The Film Companion,* called him a "splendid heavy in some films of the 20s and 30s". Amongst his films were *The Barton Mystery* (1920), *The Speckled Band* (1931), *The Triumph of Sherlock Holmes* (1935), *Fire Over England* (1937), *Underneath the Arches* (1937), *Silver Blaze* (1937), *Goodbye Mr. Chips* (1939) and *The Prime Minister* (1941). He is said to have made his first film in 1914. At one point he made a visit to America and appeared in one or two films but the Hollywood breakthrough never came.

But despite all his fame Lyn never forgot the people of the Moors. To them he was always "Dai". In 1938 he returned to his roots when a ceremony was held at the one room village school to mark his 71st birthday. The rain poured down all day but did nothing to dampen the old actor's spirits as he first planted a memorial tree and then unveiled a plaque. (A similar plaque was also unveiled at Newport Museum and Art Gallery by the Mayor but this seems to have disappeared from view.)

In his day Lyn Harding was regarded as one of the tallest actors on the stage and had a dominating stage presence. His last West End Appearance was as Abu Hassan in *Chu Chin Chow* in 1941. He was nearly 74 years old. When he was almost 80 he played the part of Owen Glendower/Owain Glyndŵr in Shakespeare's *King Henry IV, Part I,* broadcast on the BBC's Third Programme in 1947. (He was eighty-four when he read the Lesson at Ivor Novello's St. Martin-in-the-Fields Memorial Service.) In August 1950 he moved from London to Westcliffe-on-Sea, Essex. Two years later after a long illness, the man described by no less a personage than Sir John Gielgud as "a skilled player", died in a Southend hospital on December 26th, 1952. His funeral took place at the City of London Crematorium on Friday, January 9th, 1953.

On July 21st, 1967, Lyn Harding's old village school closed its doors for the last time after 100 years of teaching. Sixteen pupils were transferred to a large new school in Marshfield. (Once, on one of his periodic visits to the school, in 1939, Harding had presented the boys and girls with a box of oranges, a real luxury at the time. As the newspaper reports of the time had it, the children of St. Brides were sucking oranges for quite a while.) As for the plaque it eventually made the short journey to the village pub where it continues to keep alive the memory of David Llewellyn Harding.

ROLF HARRIS

Rolf was born in Bassendean, Western Australia on March 30th, 1930. At school his nickname was 'Ris' (after the last three letters of his surname, Harris). He attended the University of Western Australia and arrived in London in the year 1952 to study art. A six-footer, it did not take him long to make his mark. Within a year he was being seen on TV as a story-teller and artist. A children's TV regular in the 1950s, the bearded entertainer went on to star in such shows as *The Rolf Harris Show, Rolf on Saturday, Rolf Harris Cartoon Time* and *Rolf's Here! O.K?* from the late sixties to the late eighties. In the nineties, he enjoyed another helping of fame presenting *Animal Hospital.* He has also enjoyed musical success with *Tie Me Kangaroo Down, Sport* and the didgeridoo flavoured *Sun Arise,* not to mention *Two Little Boys, Jake the Peg* and his nineties cult cover version of the Led Zeppelin epic *Stairway to Heaven.* But despite his Australian persona, Rolf's father, Cromwell, worked as a turbine operator in Cardiff and his mother, Agnes, studied at Cardiff High School. The pair emigrated to Australia in 1921 before Rolf was born.

In 1910, Rolf's grandfather, George Frederick Harris, painted a portrait of Godfrey Morgan, Viscount Tredegar, and the hero of Balaclava, where he rode his horse Sir Briggs in the Charge of the Light Brigade. It can be seen at the top of the great staircase in Tredegar House, Newport. And the Welsh connection does not stop there - Rolf's sculptress wife, Alwen, to whom he has been married for forty years, hails from Meirionydd (her parents emigrated to Australia when she was a child). They have a daughter, Bindi. He has been awarded both the MBE and the OBE and he has also been made a Member of the Order of Australia.

Rolf returned to the Land of His Fathers for the final of the 1999 World Rugby Cup held at the Millennium Stadium in Cardiff. Before the match started he, accompanied by a well-known Australian folk singer, entertained the crowds with his button accordion, and a selection of well-known Australian standards. It was not the first time Rolf had sung at a sporting event. In 1982 he performed at the Opening Ceremony of the Twelfth British Commonwealth Games held in Brisbane, Queensland and regaled the spectators with *Waltzing Matilda* and a re-vamped version of *Tie Me Kangaroo Down, Sport.* Rolf has appeared several times at the Glastonbury Festival.

Rolf Harris with his trusty didgeridoo

BOB HOPE

This quintessentially American comedian was actually born in England of a Welsh mother and an English father. Bob Hope's mother, Iris Towns, married William Hope in Cardiff on April 25th, 1891. William, a master stone mason, had moved in the late nineteenth century from his Weston-super-Mare home to find work in the docks at Barry. (Iris had been born in the Welsh seaport and used to sing in the local concert halls.) For many years, the couple lived in Barry's Greenwood Street (Number 12). They subsequently moved to Newport where they lived for three years. After Newport, they moved to Eltham in Kent. It was there, at 44 Craigton Road, that Bob, their fifth son, was born (on May 29th, 1903) and Iris would sing Welsh hymns to Bob whilst he was sitting on her lap. Five years later, Iris and her six sons sailed to America, following after William who had gone on ahead to find work. They proceeded to set down roots, first in New York, and later in Cleveland, Ohio.

Leslie Towns Hope (Bob's real name) started his working life in the butcher's shop owned by his brother but was soon earning a living by dancing in music halls. He served his apprenticeship in the vaudeville halls across America where he was first known as Leslie T. Hope, then Lester T. Hope and, finally, Bob Hope, working his way up to the big time in New York. He made his film debut in the 1938 *Big Broadcast* but really struck it big in *Road to Singapore* (1940), the start of his association with Bing Crosby and Dorothy Lamour. He went on to make nearly eighty films and countless appearances on TV, radio and the stage and become an extremely wealthy man. Famous for his extensive tours to entertain the troops both in World War Two and the Vietnam War, he always referred to his mother as "mam' in the Welsh fashion. Often making trips to Britain to visit his relatives, he combined his stays with stints at the London Palladium. Already an Honorary Commander of the British Empire, in May, 1998, he was awarded an honorary knighthood by the Queen.

Bob Hope married night club singer Dolores Reade on February 19th, 1934 in Erie, near Cleveland and the couple later adopted four children. A golf addict, some of his regular partners were Presidents and ex-Presidents of the United States. Bob took part in the 1951 British Amateur Championship at Royal Porthcawl, staying at St. Donat's Castle, then still owned by William Randolph Hearst, the American newspaper proprietor. He lost in the first round. Although he achieved fame as a stand-up comic and his part in the seven *Road To ...* movies he has a pleasant singing voice and has been associated with some show stopping film songs such as *You Do Something To Me, It's De-lovely, Two Sleepy People, Buttons and Bows* and, of course, his theme tune *Thanks for the Memory*. Apart from the Road films he will be remembered for his roles in *The Cat and the Canary, The Paleface* with Jane Russell, (his most successful film), *Son of Paleface* and *Call Me Bwana* and for his film persona as that of the wise cracking, cowardly comedian who seldom got the girl, especially when Crosby was around.

Bob Hope fans all over the world held their breath on June 1st, 2000 when the much loved entertainer was admitted to the Eisenhower Medical Centre in Rancho Mirage, California, not far from his Palm Springs home, suffering from gastrointestinal bleeding. Hope needed blood transfusions to stabilise the bleeding, but happily, he left the hospital on Thursday, June 8th, apparently none the worse for wear, despite his ninety-seven years.

MARY HOPKIN

Mary Hopkin was born in Pontardawe on May 3rd, 1950. She started out on the road to musical glory by singing in her local Tabernacl Chapel. It was there she sang her first solos. When Mary sang, recalls a childhood friend, "even the Deacons sat up and took notice". At school in Pontardawe Mary appeared in Welsh language plays organised by the school's Welsh teacher, Eic Davies. He, along with the Chemistry teacher, Gwyn Davies, also translated songs from English into Welsh for Mary to sing. (Eic translated the folk anthem *Turn, Turn, Turn* made popular by The Byrds into Welsh.) Interestingly, Eic Davies's son, Huw Llewellyn Davies, the well-known rugby commentator, seemed to imply in a recent S4C programme on Mary (April, 2000) that her Welsh was borderline and that she only just scraped into the Welsh stream in school. Yet her mother and father both spoke Welsh. It was also noticeable in the same programme that whereas most of those interviewed - her mother, her childhood friends - spoke in Welsh, Mary resolutely spoke nothing but English, although she cheerfully sang songs in Welsh to her own guitar accompaniment.

After appearing on the Welsh language musical programme *Hob y Deri Dando*, Mary was signed by Joe Cambrian in 1967 for his Pontardawe based label, Cambrian Records, and recorded some four Welsh language L.P.s for him. At the time she was appearing in lots of gigs in the local area and was considering doing Music, Art and English at 'A' Level, but then her agent, Bert Veale, put her name forward for Hughie Greene's talent spotting programme, *Opportunity Knocks* about a month before her exams. Mary was not keen on this idea but reluctantly agreed to go through with it, and auditioned in a cold church hall in Cardiff. Much to her surprise she won the first programme. In fact, she kept on winning for the next six or seven weeks. More than thirty years later, she would say that it was a very exciting time, but then go on to contradict herself, by stating that she felt as if she had been taken over and become someone else's property.

Someone who was unaware of Mary's inner struggles at the time was the model Twiggy, famed for her ultra-slim figure. When she saw the first programme Mary appeared in, her initial reaction was to exclaim "what a lovely voice". Her second reaction was to get in touch with Paul McCartney and sing Mary's praises to him. The Beatle wasted no time in contacting the Hopkin household. A telegram from Apple, The Beatles' own record label, lay unopened on the mantelpiece for several days before anyone got around to opening it. Then McCartney telephoned. At first, Mary's mother thought it was someone playing a joke but the 'joke' became reality when a car arrived within a few days to take her and her daughter to the recording studio in London. Mary was later to say that it all felt just as if she were in shock. Everything seemed to be like a dream through which she was drifting. Thus did the unsophisticated girl from a small Welsh town become the Apple label's first ever female singer.

At the studio Peter Asher and Paul McCartney recorded Mary singing ten songs but Mary was not satisfied with the first recording she made of *Those Were The Days*. McCartney had offered the song to a few singers but it did not suit their voices. When they recorded it for the second time, however, she felt much better. Based on a Russian folksong, *Those Were The Days* entered the charts on September 4th, 1968 and stayed there for twenty-one weeks, reaching Number One. The song with which Mary will always be associated, ("I still have a very great fondness for that song", says Mary) it even knocked The Beatles' *Hey Jude* from its Number One position. (John Lennon is said to have come up to her in the recording studio and said "What do you mean by knocking us off the Number One?") *Those Were The Days* sold a million copies in the U.S. alone. By the end of 1970 it had sold eight million copies. The song reached Number One in twelve other countries besides the U.K. (She also sang it in Italian - a talent she used to good effect in the 1969 San Remo Festival.) *Goodbye*, written by those well-known songwriters Lennon and McCartney, did almost as well - it got to Number 2 in the singles chart in Britain and to Number Thirteen in the U.S. Her first Apple L.P. *Postcard* which also featured some Donovan tracks came out in 1969. It reached Number 3 and stayed in the L.P. charts for nine weeks.

From very early on, however, it became apparent that McCartney wanted Mary to go down a commercial route, singing "very bubbly, silly little songs" whereas the girl from the Swansea Valley would have preferred to follow her folk inclinations. Nevertheless, in the early days Mary enjoyed working with Paul. She found the songs that he chose for her "far too old or too sweet" but did not question things at the time. (It was also the case that The Beatles had been her idols ever since she had seen them in Llandudno when she was thirteen years old, and she may still have been in awe of them. It must also be remembered that all this happened just a few months after she had left school and she was still very young.) Paul McCartney and Mary parted company in 1969 - "It was pretty awful" recalls Mary. It was also the case that the shy, simple girl from a small town Welsh background with the pure voice felt out of place in the big city, finding the young Londoners rather too sophisticated for her taste.

With a new producer, Mickey Most, she continued to enjoy single success with *Temma Harbour, Knock, Knock, Who's There?* (composed by John Carter and Geoff Stephens) and *Think About Your Children* (written by Errol Brown and Tony Wilson of Hot Chocolate fame, this got as far as Number 19 in 1970). After this, a slide began to set in. The 1971 single *Let My Name Be*

Sorrow climbed to Number 46 and no higher and her last ever chart entry, the 1976 *If You Love Me* only made it to Number 32 and was gone after four weeks. Her image now was of someone "very young, very delicate", something she was not happy with. She turned down the chance to record an L.P. with Most, feeling that he had no interest at all in involving her in the music - he simply wanted her to go into the recording studio and use that "wonderfully evocative and very beautiful voice" of hers.

Mary has described *Knock, Knock, Who's There* as "one of the most appalling songs of all time". At first she had not wanted to do the Eurovision Song Contest and was only persuaded to do so against her better judgement when she was assured she would be given a 'quality' song to sing. She ended up with *Knock, Knock*. It came second in the Contest but Eurovision was really the last straw. It shot what was left of Mary's fragile confidence to pieces. For what it is worth, the much maligned *Knock, Knock* did, however, get to Number 2 in the hit parade.

More to her liking was the 1971 folk-orientated *Earth Song, Ocean Song* album produced by her future husband, Tony Visconti and featuring Ralph McTell and the Strawbs' Dave Cousins amongst the backing musicians. The album did not sell in such great numbers but she "loved it". Unfortunately, she could not afford the time to promote it properly as she was then heavily involved in summer shows. She married Visconti secretly in New York on November 20th, 1972 and they honeymooned together in the Catskill Mountains. (They would later file for divorce on November 30th, 1985 after being separated for two years.)

There followed a period of around four years in which she was, more or less semi-retired - she herself has said "I gave up the music business in 1971 because it wasn't about singing, it was about money". During this time she brought up her children but she also managed to put in a few back-up vocals on L.P.s by Thin Lizzy, Ralph McTell and David Bowie. In 1976 she went back into the studios to record *If You Love Me*, an Edith Piaf song which Visconti produced.

In 1979 she brought out *The Welsh World of Mary Hopkin* on Decca records, a compilation of her earlier Welsh-language material. She was among those taking part in George Martin's 1988 recording of *Under Milk Wood*, which the legendary Beatles producer recorded for EMI. The following year she brought out an L.P. of religious songs on the Trax label. For a brief spell in 1984 she played with Oasis. Not that Oasis. This Oasis included the songwriter and pianist Peter Skellern who had had a massive hint with the romantic *You're A Lady*, the arrangement for which drew on his Northern English roots. Before that she had been a member of another short-lived group, Sundance.

When she first shot to fame Mary looked very doll-like with her long blonde hair. (There is a TV clip in which she, together with her father, is being interviewed in Welsh. The interviewer calls her the first Swansea Valley girl to be Top of the Pops, but directs most of his questions to Mary's father, who died in 1983, hardly ever addressing Mary directly and, when he does, she answers only in monosyllables.) The image of Mary today is that of a more confident, more mature woman at ease with herself. She says she's very content with life, living the way she wants to live and no one is telling her what to do. Living in Henley-on-Thames, her hair is now cropped fashionably short.

So far at least Mary has resisted all efforts to get her to make a comeback although she did tour Great Britain with the Irish band The Chieftains in May, 1999. Recently, Mary has sung with the Welsh group The Crocketts (coincidentally, their drummer Owen, whose surname is also Hopkin, comes from Pontardawe), self deprecatingly describing her role on the record as being that of "the token '60s pop singer" and she has also begun writing her own songs with her son Morgan.

Some now regard Mary Hopkin as 'a flash in the pan' and it is true that her time at the top was relatively short, her hits relatively few. Yet there is still great interest in her - the Internet has a host of web sites devoted to her - and more than one television documentary in recent years has been devoted to her life. An honorary member of The Gorsedd of Bards - she was initiated at the Ammanford National Eisteddfod - she appeared in *Dick Whittington* with Tommy Steele. She also sang in London's St. Paul's Cathedral in 1969, appeared on TV and Radio in Japan (many of her early records sold very well in The Land of The Rising Sun). Popular in Germany, Scandinavia and Holland, she is still a Welsh icon remembered with affection by many.

SIR ANTHONY HOPKINS

Phillip Anthony Hopkins was born at 77, Wern Road, Margam, Port Talbot on December 31st, 1937, the son of baker Dick Hopkins and his wife Muriel. He was educated at Port Talbot's Central School, West Mon School, Pontypool and Cowbridge Grammar School. His grandmother on his mother's side was Welsh-speaking. He learnt very slowly in school and was termed a "very solitary child", but demonstrated precocious talent as a pianist. When he left Cowbridge, aged 17, his sole '0' Level was in English.

The picture that emerges from Michael Feeney Callan's 1993 biography of Hopkins is that of a difficult, obsessed, driven, tormented personality who, for many years, saw his compatriot Richard Burton as his arch-rival. (Indeed, many critics, not to mention Hopkins's fellow Welshmen, were continually comparing him to Burton. Unlike Burton, however, Hopkins was not interested in Welsh rugby, or the Welsh language, all the totems of Welshness which Burton wore so easily - although, for a time at least, he threatened to emulate Burton in his drinking prowess.) On the downside, Hopkins could be famously awkward, both with directors and his fellow actors and, on occasions, stupefyingly rude - especially when under the influence of drink.

In the Introduction to his book, Feeney Callan wrote that: "Hopkins's deep and disturbed character initially intrigued me, finally mesmerised me. Even as I conclude this work, with analysis locked in a typewriter, he moves with the coruscation of a jewel. In this sense, Sir Anthony Hopkins is truly what a star should be: dazzling, beguiling, comprehensible, yet abidingly remote".

The star to be's first acting role was a one-line, walk-on part at the Port Talbot YMCA building in 1955. He played the part of a Roman soldier in a Biblical play called *Emmanuel*. Sensing that acting was where his future might lie, Anthony applied for and won a scholarship to the Cardiff College of Music and Drama, where he studied for two years. A job as Assistant Stage Manager with the Arts Council followed and then, in February, 1958, he was called up into the Royal Artillery where he worked for two years as a clerk.

RADA trained (from September, 1961 to July, 1963), he spent a few years in rep with various companies before, in October, 1965, he began working with Laurence Olivier and the National Theatre. There he worked his way up, playing Coriolanus in 1971 and Macbeth in 1972. A combination of other roles and his personal demons led to an absence of fourteen years before he returned to the National in 1985, playing Anthony with Judi Dench as Cleopatra. He then starred in David Hare and Howard Brenton's play *Pravda* as the South African Lambert Le Roux. In 1986, he became the first actor ever to play the role of Lear one hundred times on the London stage. Soon, he was being spoken about as the logical successor to Burton and Olivier. Since then, however, his stage performances have been few and he has tended to concentrate on his film work. Hopkins appears to have always struggled with Shakespeare, claiming to actively dislike appearing in the Bard's plays. Yet he racked up over one hundred performances as King Lear and as Anthony in Anthony and Cleopatra. Perhaps the damage was done when he walked out on a 1972 National Theatre production of *Macbeth* in which he was playing the title role.

His first real cinema film was the 1958 *The White Bus*, a short directed by Lindsay Anderson. The roll call of his subsequent films includes the crazed ventriloquist in *Magic* (1978), the doctor in *Elephant Man* (1980), Captain Bligh in *Mutiny on the Bounty* (1984), the shop manager, Frank Doel in *84 Charing Cross Road* (1986), the monstrous killer Hannibal Lecter in *The Silence of the Lambs* (1990), Henry Wilcox in *Howard's End* (1991), Vampire-buster Van Helsing in Bram Stoker's *Dracula* (1992), directed by Francis Ford Coppola; the butler in *The Remains of the Day* and C.S. Lewis in *Shadowlands* (both 1993) and the disgraced President Nixon in *Nixon* (1995).

Other Hopkins films include *The Lion in Winter* in which he played the young Prince Richard later to become Richard the Lionheart. He broke his arm whilst riding a horse during filming. In *When Eight Bells Toll* he was the secret agent Philip Calvert and in *All Creatures Great and Small* he was the vet Siegfried Farnon. In *A Bridge Too Far* he was Lieutenant-Colonel John Frost. He appeared in Steven Spielberg's *Amistad* and also in *Meet Joe Black* and *The Edge*. He played Don Diego de la Vega - the original Zorro - in the 1998 film *The Mask of Zorro*.

His performance as the cannibalistic Hannibal Lecter in *Silence of the Lambs* won him not only the British BAFTA Best Actor Award, but also the prestigious Hollywood Oscar for Best Actor. (Only the second Welshman ever to achieve this honour, Hopkins followed in the footsteps of Ray Milland who was awarded the trophy for his performance as the drunken alcoholic writer in the 1945 film *Lost Weekend*. This and his subsequent knighthood saw him finally climbing out of the shadow of Burton.)

In September, 1967, he married his first wife, actress Petronella 'Peta' Barker, the daughter of comedian Eric Barker but things turned sour because of Hopkins's drinking and, after a two-year separation, the couple were divorced on March 14th, 1972. Hopkins' and Petronella's daughter, Abigail, was only fourteen months old when her parents broke up. (Hopkins married his second wife, Jennifer Lynton, the associate producer's secretary on *When Eight Bells Toll*, on January 13th, 1973 at the Methodist church in Barnes.) At about the time of his first marriage and even before he had begun drinking heavily.

In October, 1974, he played Dr. Dysart in *Equus* on Broadway. The play's opening night took place on October 24th at the Plymouth Theatre and was witnessed by, amongst others, Rachel Roberts and Sybil Burton (Ironically, Sybil's former husband, Richard, took over the Dysart role from Hopkins and subsequently played the part in the film version.) Hopkins then moved to Los Angeles where he continued to play the 'roaring boy', expending most of his energies on drinking, much of it solitary. It was there that, on Monday, December 29th, 1975, he decided to bring an end to some fifteen years of solid drinking, claiming that God had spoken to him as he left a less than savoury bar in Westwood, a suburb of Hollywood. He apparently heard a voice telling him that it was all over and that he could now start living again. Soon afterwards, in an effort to get to grips with his drinking, Hopkins made contact with "a self-help group for alcoholics" and threw in his lot with Alcoholics Anonymous. He has kept away from the booze ever since.

Besides being an accomplished pianist, Tony Hopkins is also a gifted mimic - he would have his fellow boarders at Cowbridge Grammar School in tears with his take-offs of their teachers after 'lights-out'. According to fellow Welsh actor Matthew Rhys, he does amazing impressions of Marlon Brando, and he has also been known to 'do' Rod Steiger, Richard Burton, James Cagney, Laurence Olivier and the like. When he 'does' them it is not just their speech, but also their way of walking, their little idiosyncrasies and even their attitudes that come to life. He does a 'spot-on' Tommy Cooper and, by all accounts, he has a great regard for the manic comedian, once going so far as to state that he had based part of his Hannibal Lecter character on Cooper's crazy routines.

In a nod to his Welsh roots he played Dafydd ap Llewellyn in Michael Winner's 1989 film of Alan Ayckbourn's *A Chorus of Disapproval* and took the part of the First Voice in the 1988 recording of *Under Milk Wood*. Hopkins made his first TV appearance in a small, non-speaking part in Emlyn Williams's *The Corn is Green* in 1956. His TV credits include *The Looking Glass War, War and Peace, Kean, Othello, Blunt, Heartland, Great Expectations, Selected Exits* and narrating *Visions of Snowdonia* for BBC2 in May, 1997.

A long-time resident in the United States (he lives in Los Angeles and, very early on in his career, had set his sights on success in America), Hopkins has been showered with awards. He received Best Actor Award for his role as Pierre Bezuhov in *War and Peace* from the Society of Film and Television Arts. He was named Best Actor by the New York Drama Desk for his performance in *Equus*. He was awarded the CBE in 1987 and knighted by the Queen on January 1st, 1993.

In 1998, he gave a million pounds of his own money to the fund to save Snowdon for the nation. In December, 1998, it was reported that he had announced his decision to leave the world of acting behind him. He later denied this, claiming that he had been misinterpreted. In the event he appeared as the anthropologist Ethan Powell in the 1999 film *Instinct* and also in the 1999 film version of Shakespeare's *Titus Andronicus* when he played the title role.

In April, 2000 he came under fire for promoting Barclays Bank in a series of T.V. advertisements, especially in view of the fact that the banking giant was busily closing local branches throughout Wales and the UK. The National Assembly for Wales Member for Neath, Gwenda Thomas, wrote to the theatrical knight asking him to back the campaign to keep Barclays local branches going but, at first, received no reply. Just as that particular 'storm' appeared to be subsiding more criticism was heaped upon Hopkins's head. This time he was accused of betraying the Welsh nation, of being untrue to his roots and of acting like a hypocrite. The reason for all this opprobrium was his decision to take out US citizenship in Los Angeles's Federal Building on Wednesday, April 12th, 2000. Present at the swearing-in ceremony were his mother Muriel, who had left her Newport home two years before, Hollywood director Steven Spielberg and film actor John Travolta. (Jennifer Hopkins was not present, the actor being reportedly estranged from his second wife.)

The Western Mail for one was not amused and waxed indignant at the actor's change of allegiance but its sister paper *Wales on Sunday* and *The South Wales Argus* both took a more relaxed view. As it is, Hopkins's knighthood will now no longer be valid in the States. He still, however, retains his British passport. An irate AM Gwenda Thomas took a second swipe at the thespian in as many weeks and demanded that the Freedom of the Borough of Port Talbot awarded to Sir Anthony six years previously be revoked. Others pointed out that he had been more than generous with his money as far as Wales was concerned. Quite apart from his efforts on behalf of Snowdon he had also donated money to the Welsh College of Music and Drama and presented Port Talbot YMCA with the not insubstantial sum of £20,000.

Hopkins eventually broke his silence on the issue to reveal that he had expected such an outcry and a negative reaction in certain quarters once the news of his decision leaked out. He also replied to Gwenda Thomas's original letter about Barclays Bank, stating that he was simply an actor and not responsible for running the bank. If such criticisms ever did get to him he had a ready made safety-valve at his disposal. The newly-minted 'American' has been quoted as saying: "I have a solitary life. When I have time off, I like to wander off, go into the mountains. I have a fantasy that I'd actually vanish into the hills one day and never be seen again. It's a loner's life and I love it".

Still the criticisms continued, but this time they came from an unexpected quarter. When film work began in Florence for *Hannibal*, the sequel to *The Silence of the Lambs*, two of the city's political parties, The Popular Party and The Greens, protested vehemently that some of Florence's best known landmarks were being used, pointing out that the film was intrinsically violent and would give the wrong image of Florence. But, along with many other Florentines, the mayor of the city remained unmoved and positively welcomed the publicity the film-makers were bringing to his town.

DONALD HOUSTON

Noted for his fine speaking voice, Donald Houston shot to fame playing opposite Jean Simmons in the 1949 film, *Blue Lagoon* which was filmed on the south sea islands of Fiji. With his blond hair, blue eyes and muscular broad shoulders, he looked like a Celtic deity and must have thought he was made for the part. It helped that he was a rugby player and six feet tall and also a fine swimmer and diver. In the event, Houston landed the part against fierce competition from some four thousand other hopefuls. He was twenty-three years old.

Other notable film appearances include: *A Run For Your Money* (in 1949 with Meredith Edwards), *Room at the Top* (1958), his 'Taffy' Evans in *Doctor in the House* (1954 and, incidentally, his favourite film) and Dr. Watson in *A Study In Terror* (1965). He was also to be seen in sixties films *The Longest Day*, *633 Squadron* and *Where Eagles Dare*. His film career continued into the 1980s - in *The Sea Wolves* he appeared with brother Glyn - but this proved to be one of his last outings before the camera.

Friendly with Stanley Baker, Richard Burton and Harry Secombe, Houston preferred the theatre to working in films. He played Peter Quilpe in T.S. Eliot's *The Cocktail Party*, a role he performed first at the Edinburgh Festival and subsequently at the New Theatre (now renamed the Albery) in London's West End, sharing the stage with Rex Harrison and Irene Worth. In 1956 he played the part of the Onlooker in Dylan Thomas's *Under Milk Wood* which transferred to the New in 1956. In New York, however, it lasted less than a month. He was in *Under Milk Wood* again in 1957 and joined the Old Vic Company for the 1959/60 season, taking roles in plays by Shaw and Shakespeare. In the early 1970s he could be seen in a couple of TV series:

Now Take My Wife and *Moonbase Three.* He appeared with Siân Phillips in a 1959 BBC TV production of *Treason*, a translation of Saunders Lewis's *Brad.*

Donald Houston was born in a Tonypandy terraced house on November 6th, 1923. His mother died when he was six years old and he, his brother Glyn and sister Jean were brought up by their grandmother. Houston's father, Alec, a Scotsman, had been a professional football player with Swansea and Dundee and, at one time, it had been Donald's greatest wish to play the game professionally himself, but acting claimed him for its own.

As a boy Houston's pure soprano voice earned him a a place with the Tonypandy Ebenezer Chapel Choir. Whilst still only fourteen he heard that a boys' travelling theatre company was looking for a singer and decided to audition but discovered that they wanted an actor instead. Undeterred, he auditioned and beat a thousand boys for the prize of taking part in a six-week tour. It was in Penzance in 1940 that he first set foot on stage with the Oxford Company of the Pilgrim Players (amongst whom was Meredith Edwards). The company performed religious shows in venues as diverse as the local air raid shelter and St. Paul's Cathedral.

Next stop was the Oxford Repertory Company for a leading part in *Charley's Aunt* before joining the RAF. During the war he was a wireless operator and an air-gunner. He was invalided out and it was back to Tonypandy and down the pit (Cambrian Colliery at Clydach Vale) under the 'Bevin Boys' scheme.

He was still digging coal when he took the leading role in Emlyn Williams's *The Corn is Green* at the Oxford Playhouse. He left the pit and began to tread the boards in London and Oxford. The West End beckoned and then came the screen test for the *Blue Lagoon* and the part of Michael, the lead opposite Jean Simmons.

He met his wife Brenda Hogan in 1947 whilst working in Sir Basil Dean's stage production of *Dr. Jekyll and Mr. Hyde.* Two years later they were married, a marriage that was to last forty-two years but would end in separation.

In the last six years of his life he became something of a recluse retreating behind the walls of his Portuguese cottage near Coimbra. It was there he died on Sunday, October 13th, 1991 at the age of sixty-seven. The week before he had complained to his neighbours of stomach pains. He felt better and the pains appeared to have gone but, on the Saturday, he became ill once more and died the following day. Both Brenda and Donald's brother, Glyn, flew out to attend the funeral held in Portugal.

GLYN HOUSTON

Born in 1926, Glyn Houston, younger brother of Donald, has appeared in films with the likes of Clark Gable, Michael Caine, Robert Mitchum and Alan Ladd and once even played Joan Collins's boyfriend. Considered by some to be "self effacing" and "taciturn", he often played minor roles in British films

such as the soldier in *Private's Progress* and the part of Phillips in *The Cruel Sea.*
He was also seen in *The Blue Lamp* (as a London barrowboy), *Girdle of Gold,*
Stryker of the Yard, The Happiness of Three Women, The Sea Shall Not Have Them,
Tiger Bay, Sink the Bismarck and *The Seawolves.*

Glyn Houston

In 1946 Glyn was with the army in the Far East and was sent out with his unit to stop looting and rioting. As the Forces' Entertainments Unit, ENSA, was coming to an end the authorities were looking to form a new entertainments party called CSE (Combined Services Entertainment) and Glyn decided to audition. He tried his luck at a theatre in Singapore in front of an audience of Top Brass show people, claiming he was a stand-up comedian, whereas, in reality, he only knew about three or four jokes. He duly did the three or four gags and then said, "it goes on like that for about twenty minutes".

To his own surprise he got the job, became one of the group known as 'Four in Harmony' and travelled all over the East from Madras to the borders of Tibet. In fact, the unit he was in claimed as one of its members the comedy writer Jimmy Perry who based the hit comedy show, *It Ain't Half Hot Mum,* on his experiences touring in India. So it was only fitting that Glyn himself would later appear in a 1980 episode of the show.

Remarkably, he appeared as Morgan, the chauffeur in Eynon Evans's *The Wishing Well,* not just as part of the touring company, but also in the West End stage version, the film of the play, entitled *The Happiness of Three Women,* the television production and also, he thinks, when the play was broadcast on radio. Part of the cast of the musical *Pickwick,* he began his TV career in the 1960s in *The Splendid Spur,* a "rousing escapade" of the English Civil War which went out live. He followed it up with a leading role as Hywel Bennett's probation officer in Dennis Potter's 1966 TV play *Where The Buffalo Roam* set in Swansea. He played the eldest son of the Morgan family in BBC TV's 1960 production of *How Green Was My Valley.* Glyn's best TV performance is probably *Better Days* in which he plays a retired miner who moves from the valleys to live with his son in Cardiff.

He played Lord Peter Wimsey's manservant Bunter in the BBC1 television adaptation of Dorothy L. Sayers's stories which ran from 1972 to 1974. He appeared in two Doctor Who stories: *The Hand of Fear* in 1976 in the role of Professor Watson and *The Awakening* in 1984, playing the part of Colonel Wolsey. He has also been seen in *Are You Being Served?* and *Minder*. He played the old miner Uncle Vernon in *A Light In The Valley*, the Michael Bogdanov produced community film about present day life in the Rhondda shown on BBC1 Wales on Tuesday, December 8th, 1998. In another Bogdanov production *A Light On The Hill* screened on BBC One Wales on Wednesday, March 15th, 2000, Glyn took the part of the farmer Lewys Jeffries who died in the opening takes and, from then on, is only seen in flashbacks. Glyn also played a 100-year-old in Bogdanov's *Cardiff in The City*, the third in the trilogy.

Despite his strong Rhondda Valley connections, Glyn is currently living in Weybridge, Surrey. He returned to the land of his birth on Saturday, May 13th, 2000 to unveil the South Wales Miners' Memorial at the Rhondda Heritage Park in Trehafod.

JACK HOWELLS

In 1963, Jack Howells won the Oscar for Best Short Film with his *Dylan* narrated by Richard Burton, the only Welsh film maker (so far, at least) ever to achieve this feat. Dylan, a 1962 joint production by TWW (Television Wales and the West) and the BBC was two years in the making. After winning his Oscar Howells went to a Los Angeles movie theatre to watch his film again. He later confided in Carwyn James: "I confess to a private Welsh thrill when I saw its title blazing outside in lights. Such is the power of the Oscar. And I listened to as Welsh a piece as you could wish - no concessions to America".

Born in Abertysswg in 1913, the son of a miner, Howells was educated at Lewis Boys School, Pengam but moved from the Rhymney Valley when he was twelve. During his time at Cardiff University he was President of the Students' Union. He was a schoolteacher for a time before working under Donald Alexander in Soho Square at the Documentary and Technicians' Alliance, mostly as a writer and at Pathé's London cutting rooms. He then moved on to Associated British Pathé, where, together with Peter Baylis, he made his first film, *The Peaceful Years* (1948) and then *Scrapbook for 1933* the following year. He then went solo with *Here's to the Memory* (1951). Together with Jay Lewis he co-scripted the 1953 *Front Page Story* with Jack Hawkins in the main role of news editor. In that same year he scripted the *Skid Kids*.

The 1965 *The World Still Sings* was a documentary on the Llangollen International Eisteddfod. His *Nye* shown on TWW that same year was not only voted the best Welsh TV production of that year but also the best Welsh TV documentary of 1965. *Penclawdd Wedding* was a 1974 HTV film with a running time of twenty-seven minutes. Also in 1974, and for HTV, *Return to Rhymney* went back to his roots. In 1980, he made *Let Us Sleep Now,* a tribute to those artists and poets who fought in the First World War. Amongst his friends Jack Howells counted Shelley Winters (she is said to have been reduced to tears after seeing him receive his Oscar) and Charlie Chaplin. He died in the morning of Thursday, September 6th, 1990 at the Marie Curie Hospice, (for patients terminally ill with cancer) Home Towers, Bridgend Road, Penarth. He had been admitted to the hospice the previous Friday. The funeral service took place at the Roath Court Funeral Home Chapel on Friday, September 14th and he was cremated shortly afterwards at the Thornhill Crematorium.

GARETH HUGHES

William John Hughes - later to achieve fame as, the now obscure, Gareth Hughes was born in Llanelli on August 23rd, 1894. He was educated at the town's Coleshill School where he took part in such school productions as *The Merchant of Venice,* playing the part of Shylock. Hughes was obviously interested in the theatre at an early age. An article he contributed to the school magazine described a visit to the Royalty Theatre in Llanelli in 1909 to see F.R. Benson's Shakespearian company perform *Julius Caesar.* (Incidentally the Royalty enjoyed a somewhat chequered career, it became Haggar's Theatre and then The Hippodrome before it was turned into a Bingo Hall. Even that no longer exists, having been knocked down to create space for a supermarket.)

Hughes never forgot his old school. In 1912 he lent costumes to it for a production of *As You Like It* and visited it again to talk to the boys when he made a brief return to his home town in the early 1960s. In his time, Hughes enjoyed fame as a silent film star. (He never really appeared with any big-name directors and most of his films are now forgotten except by film buffs, yet in his time he brought his own piece of glory to his native land. Some of the actors he appeared with, however, did have names that still resonate down the years: Bessie Love, Adolph Menjou, Pola Negri and Lionel Barrymore. He also became friends with the likes of Jack Dempsey, the World Heavyweight Boxing Champion.)

A Welsh speaking Welshman, Hughes left Llanelli when he was thirteen years old and joined a strolling band of Shakespearian actors. Somewhere along the line he acquired the name of Gareth and, before long, he was himself playing big parts on the stages of London and New York. In 1911, he took the plunge and decided to emigrate to America. It proved to be a wise decision. By 1920 he was one of the Broadway big names and well known for his parts in Shakespeare's plays. But the siren calls of the silver screen grew ever louder and he journeyed west to California and Hollywood. At the height of his movie popularity he was being paid as much as $2,000 a week. In thirteen years, from 1919 to 1932, he made forty films, (most of which were of a sentimental nature) was a Hollywood regular and was employed by such studios as Fox and MGM; often appearing with the well known female stars of the day.

By the mid-1920s, he had become an American citizen, but there were minus points to be considered. Standing a mere five feet five inches and weighing in at only eight and a half stone, he was a comparative weakling. This lack of physical presence, combined with his rather youthful looks, meant that he was, more often than not, typecast as naive young men or 'glamour boys' with little to show for themselves, apart from their glamorous faces. In his book *Wales and Cinema - The First Hundred Years,* published by the University of Wales Press, David Berry says that "Generally, Hughes seemed more at ease as lonely helpmate and lover or flawed innocent than as worldly man-about-town". Berry also quotes from the 1954 book by Fulton Ousler, *Lights Along The Shore,* in which Ousler describes Hughes as "the charm boy to end all charm boys" and "a petted darling of a precious set". Such quotes, make it clear that Gareth Hughes was not without talent but, unable, or unwilling, to make the move to more mature roles which would challenge him, his film career inevitably began to slide.

He took the decision to leave the film world and return to the stage, having always preferred the theatre to the world of cinema anyway. His last film was the 1931 *Scareheads.* (There is no evidence, however, to suggest that the coming of the 'talkies' put paid to Hughes's film career.) Eventually, he 'dropped out' altogether in the the 1930s to become a priest, ministering to the Paiute Indians on their Nevada reservation at Pyramid Lake. (His last theatre performance was in 1938 in *The Merchant of Venice* which ran for twenty weeks at the Hollywood Playhouse.) The Indians called him Brother David. From earning a fairly substantial amount of money every week, 'Brother David' now found himself with very little money at all, having given away almost everything he possessed and, the supreme sacrifice, perhaps, having burnt the press cuttings which he had been collecting for the past twenty-six years. What money he did have he gave to the Indians, all he kept for himself were some special books and pictures.

Hughes's desert 'parish' included three small mission churches. He was provided with a spanking new Sedan car but traded it in for a secondhand station wagon. This he used every day to ferry water and, when the occasion demanded, it also doubled up as a bridal coach and, in sadder times, a hearse. It was a tough life and Hughes had a hard fight on his hands struggling against the everyday crime, ignorance and superstition which he found all around him, but he grew to love the Paiute Indians, calling them his "children".

In 1958 he decided to return to Llanelli intending to spend his declining years in the town of his birth but soon found that the damp and cold Welsh weather no longer agreed with him. After five months, he packed his bags and returned to the warmth of his adopted homeland. In the early sixties RKO Pictures toyed with the idea of making a film about his life and his time with the Indians called *The Desert Padre,* but he turned down all offers.

He spent his last years at the Motion Picture Home in Woodland Hills, California where he died on October 1st, 1965 after a long illness. He was buried in Reno, Nevada. The words 'Brother David' are inscribed upon his tombstone. Gareth Hughes seldom appeared in big productions, and when he did, his name was not the one in lights. Yet he brought comfort and succour to many, both in his film performances and in real life. Perhaps his greatest production of all was the one he himself played out, far from the spotlight of publicity, tending to the needs of his beloved Paiute Indians.

RHYS IFANS

Rhys Ifans was born in Haverfordwest, and was only a baby when his family moved to Ruthin. He attended a Welsh-speaking school in Mold (Maesgarmon Comprehensive) where he passed six 'O' Levels. Aged eighteen, he failed to turn up for his 'A' Levels in Welsh, British Constitution and Art, even though both his parents, Eirwyn and Beti, were teachers. Not surprisingly, he was awarded three 'Fs' for grades. After leaving school, he did a little work backstage at Theatre Clwyd before moving to London and the Guildhall School of Music and Drama where he studied for three years. He left the Guildhall to work in theatre in Chichester and then worked in Cardiff for S4C before going back to London. Now 29, he enjoys a reputation as something of a hell raiser. He was Eddie in *You're Dead* with John Hurt. He played one of the Lewis twins (Jeremy Lewis) in Kevin Allen's *Twin Town*. (Rhys was first noticed by Kevin at a National Theatre production of *Under Milk Wood* when playing the Second Voice.) Rhys recommended his brother Llyr for the role of second twin in *Twin Town*.

Rhys Ifans

Ifans has appeared in Karl Francis's *Judas and the Gimp* and *Streetlife* and in Anthony Hopkins's *August*. He also played the two brothers in The *Deadness of Dad* which won the prize for Best Short Film at the Galway Film Festival in July, 1997. On Welsh language TV he was one of The Franks and he has been seen in *Shakespeare Shorts* on the BBC. He was also seen in Lynda La Plante's ITV thriller, *Trial and Retribution*. He played Meirion in S4C's 1994 *Rhag Pob Brad*.

His theatre appearances include *The Idiot* at the Guildhall in London and he worked for the National Theatre for eighteen months. He has also worked for the Manchester Royal Exchange. Ifans was in *Badfinger* at the Donmar Warehouse in London.

He made his film debut in a minor role in the Anthony Hopkins directed *August* in which he did little else but ride a bike and mouth phrases like "Trouble at quarry". Elsewhere on the big screen he was in *The Sin Eater* and appeared with Meryl Streep, Michael Gambon and Catherine McCormack in the 1998 film, *Dancing at Lughnasa*, based on a play by Brian Friel. His other films include *Rancid Aluminium*, playing London businessman Peter Thompson, *Heart*, as the writer Alex, *Janice Beard: 45wpm* (in which he played a double agent) and *Notting Hill* with Julia Roberts and Hugh Grant (all 1999). In *Notting Hill*, he played Spike, Grant's less than salubrious Welsh flatmate, who threatens to steal the show from the two main leads. (Interestingly, Richard Curtis's script had Spike down as a Scotsman but Ifans managed to persuade director Roger Mitchell to let him play the part as a Welshman.) The film critics raved over his performance and the part earned him cult status.

His first Hollywood film was *The Replacements* a football comedy where he starred alongside Keanu Reeves. His second Tinseltown outing came in *Little Nicky* in the role of a demon, the son of Harvey Keitel's Satan.

Two interesting things about Rhys Ifans are: he met his current girlfriend - fashion PR executive Jess Morris with whom he now lives in London - whilst the two of them were trapped in a hotel lift in Milan, and he changed his name from Evans to the more Welsh sounding Ifans when he was thirteen years old. (His actor brother, Llyr, stayed true to the original Evans.)

Famously called a "Taff in Pants" (after his role in *Notting Hill*) Ifans appeared in school productions such as *The Wizard of Oz* (he played The Tin Man) and *Oliver* (he took the lead role). His film *Rancid Aluminium* was, however, universally panned by the critics. Some people even began to doubt Rhys's ability to pick out a good film role. Rhys's appearances in the 2000 British films *Love, Honour and Obey* (as a gangster) and as super-DJ Eyeball Paul in the Harry Enfield film *Kevin and Perry Go Large* received similar short shrift from the critics. *Janice Beard:45 WPM* was also shot down in flames in no uncertain manner. (This particular putdown was adding insult to injury as, whilst filming Janice, Rhys had fractured his ankle, causing him to be absent from filming for a week. But no exciting stunts were involved - the man from Ruthin simply missed his footing when stepping down from the catering bus and fell awkwardly.) Undaunted, Rhys featured in the video of Tom Jones and the Stereophonics' version of *Mama Told Me Not To Come*.

DAVID JASON

Del Boy Trotter - the role indelibly associated with the name of David Jason. David is also well known for his portrayal of Pop Larkin in Yorkshire TV's *The Darling Buds of May* first shown on April 1st, 1991 and also for his role in another Yorkshire TV series - that of Detective Inspector Jack Frost - in *A Touch of Frost*, first shown on December 6th, 1992.

Born David John White on February 2nd, 1940, in the North Middlesex Hospital, the son of Arthur White and his Welsh wife Olwen, he was one of two twins, but his other twin, Jason, died after only two weeks. David White, the surviving twin, attended Northside School and, after leaving school, joined an amateur theatrical group known as The Incognitos. He started working life apprenticed to become a garage mechanic but abandoned this twelve months later to train as an electrician. Aged twenty he found himself made redundant by the London Electricity Board but determined to set himself up in an electrical business of his own.

Meanwhile, David was putting in such consistently high performances with The Incognitos - both comic and serious - that it seemed only a matter of time before he would transfer his talents to the professional stage. His big chance came when his brother, Arthur White, picked to play the South Sea Island butler in Noel Coward's *South Sea Bubble*, withdrew at short notice having been offered a part in the TV programme *Z Cars*. So David stepped into Arthur's shoes making his professional debut for Bromley Rep on April 5th, 1965 and followed this up with a part in *Under Milk Wood* at the Vanbrugh Theatre in London which ran for four weeks. His second play with the Bromley Rep was a farce called *Diplomatic Baggage*.

When David first entered the acting profession he could not call himself by his real name David White, as Equity already had an actor of that name on their books. It was the same story with his second choice David Whitehead, and so he elected to call himself David Jason, consciously or unconsciously, perhaps, perpetuating the name of his dead twin brother.

The first series of *Do Not Adjust Your Set* was shown on December 26th, 1967. It ran for three series, ending on May 14th, 1969 and David made his mark here in his role as Captain Fantastic. The show also starred Michael Palin, Terry Jones and Eric Idle. London Weekend TV's *Hark at Barker* where David played Ronnie Barker's aged gardener Dithers was first shown on April 11th, 1969. David co-starred in three episodes of *Porridge* in 1975 and 1977 as the ageing prisoner Blanco Webb.

Open All Hours was first shown in February 1976 and David soon made his mark as shop owner Arkwright's (played by Ronnie Barker) put-upon nephew Granville. The show ran for four series and ended in 1985. The immortal Derek 'Del Boy' Trotter, star of *Only Fools and Horses*, first hit the nation's screens on September 8th, 1981. There were seven series of the much loved Trotters' adventures but the last time David was seen on screen as Del Boy was in the 1996 Christmas specials.

On September 4th, 1985, David opened in *Look No Hans!* at the Strand Theatre in London's West End. In 1988, he won the BAFTA Award for Best Actor for his role as Skullion in Channel 4's *Porterhouse Blue*.

Apart from his other, more familiar comic creations, Jason is also the voice behind such cartoon characters as Dangermouse, Count Duckula, The Big Friendly Giant and Toad of *Wind in the Willows* fame. He has been a gardener in *Crossroads*, taken over the starring role from Michael Crawford in *No Sex Please - We're British*, (a role he played for eighteen months), supported Bob Monkhouse on radio, acted in farce with Brian Rix and wowed audiences in the London theatre.

His film career to date has been less successful. In the 1972 film version of *Under Milk Wood* he was No Good Boyo. He made his big screen debut as a leading man in the ill-fated, low budget 1973 British film *White Cargo*. Originally titled *Albert's Follies*, it was panned by the critics. A qualified diver, David Jason goes scuba diving in the Cayman Islands and also flies gliders by way of relaxation. The role of real life Captain Frank Beck (who led his men against the Turks at Gallipoli in August, 1915) in *All The King's Men* shown on BBC1 on Sunday, November 14, 1999 was a new departure for him. His long-time Welsh girfriend and partner, Myfanwy Talog, died of cancer in March, 1995.

KARL JENKINS

With his trademark bristling moustache Karl Jenkins looks every inch the Viking warrior. Hardly surprising really when you consider that his Swedish grandfather met his Welsh grandmother whilst she was selling Penclawdd

Karl Jenkins (Sheila Rock)

cockles in Newport, Gwent. (His ship had docked in the town at the time.) Karl himself was born in Penclawdd near Swansea. His mother died when he was five and he was raised by his father (an organist and choirmaster) and his aunt, Evelyn Hopkins. The young Jenkins grew up surrounded by music. At the age of six he learned to play the piano and then progressed to the oboe at Gowerton Grammar School where he also learned to play the saxophone. He was principal oboe with the National Youth Orchestra of Wales. He was educated at Cardiff University and then, aged twenty-one, went to the Royal Academy of Music. He would study by day and then, when night came, 'moonlight' at Ronnie Scott's Jazz Club.

In the early 1970s Karl co-founded the experimental jazz band Nucleus which went on to win First Prize at the Montreux Jazz Festival. He played keyboards in the group which was described by the *Virgin Encyclopedia of Seventies Music* as "the doyen of British jazz-rock groups". *The Encyclopedia* then went on to say that the group's first three albums (on which Karl Jenkins played) would form an integral part of any comprehensive rock or jazz collection. His oboe backed vocalist Linda Hoyle in her 1971 album *Pieces of Me*. Jenkins left Nucleus in 1972 to join the progressive rock/jazz group Soft Machine which was first formed in 1966. He stayed with them through various incarnations, writing and playing before deciding to branch out on his own.

In 1997 he wrote the children's operetta *Eloise* which was first performed by the West Eleven group in Notting Hill Gate. (The libretto was written by his wife, Carol Barratt, who is herself a composer.) It was later performed by Gowerton School at Swansea's Taliesin Arts Centre in December, 1998 as part of the school's celebrations of its twenty-five years as a Comprehensive.

People have written to Karl saying that *Adiemus - Songs of Sanctuary* and his music in general has changed their lives. It sold over one million copies throughout the world (it went platinum in Finland) and reached Number One in the classical FM Charts maintaining that position for a number of months. It was also used as the theme music for the 1996 Five Nations Rugby Tournament and also the animation series *Testament* which was shown on BBC2. It was performed 'live' at London's Battersea Power Station in December, 1997.

Jenkins himself has said that his music comes from a classical base. He always uses acoustic instruments, but his jazz and rock background allows him to combine all these influences in his work. He does not consider himself to be a classical composer as such but feels that he has gone back to his classical roots. He describes his work as "spiritual music for a secular age" and has said that "I write music that connects with a lot of people and gives them, they say, some spiritual solace".

He uses words as sounds instead of meaning, as witness the Cheltenham and Gloucester Building Society advertisements. Known for his experimentation he has invented a kind of language of his own. He uses vocals as instrumental sound - the whole sounding vaguely like Latin which gives it "a kind of spiritual feel".

Besides writing the music for many television advertisements - companies such as De Beers, Levi Jeans, Delta Airlines and the Renault Clio have all used the 'Jenkins sound' - Karl Jenkins has also composed *Cantata Mundi*. His own personal tastes include classical music, jazz and some popular music and he cites Cream as a favoured band. He originally composed using traditional pen and paper but has since moved onto computers. His *Fanfare for Four Trumpets* was written to celebrate the Ceremonial Opening of the National Assembly of Wales on May 26th, 1999. To herald the arrival of the Queen and the Duke of Edinburgh, the *Fanfare* was played throughout the day. He was made an honorary Fellow of the Welsh College of Music and Drama in July, 1999. (The Fiftieth Anniversary of the founding of the College.)

BBC Wales especially commissioned the composer to produce *Dewi Sant*, a new choral and orchestral work for its Millennium celebrations. It was given its world premiere on March 1st, St. David's Day, 2000. Conducted by Jenkins himself the work was performed by the National Orchestra of Wales and recorded at St. David's Hall. Divided into seven movements, *Dewi Sant* takes up the triple theme of the saint's last sermon - Be Joyful, Keep the Faith and Do the Small Things. Broadcast on BBC2 Wales on Sunday, March 5th, 2000 the work was sung in three languages - Welsh, Latin and English and narrated by rising star Ioan Gruffudd. Reviewing it in the following Saturday's *Western Mail*, Dewi Savage called Jenkins's latest work "an inspiring journey" and warmed to "the valedictory penultimate movement" which he found "particularly brilliant".

GLYNIS JOHNS

The blue eyed, blonde haired daughter of Mervyn Johns, husky voiced beauty Glynis Johns was born in Pretoria, South Africa on October 5th, 1923 and was on stage from the age of twelve. Her first film was the 1936 *South Riding*. Other films include *Perfect Strangers, An Ideal Husband, The Card, The Beachcomber, The Sundowners*, (for which she was nominated for an Academy Award) *Mary Poppins* (she played the suffragette mother), *Lock Up Your Daughters* and *Vault of Horror*. She was in the 1949 film *Third Time Lucky* and played Mary Tudor in the 1952 film *The Sword and the Rose*. In the 1972 film version of *Under Milk Wood* she was Myfanwy Price. On stage she has appeared in *Major Barbara, Too True To Be Good* and *A Little Night Music* (for which she won a 1973 Tony Award). She made her New York debut at the Plymouth Theatre on January 30th, 1952 playing the title role in Enid Bagnold's *Gertie*. She played the woman accused of murdering her husband in Terence Rattigan's last play, *Cause Célèbre*. She was still appearing on TV and in films in the '80s and '90s - that distinctive voice was heard again when she guest starred as Mrs. Helen Chambers, Diane's mother, in an episode of the Boston bar-room comedy *Cheers*.

MERVYN JOHNS

Mervyn Johns was born in Pembroke on February 18th, 1899. His original intention was to become a doctor and he began his studies at the London Hospital, but it soon became clear to him that he was not sufficiently tough for this profession and so he decided to switch to acting. It proved the right choice. In his time at RADA he took not only the Gold Medal but several other awards as well.

He made his first appearance on a London stage in 1923 when he played a small part in *The Elopement*. There then followed a South African tour (where, towards the end of 1923, his daughter Glynis was born). For the next ten years Johns spent most of his time in touring productions or taking the leading roles in provincial repertory companies. He enjoyed his first long run at the Little Theatre in Bristol and it was during this time that, directing and acting, he began to hone and polish his craft.

His first film role was in the 1934 *Lady in Danger* and the films for which he will probably best be remembered are Hitchcock's *Jamaica Inn*, *Next of Kin* where he plays a Nazi spy, the war film *Went the Day Well*, the Welsh-based *Halfway House* where he played an innkeeper returned from the dead and the 1945 Ealing fantasy chiller *Dead of Night*. He also played the minister in *Valley of Song* and amongst his seventy or so other films were: *Moby Dick*, *The Rebel*, *55 Days at Peking*, *Day of the Triffids* and *The Heroes of Telemark*.

Johns made his greatest impact on stage in the 1940s, playing Sir Patrick Cullen in Shaw's *The Doctor's Dilemma*, Shotover in *Heartbreak House* and replacing Michael Redgrave as the Duke in *The Duke in Darkness* by Patrick Hamilton. In 1949 he was Jeeter Lester in *Tobacco Road* which enjoyed a long run at the Playhouse Theatre. In *Pen Don*, he played Emlyn Williams's twin brother.

In the 1950s Johns was relatively quiet, between 1952 and 1961 he did not appear on a West End stage and made comparatively few films although one of them, the 1951 version of *A Christmas Carol* with Johns as Bob Cratchit and Alaistair Sim as Scrooge achieved near cult status in America, being a regular feature of Yuletide TV in New York for a great many years. He broke his stage 'duck' by playing Ben Morton, the head of the Morton family, in Gwyn Thomas's *The Keep*, at the Royal Court in 1961. Even then he was not settled and announced he was going to live in South Africa with his wife. When she died in 1970 he returned to Britain and occasionally performed but it was clear that he was no longer really interested.

He retired to Denville Hall, the showbiz retirement home, and it was here that he met Diana Churchill, the former actress now wheelchair-bound and suffering from multiple sclerosis. She had been a widow for the past twelve years but a spark was struck and they married in 1976. (The widow of Barry K. Barnes who died in 1965 and had co-starred with her in comedy thrillers in the late 1930s, Diana died in 1994.) A year later, they were both to be seen in an episode of *The New Avengers*. He also appeared on TV in *Shoestring* in 1983. (Earlier, in July, 1964, he had appeared as the detective Father Brown in a BBC production *The Quick One*.) Mervyn Johns died, aged 93 years of age, at Denville Hall on Sunday, September 6th, 1992.

ALLAN JONES

In an ocean of Marx Brothers mayhem he stood out like an island of calm and sanity, even managing to find a few precious moments to sing, whilst the Brothers Marx were otherwise engaged. His name was Allan Jones and he was born in Old Forge, near Scranton, Pennsylvania in the United States of America on October 14th, 1907, the son of Welsh parents. His father was a miner from Cwmbach in the Cynon Valley and the young Jones followed in his father's footsteps, also working down the mines for a time. After leaving school he used his savings and a scholarship he had gained to study music at Syracuse University and also in Paris. When he returned to America he appeared in stage musicals and sang on Broadway, (he had his first big part as Boccacio in the operetta of the same name by Suppé in 1931 and he was in the 1933 musical *Roberta*) before trying his luck in the Hollywood of the mid-1930s.

Once arrived in Los Angeles it did not take him long to make his mark as a romantic lead who also sang tenor in such films as *Showboat* and *The Firefly*. (On this occasion in 1937 Jones was able to steal a march on his main rival Nelson Eddy by appearing with the latter's regular singing partner Jeanette MacDonald.) It was in *The Firefly* that he first sang the *Donkey Serenade* by Rudolf Friml which was to be his theme song ever afterwards. He also provided what the film historian Ephraim Katz called "the rather wooden romantic interest" for the two Marx Brothers films *A Night At The Opera* in 1935 and the 1937 *A Day At The Races*.

Other films Jones appeared in were his first, *Reckless* in 1933 (he had a minor role in this Jean Harlow vehicle which also featured James Stewart and David Niven), *Rose Marie* in 1936 and *The Great Ziegfeld* (1936) in which he did not actually appear himself but dubbed the singing voice for Dennis Morgan. Other Thirties films he could be seen in were: *Showboat* (other stars of this 1936 film included Irene Dunne and Paul Robeson), *Everybody Sing* (1938 - he played opposite Judy Garland) and two 1939 movies, *Honeymoon in Bali* and *The Great Victor Herbert*.

Allan Jones made his best films in the 1930s. In the 1940s the studios used him in a total of thirteen films but it was mostly a case of quantity, not quality. For the record the films are: *One Night In The Tropics* (1940 - once again he found himself playing the 'straight man' to comedians, the jokers this time being Abbott and Costello), *There's Magic in Music* (1942), *True to the Army* (also 1942), *Moonlight in Havana* (1942), *Rhythm of the Islands, Larceny with Music, Crazy House, You're A Lucky Fellow Mr. Smith, When Johnny Comes Marching Home* (all 1943), *Sing A Jingle* (1944), *The Singing Sheriff* (1944) and *Senorita from the West* and *Honeymoon Ahead* (both 1945)

Jones continued to make films in the 1950s: *All My Love, Donkey Serenade, The Lonesome Road, The Monkey and the Organ Grinder* (all 1950), *Only A Rose, Over and Over, Questa o Quella, Take Me In Your Arms* (all 1951) and, in 1952, *The World Is Mine Tonight*.

Away from the world of Hollywood, Jones appeared on Broadway in

Bittersweet (1934) and in the same year he featured in *Music Hath Charms*. In 1942 he sang in *The Chocolate Soldier* and, two years later, he could be heard, again on Broadway, in *Jackpot*.

After an argument with Louis B. Mayer, the head of MGM, Jones turned his back on Hollywood in 1945 and switched his attention to playing the nightclubs. (Apart from the clutch of 1950s films already mentioned he only ever made two films again - the 1965 *A Swinging Summer* and the 1967 *Stagecoach to Thunder Rock*, neither of which is ever likely to find its way into the hundred best movies of all time list.) He toured the States in the 1950s singing in the musical *Guys and Dolls* and toured again with the *Man of La Mancha* in the 1970s, receiving an award for his interpretation of the main role of Don Quixote. In the 1970s he also played the Northern England clubs.

Shortly after returning from touring Australia, he died in New York City of lung cancer on June 27th, 1992. He was married four times: to Marjorie Buel in April, 1929 (they later divorced), Irene Hervey (June 26th, 1936 to December 28th, 1957 when they divorced), Mary Florsheim Picking (from 1958 to 1964, divorced) and to Esther Marie Villavincie from 1967 to his death.

Allan Jones's son Jack Jones, by his second wife, actress Irene Hervey, took up where his father left off and became an internationally famous popular singer. Once linked romantically with British actress Susan George, he has won two Grammies for his singing and is frequently to be found singing in nightclubs, recording albums and appearing on T.V. Jack was born on the same day that his father recorded the song which would always be associated with him - Donkey Serenade (Many consider the film in which this song featured - *Firefly* to be Jones's best). From then on it would become one of Allan Jones favourite quips to joke that he called his son Jack because it was short for 'jackass'.

CATHERINE ZETA JONES

This Swansea born beauty was born just plain Catherine Jones on September 25th, 1969. (The 'Zeta' is said to have been inserted to distinguish her from other Catherine Joneses, but apparently comes from her grandmother, called Zeta after a cargo ship of the same name sailing out of Swansea harbour.) Her father, David, was a sweets salesman and she was born and raised in Treboeth, east Swansea before the family moved to West Cross and then to Mayals, a sought after area of the city. A veteran of stage appearances from the age of four - she appeared in social clubs and workingmen's institutes - the young Catherine won a Butlin's Star Trail junior talent contest in Minehead at the age of ten. One year older and she was appearing on stage in *Annie* at the Victoria Palace in London playing the part of an orphan. When she was thirteen she was British Tap-Dancing Champion. Educated at Swansea's private Dumbarton House School, she was getting ready to do her 'O' Levels when she was asked to go on tour with *The Pyjama Game*. Her headmaster, Aled Davies, is reputed to have said to her "Go, you're going to be a star, not a professor". But it was a part in the successful musical *42nd Street* which launched her on her road to success.

The girl from the Mayals district of Swansea made a memorable TV appearance when only nineteen as Mariette, Pop Larkins's nubile young daughter in *The Darling Buds of May* which ran from 1991 to 1993 and also produced a 1992 Christmas Special. She was Victoria Chapman in *The Cinder Path*, a mini-series based on a story by Catherine Cookson.

Her films to date include the part of Scherezade in the film of the same name, *The Return of the Native, Christopher Columbus, Catherine the Great, The Discovery, Splitting Heirs* and *Blue Juice* but none of these brought any real critical acclaim or led to long queues at the box office. She moved to Los Angeles to kick-start her flagging career in films. Her first American film was *The Young Indiana Jones Chronicles*. She then starred in the two-part mini-series *The Titanic* and with Billy Zane in the 1997 film *The Phantom.*

In the 1998 film *The Mask of Zorro*, she played the part of Elena de la Vega, the daughter of the original Zorro (Anthony Hopkins). Speaking about the film to Ray Gravell on S4C, she said: "I sing, I dance, I act. I always felt really restricted in Britain. *Zorro* is an important transition in my career." The following year she co-starred with Sean Connery in *Entrapment,* playing Gin Baker, an insurance agent, out to catch Connery's art thief. She starred opposite Liam Neeson as a "wild bisexual" artist in *The Haunting of Hill House* released in the USA in the summer of 1999 and in Great Britain in September, 1999.

Miss Zeta Jones has been romantically linked with a number of males ranging from the Simply Red singer Mick Hucknall to ex-Blue Peter presenter John Leslie, not to mention John Peters the film producer and the actors Paul McGann and Angus McFadyen (*Braveheart*). There have even been rumours that her relationship with Sean Connery overstepped the bounds of professionalism. However, the talk of the papers in the summer of 1999 was her romance with *Fatal Attraction* star Michael Douglas. (After meeting at the Deauville film festival in August, 1998 they had been seen together in Majorca and in London and, on July 1st, 1999, she described theirs as being "a very special relationship"). It was confidently expected that the couple would marry once Douglas had secured an, expensive, divorce from his wife, Diandra. Notwithstanding the whirlwind romance Zeta Jones continued to remain close to her family - her father and brothers taking an active role in administering her affairs.

The pair spent Christmas 1999 together in a Swansea hotel, Douglas renting the three top suites at the city's Swansea Marina Marriott Hotel, and the couple visited local beauty spots as well as spending time with singer Bonnie Tyler at her Swansea Bay home on Christmas Day. Their stay proved to be something of a minor triumph for the two, as previously they had fooled the world's media into thinking all was not well between them - Zeta Jones having flown into Heathrow alone and rumours circulating that

Douglas would be staying in America. However, Douglas flew into Cardiff Airport by himself on Christmas Eve and the lovers were re-united. Their soap opera romance continued when it was announced on Michael Douglas's Internet Website that he had proposed to Catherine at his Aspen, Colorado home on New Year's Eve, 1999 and that she had accepted.

Speculation immediately started as to when and where the marriage would take place. Would it be on September 25th, the gilded couple's joint birthday? Would it be in the small Swansea church of St Clyne's or in one of Michael Douglas's plush homes - perhaps his villa in Majorca? A castle in Scotland was mentioned but promptly denied by Michael Douglas. Even Newport's Celtic Manor was rumoured to be the place, although the hotel soon scotched any such speculation. The newspapers also had a field day regarding Roman Catholic Zeta Jones's wedding dress and who would design it. Meanwhile the Zeta publicity mill ground inexorably on. It was reported that she had rejected a role in an Oliver Stone directed Kevin Costner film, to prepare for her wedding, and that she had formed her own production company - Zeta Films - to make up to twelve movies. She was also to appear in TV commercials advertising a hair shampoo. There were also reports that she would sign a pre-nuptial agreement guaranteeing her future husband's fortune. The couple's forthcoming baby also hogged the headlines. Some Welsh people even went so far as to bet on which name it would be given. One woman dreamt that Jamie would be the chosen name and backed her dream accordingly.

Of late, Zeta Jones, now very wealthy in her own right, has become increasingly quotable. Some of her comments include: "I don't mind saying 'obey' as long as he says it" (referring to her coming wedding to Michael Douglas) and "I really want to grow old gracefully. I want to be Anne Bancroft in *The Graduate,* seducing the new Dustin Hoffman". Meanwhile the Swansea star has begun to pick up some 'gongs'. In May, 2000, at the 2000 Blockbuster entertainment Awards held in Los Angeles she was named as Favourite Action Actress for her part in *Entrapment.*

Zeta's baby - 7lb. 7oz. Dylan Michael Douglas - was born in the early hours of Wednesday August 9th, 2000 in the Cedars Sinai Medical Centre in Los Angeles. It was a week overdue and had been induced.

GRIFF RHYS JONES

The name is, unmistakably, Welsh, the birthplace scarcely less so. Griffith Rhys Jones was born in the capital, Cardiff, at the city's Royal Infirmary on November 15th, 1953. His parents were the eminently Welsh Elwyn Rhys Jones, a North Walian surgeon, and Gwyneth Margaret Jones, from the Rhondda and a nurse at the hospital where he was born. He was only six months old when the family left Cardiff for the south-east of England. Regarding his own Welshness, he is quoted as saying "I was born here, but I am not really Welsh. I suppose, I'm a bogus Welshman". Educated at Brentwood School, he read History and English at Cambridge University. He started out producing radio programmes like *Weekending* and *Top of the Form* for the BBC. His big TV break came in 1979 with *Not the Nine O'Clock News* when he was twenty-six. Then he became one half of the well known Smith and Jones duo, together with Mel Smith. (Most of the jokes, sketches etc. for the Smith and Jones shows are provided by Griff). Away from comedy, he regularly presents the BBC1 programme *Bookworm*.

He played Hildy Johnson in *The Front Page* at the Donmar Warehouse Theatre in London, in December, 1997. His other stage performances include *Plunder, The Alchemist* and *Charlie's Aunt* (his performance in this won him a Best Comedy of the Year Award). In 1991, he directed *Twelfth Night* for the RSC and he has also appeared in opera at Covent Garden. He was made an honorary fellow of the Welsh College of Music and Drama in July, 1997.

His portfolio includes stage appearances in *The Wind In The Willows* and such TV programmes as *Not the Nine O'Clock News* - which first brought him to national prominence, *Alas Smith and Jones* and *The Best of Smith and Jones*. In 1987 he featured in Channel 4's *Porterhouse Blue*. His film credits include *Morons From Outer Space, Wilt, Shattered* and *Up'n'Under*, the 1998 film written by John Godber where he appeared as a radio commentator. He was in the film *The Testament of Taliesin Jones*, playing a headmaster. In June, 1999, his comedy sketch show *Griff Rhys Jones* was broadcast on Radio 2.

Griff Rhys Jones

GWYNETH JONES

Gwyneth Jones

It's a long road from Pontypool's Twmpath Secondary Modern School to performing in the world's leading opera houses but it is one that Dame Gwyneth Jones with her "strong, vibrant voice" and "handsome stage presence" has travelled successfully. She was born at Pontnewynydd, near Pontypool on November 7th, 1936. Her father was Edward George Jones and her mother Violet's maiden name was Webster. At the age of three her mother died. After leaving school she belonged to the Abersychan and Pontypool Cooperative Choir and was employed in a secretarial capacity at the Pontypool Foundry and Engineering Company. (Coincidentally, the firm closed down after Gwyneth moved to London to study.) She was still a teenager when her father died just two hours before she learnt that she had been accepted as a student at the Royal College of Music. She went on to train at the Royal College of Music in London, the Accademia Chigiana in Siena, Italy and the Zürich Internat.

She made her Welsh National Opera debut as Lady Macbeth on September 23rd, 1963 at the New Theatre in Cardiff and, as a mezzo-soprano, she sang for the first time at the Zürich Opera House in 1962 in Gluck's *Orpheus*. She has been a Principal Dramatic Soprano at the Royal Opera House, Covent Garden since 1963; at the Vienna State Opera since 1966, the Deutsche Oper, Berlin since 1966 and the Bavarian State Opera since 1967. She has performed in Hamburg, Berlin, Munich, Bayreuth, Salzburg, Vienna, Milan, Verona, Tokyo, Rome, Geneva, Chicago, New York, San Francisco and Buenos Aires.

Known for her Wagner roles (but she is not just a star of Wagnerian operas she is just as comfortable singing the works of Richard Strauss, Beethoven, Puccini and Verdi) she has performed to acclaim at Bayreuth's Festspielhaus. A dramatic soprano, she has played Brünnhilde many times. She sang Fidelio in Beethoven's opera both for the WNO and Covent Garden. She was Leonore in Verdi's *Il Trovatore* - she took over the role from Leontyne Price and was an immediate success. Well known in Germany her roles (in German) include Salome, the Marschallin in *Rosenkavalier*, Helen of Egypt, Ariadne and the Dyer's Wife (in operas by Richard Strauss); Elektra, Isolde, Brünnhilde, Sieglinde, Elizabeth and Venus (in operas by Richard Wagner). Her Italian roles include Leonore, Lady Macbeth, Tosca and Butterfly.

In 1988, aged fifty-one, she returned to the Royal Opera as Turandot to mark the twenty-fifth anniversary of her debut there and, in honour of the occasion, she was awarded the Royal Opera's Silver Medal. Other, less famous venues she has performed at are Wormwood Scrubs prison where she regaled her 'captive' audience with a selection of folk songs from Wales and some of her favourite operatic arias, Pontypool Leisure Centre, a return to her roots in April, 1977 and Newport in 1989 as part of a private Memorial Service for well-known local musician Dorothy Adams-Jeremiah, in whose choir Dame Gwyneth had once sung.

Awarded a CBE in 1976 and made a Dame Commander of the British Empire in 1986, Dame Gwyneth is married (her second marriage) to a Swiss businessman, Till Haberfeld, with one daughter. A true Great of the World of Opera she has made many recordings and appeared on both radio and television. Writing in the *Western Mail* on Saturday, February 22nd, 1997, Rian Evans summed up the feelings of many regarding Dame Gwyneth, praising her strong stage presence and admiring her physical tributes: "The radiant beauty and warm personality has made her adored by audiences, but she caused her biggest stir when singing Brünnhilde, the Valkyrie warrior-maiden, clad in Avenger-style black leather, female strength and fearlessness personified. It is in Wagner roles that Gwyneth Jones has inspired her greatest following."

Writing in the same paper on the same day, her colleague Mike Smith was equally impressed, claiming that one withering look from Pontnewynydd's favourite daughter, in her role as Ortrud in Wagner's *Lohengrin* was enough to chill the bravest antagonist. The audience at The Royal Opera House in Covent Garden certainly seems to have thought so, deluging her with daffodils, raising the roof with their boisterous bravos and generally letting the singer know that it is not just in Germany where she is most admired.

MAI JONES

Nowadays, *We'll Keep A Welcome In The Hillsides We'll Keep A Welcome In The Dales* may be regarded as rather unfashionable, sentimental even, but there was a time when it was looked upon as almost a second Welsh national anthem and an indispensable part of any Welsh musical gathering. The woman who wrote the music for this, her most famous song, was Gladys Mary Jones who was born in Newport in 1899. She was the daughter of Thomas John Jones, the station and depot master at Pontypool Road Railway Station and Beatrice Jones. Mai was 'discovered' by the Welsh composer Dr. Vaughan Thomas, when, aged eight, she played the piano at a National Eisteddfod. She was appointed the official pianist at the 1924 Pontypool National Eisteddfod. She studied in Cardiff at the University College of South Wales and Monmouthshire (where she was awarded the Caradoc Music scholarship for composition and piano) and the Royal Academy and her first song *Blackbirds* was published in 1925. She enjoyed another hit two years later with *Wondering If You Remember* which was first performed at the London Coliseum and was later incorporated into the stage musical *Gypsy Princess*. As part of the musical act 'The Five Margarets', she did the rounds of the London theatres.

As well as playing the piano, Mai Jones also sang and played the accordion. She started out as a professional musician playing the piano for a concert party. In 1928 she could be heard on the radio from London's Savoy Hill broadcasting songs and impressions with Jack Payne and his band. She made her first broadcast from Cardiff in 1932 and spent the next eight years working the music halls and the radio stations. Her first BBC jobs took her to Belfast, Birmingham and Bristol. Together with Lyn Joshua (the son of the revivalist Seth Joshua) she wrote the song *You Can't Stop Us Singing* which was featured in the 1940 mining film *Proud Valley*.

Mai Jones was asked to devise a radio show for Welshmen serving in His Majesty's Armed Forces and came up with the idea of *Welsh Rarebit* which, at its peak, attracted as many as twelve million listeners. The show's first performance took place on July 19th, 1938 and went on to become extremely popular, not only in Wales, but throughout the United Kingdom. Among those she 'discovered' during the programme's heyday were Swansea comedienne Gladys Morgan, comedian Stan Stennett and singer-cum-comedian Harry Secombe. Even without *We'll Keep A Welcome*, Mai's place in Welsh popular entertainment history would be assured as she it was who produced one of the BBC's most popular radio programmes ever to come out of Wales - the aforementioned *Welsh Rarebit*. No mean feat at a time when a woman's place was still popularly thought to be in the home. There was also the little matter of her perhaps being thought too connected with popular entertainment to take the job. At the time of her appointment to produce

Welsh Rarebit, there were doubts about her suitability because of her sex, and Alun Watkin Jones, Head of Programmes in Cardiff, is alleged to have said of her: "She's Music Hall stuff". This cut no ice with his superior, Rhys Hopkin Morris who replied "that's exactly what we want" and Mai got the job. (According to John Davies, however, Hopkin Morris found "Mai's habit of calling everyone 'darling' profoundly distasteful", although the fact that she "only had a slight knowledge of Welsh ... was not considered a major impediment". In the event, Mai did not become a permanent member of the BBC staff in Cardiff until May 15th, 1945.)

Described by Harry Secombe as "a lady of tremendous energy and talent" she did not only produce *Welsh Rarebit*. She also conducted the orchestra and, just to emphasise the family connection, her husband Dai was the show's engineer. As if all this was not enough, Mai also wrote the music to the programme's theme song, which just happened to be Wales's unofficial national anthem *We'll Keep A Welcome* (the words of the song, first published in 1949, were written by James Harper and Lyn Joshua, and it was first associated with the Lyrian singers who performed it on the programme, but Harry Secombe was later to make it his own. It was first performed on *Welsh Rarebit* on February 29th, 1940).

As a measure of Mai's achievements it should be remembered that *Welsh Rarebit* was not just popular during the War years. When peace was restored in 1945 it was broadcast on the Welsh Home Service where it pulled in audiences of up to fifty-nine per cent. It was so successful that it was broadcast on the Light Programme for a March, 1948 series and also in February, 1949. According to John Davies it proved to be more popular in Britain as a whole than *Take It From Here* which featured the popular comedian Jimmy Edwards. There was even a television version broadcast in August, 1952 but this proved to be not so successful.

During her time at *Welsh Rarebit*, Mai was to discover many stars in the making, but one 'big fish' got away as Harry Secombe recorded in his autobiography. Shirley Bassey auditioned for the programme but, instead of being invited back again was simply told to "go home, love". (Regarding this episode, Shirley Bassey's biographer, Muriel Burgess, was rather unkind to the woman *The Western Mail* called "playwright-producer and composer extraordinary". According to Muriel, Shirley was actually auditioned by Wyn Calvin who later went on to become a comedian and well-known pantomime dame. Calvin thought that Bassey had a wonderful voice, but sitting in the control box was Mai, described by Burgess as: "a highly respected senior producer. A gaunt, forty-ish blonde, she was serious about music and liked to surround herself with up and coming young musicians".

Again, according to Burgess "the formidable Miss Jones" was not impressed with the song which Shirley chose to perform - *Stormy Weather*, or with the fact that the young hopeful could not read music. When Calvin saw "the faint expression of distaste on Miss Jones' face" he knew Shirley's cause was lost. "That model of rectitude, Miss Mai Jones", as Muriel Burgess put it, had seen to that. Ironically, some forty odd years later, Shirley would sing Mai's song *We'll Keep A Welcome In The Hillsides* at the 1999 Rugby World Cup held in Cardiff. Other popular radio shows Mai produced for the BBC in Wales were *Merry-go-Round*, *Silver Chords* (which featured her own Newport choir singing songs of a religious nature on a Sunday), *Souvenirs* which, as its name implied, was a pot-pourri of musical 'standards', *Welsh Half Hour* and *When The Day Is Done*, a cheerful mixture of songs from the musical shows. (In his book *Broadcasting and the BBC in Wales*, John Davies describes Mai as "indefatigable" and "a brilliant pianist".)

She married Davey Davies, a BBC programmes engineer, in 1947. Wil Ifan, Archdruid of Wales at the time composed a Welsh hymn which was sung at the wedding. She fell ill in 1958 and, shortly afterwards, retired from the BBC. But even when she was lying in Panteg Hospital, Mai summoned up the energy to leave her hospital bed, and take part in Harry Secombe's *This Is Your Life*. Once on air she was quite happy to tell the assembled viewers that she had been the first person to realise that Harry was not just a crazy comedian, but he also had a voice worth cultivating.

Mai Jones died suddenly at her home in 19, St. Mark's Crescent, Newport on Saturday, May 7th, 1960, aged sixty-one. Reporting on her death *The South Wales Argus* recalled Mai's musical philosophy. She had respected all kinds of music, and she had been firmly of the opinion that light music should not be treated in a slipshod manner, just because it was light music. On the contrary, she believed that: "Light music requires as much pains, trouble and study as if it were a concerto in the Queen's hall ... revue music in Wales suffers because there are no lyric writers. They either burlesque the Welsh or write about subjects that do not interest the Cymry."

The funeral service was held on May 11th at the Welsh language Mount Zion Congregational Church, in the aptly-named Hill Street in Newport, where Mai had been the organist for thirty years. Crowds lined the streets outside. Amongst the packed congregation were well known Welsh comedians of the time: Ossie 'I must 'ave 'ush' Morris and the renowned pantomime dame Wyn Calvin, the Caerphilly playwright and actor Eynon Evans and *Welsh Rarebit* compere Frank James and Alan Taylor (later of TWW's *Mr. and Mrs.* fame). Welsh radio and television personality Alun Williams was also present. Flowers were sent by Harry Secombe, and by two other Welsh comics Stan Stennett and Swansea-born Gladys Morgan, she of the maniacal laugh. Mai's brother-in-law, the Rev. Evan Davies, conducted the service in both Welsh and English and Mansel Thomas, Head of the BBC's Broadcasts in Wales played the organ. Mai was then buried at Newport's St. Woolos Cemetery in the same grave as her parents.

And that might have been that, if it had not been for the inquest held on Monday, July 19th, 1960 and presided over by Mr. Glyn Evans, the Newport Deputy Coroner where a picture of another Mai altogether emerged. Dr. Geoffrey Samuel Andrews, the consultant pathologist at St. Woolos Hospital, Newport told the court that Mai had died from acute alcoholic poisoning, but neither he nor the Forensic Science Laboratory at Llanishen, Cardiff could find any explanation for the fact that, at the time of her death, Mai Jones's blood contained no less than sixty per cent carbon monoxide. Indeed, when the postmortem examination took place on May 9th one blood sample was found to contain one hundred per cent carbon monoxide. Even after a week had passed there was still sixteen per cent concentration of carbon monoxide in her blood, but, Dr. Andrews concluded, the concentration of alcohol in Mai's body was sufficient by itself to cause death.

When Mai's husband, Davey Davies took the stand he was seen to tremble violently from time to time. He told the court that she had been working under great pressure and had had several nervous breakdowns. She had attended St. Cadoc's Hospital, Caerleon as an in-patient at various times. She had come out of hospital in March, 1960 but complained later of weakness. On the day of her death they had breakfasted together and discussed plans for the future. She had seemed "full of enthusiasm" for her future with the BBC and expressed a wish to write more music but, around noon, she had taken a rest.

Later a taxi took them to Bridge Street to do some shopping. (Mai was reputed to go everywhere by taxi - indeed, one of the floral tributes at her funeral came from Silverline Taxis in Newport. Not surprisingly, therefore, The Joneses were on first name terms with the driver who drove them on that fatal day as he had often driven them around the town.) Once in Bridge Street they did their shopping and then went to the *Bridge Hotel* (closed in August, 1973 and then demolished) for a drink. Davey had a beer and Mai drank whisky.

The taxi driver, who arrived late in court, claiming that his employers had not told him about the hearing, said that before Mai left the house she drank half a cup of whisky. He picked her and Davey up at the *Bridge Hotel* about ten to three in the afternoon and, on the way back, she was "laughing and joking and said she had bought a chicken" but then went rather quiet. When they reached the house Mai collapsed on the pavement. He tried to give her some water but she was dead by the time the doctor arrived. He then had to leave as he was late for another call.

Police-sergeant J. Webb said he had found nothing wrong with the taxi's exhaust system and Detective-sergeant Valentine Shortridge said he had examined the gas appliances both at the *Bridge Hotel* and Mai's home and was certain no accidental leaks had occurred.

Summing up, the coroner was critical of the behaviour of the taxi driver feeling he could have done more to help Mai's husband, but stated that he did not intend to speculate how the carbon monoxide had got into Mai's blood. He found that "she drank to buck herself up when she was feeling tired or depressed" and was satisfied that she died from "taking alcohol to excess over a period of time".

TERRY JONES

Terence Graham Parry Jones's father was a bank clerk and his mother a housewife. He was born in Colwyn Bay on February 1st, 1942, but moved away, when he was four and a half, to the Home Counties where he was brought up. Educated at Esher Church of England Primary School, Guildford's Royal Grammar School and Oxford's St. Edmund Hall, Terry Jones will forever be associated with the anarchic *Monty Python's Flying Circus* which graced our screens from 1969 to 1974. The first thing he ever wrote that was performed was for Ken Dodd - 'A Policeman's Sports' routine - which was shown on TV. His great comic heroes are Buster Keaton and Jacques Tati. He did student revues at Oxford where he met Michael Palin. He wrote for the 1960s comedy show *The Frost Report,* and appeared in *Do Not Adjust Your Set* with Michael Palin, Eric Idle and David Jason. He started out his showbiz career scriptwriting with Michael Palin and together the duo provided material for such stars as Kathy Kirby, Ken Dodd, The Two

Terry Jones

Ronnies, and Marty Feldman. Jones and Palin were to work together again on BBC 2's *Ripping Yarn* series. Jones himself was seen in the films *Monty Python and The Holy Grail* (which he co-directed) and *The Life of Brian* which he co-wrote and directed. He went on to direct *Personal Services* and *The Meaning of Life.* Jones wrote the scenario for and also acted in the film of *Erik the Viking.* A man of many talents, he has written eight books for children, fronted a documentary series on the history of the Crusades and written a book on Chaucer. In the latest edition of *Who's Who,* he describes himself as "a writer, director and performer". In 1996 he adapted and directed a film of *Wind in the Willows* in which he also starred as Toad. The French film *Asterix and Obelix Take On Caesar,* released in this country in April, 2000, featured Terry in a dual role: He not only provided the English dialogue for the film but also dubbed the part of Gérard Depardieu as Obelix.

TOM JONES

The man the newspapers love to describe as "a hip-swivelling legend" was born Thomas John Woodward (the Jones would come later) at 57, Kingsland Terrace, Treforest in the old county of Glamorgan on June 7th, 1940, the son of Thomas Woodward, a miner, and his wife, Freda. He was educated at Treforest Primary School and Treforest Central School. From an early age it became apparent to those around him that he was blessed with a musical talent and he would often give impromptu performances at family gatherings. Tom was about eleven when he first met Melinda (Linda) Rose Trenchard the girl whom he would later marry. (She had attended a Catholic junior school, he a Protestant one.)

Not academically inclined he left school at fifteen to start work learning to make gloves at a leather goods factory, then left to become a machinist in the local paper mill, but soon switched to working on a building site as a hod carrier. At nights he would sing in clubs and pubs (for his first paid gig in 1957, when he was aged just sixteen, Tom received the princely sum of just one pound), calling himself Tommy Scott, to earn some extra money. When not singing or working he was one of the local teddy-boys which often led to involvement in street fights, the odd broken nose and, on one occasion, his being knocked through the glass door of a local chip shop.

On March 2nd, 1957, Tom and Linda were married at the Registry Office, Courthouse Street, Pontypridd. They were both sixteen. Six weeks later, their son Mark was born. Still trying to make it big on the local music scene Tom now linked up with a group called The Senators, becoming their new lead singer. His first big break came when the Tonypandy-raised Gordon Mills saw him perform at The Top Hat Club in Cwmtillery, near Abertillery. As a songwriter, Mills had written hits for Johnny Kidd and The Pirates (*I'll Never Get Over You* and *Hungry for Love*) and The Applejacks (*Three Little Words*). He had also been a pop musician himself - once a member of The Morton Frazer Harmonica Gang, he had sung with The Viscounts whose hits included such winners as *Who Put The Bomp* and *Mama's Little Baby Loves Shortening Bread*. Mills liked what he saw, renamed Tommy Scott as Tom Jones and his group The Playboys and brought them to London. (Up until then the band had been managed by 'Myron' (John Glastonbury) and 'Byron' (Raymond Godfrey) who arranged for the group to record with Joe Meek of Telstar and The Tornadoes fame but the record 'bombed' badly.)

Jones and the group found London hard going at first and struggled to survive, living off demo discs and the occasional gig. At one stage things were so bad that Tom reportedly even thought about throwing himself under the wheels of a London Underground train. Their first record *Chills and Fever* failed to set the charts alight but *It's Not Unusual*, released in January, 1965 changed Tom Jones's life. Originally offered to Sandy Shaw, her people had turned down the Gordon Mills and Les Reed penned song, but they lived to regret their decision as it sold over 800,000 copies and reached the coveted Number One spot. (Fittingly, it achieved this feat on St. David's Day, 1965.)

Tom Jones

The Playboys now became The Squires but they soon found themselves surplus to requirements as Tom left them behind (some have alleged he abandoned his erstwhile comrades) to go his own way - their last appearance together was at Prince Charles's Investiture in Caernarfon Castle in 1969. Now a solo singer, the hits continued to flow for Tom including the famed Jones anthems *Delilah* and *Green, Green Grass of Home*. (These two have now become such a part of Welsh folklore that they are sung everywhere the Welsh gather, especially on big rugby occasions. Curiously, *Delilah* is also the song for the supporters of Stoke City Football Club.) By the '70s the Jones boy's records were selling all over the world and he was going down a storm in the U.S., earning vast sums of money packing them in such venues as Las Vegas. He played the cabaret circuit so well (including weathering a constant bombardment of women's underwear thrown at the stage whilst he was performing), that by 1975 he decided to move his home to the States for tax reasons. After the death of Gordon Mills of cancer in July, 1986 it was thought by many that Tom's career would take a nosedive, but under the new management of his son, Mark, he secured his first UK hit for fifteen years with *The Boy From Nowhere* in 1987. He followed this up with the 1988 smash *Kiss* by Prince on which he was backed by The Art of Noise.

Once thought of as irrelevant and saddled with a clichéd image of a certain kind of outdated 'macho' Welshness, Tom has managed to turn an incipient decline around and become 'hip' again. Things began to hum once more when he made a sensational guest appearance at the 1992 Glastonbury festival and when he played a pivotal role in the 1997 charity single version of Lou Reed's *A Perfect Day*. His rendition of the Randy Newman song *You Can Keep Your Hat On* in the hit British movie *The Full Monty* certainly did him no harm. Nor did his barnstorming performance of the same song with teen idol Robbie Williams in front of the Brit Award TV cameras. At Wembley Stadium on Sunday, April 11th, 1999 he performed *Delilah* in front of a capacity crowd - a fitting prelude to what would prove to be a stunning last-minute Welsh rugby victory over England. His 1999 *Reload* album featured him singing with the likes of Robbie Williams, The Pretenders and The Cardigans and gained him many fans amongst the younger generation who had previously been inclined to dismiss him as an old Welsh crooner.

After succeeding in re-inventing himself the one time tearaway has now become a kind of genial 'elder statesman' of Welsh rock duetting with Cerys Matthews of Catatonia, James Dean Bradfield of The Manic Street Preachers, and being backed by The Stereophonics on a new version of The Old Three Dog Night song *Mama Told Me Not To Come*. He even sang together with Welsh opera star Bryn Terfel. Cerys was so taken with her new singing partner, (on the old standard *Baby, It's Cold Outside*) she was reported as saying: "Old Tom's still got it. He's an amazing man with a golden voice." Not everyone was so complimentary, however. Reviewing *Reload* in *The Guardian*, Caroline Sullivan accused him of ignoring the subtleties of the songs selected by his duetting partners, and simply charging in, singing with all the finesse of a buffalo. Worse, Jones's mighty voice completely overpowered the vocal efforts of the majority of his collaborators. But even Sullivan finished her review by pointing out that *Reload* was number one in the midweek charts, and it would be churlish to begrudge Tom his success.

A tale of two waxworks could be said to sum up Tom Jones's roller-coaster career to date. In 1979, Madame Tussaud's in London melted down his waxwork judging that the singer's best days were over, but twenty years later the famous company was proud to announce that their Las Vegas branch was unveiling a new waxwork image of the Pontypridd star.

Away from his singing, Tom's sexual attraction to women is legendary. Apart from the hundreds of one night stands with willing fans he is said to have had, some of his more well publicised affairs are flings with ex-"Supreme" Mary Wilson and Miss World, Marjorie Wallace. Through it all Linda has remained his wife, in name at least, all the while shunning the showbiz lifestyle as much as possible. (However she was there with him when he performed in front of Pope John Paul at the Vatican in December, 1999.)

Tom's sexual dalliances have sometimes cost him money. One of his 'conquests', Katherine Berkery pursued Tom through the courts after a night of passion in New York led to the birth of the singer's son Jonathan on June 27, 1988. At first the singer vigorously denied any connection, but DNA tests proved he was the father and a New York judge found against him. Tom then agreed to pay Katherine Berkery and her son a monthly allowance.

Apart from singing Tom has made the occasional foray into the movie world. He played himself in a cameo role in *Mars Attacks* and was again himself in the Anjelica Huston vehicle *Agnes Browne*. Other screen roles he has been associated with are the 1979 TV movie *Pleasure Cove* (a pilot for a TV series which failed to make it), *Complex World* (1992 in which he played a cameraman) and *The Jerky Boys* (1995) none of which really took up too much of the film reviewers' time.

But it is for his musical talents that the Voice from the Valleys will be remembered. In March, 1999 Tom, who lives in a mansion in Bel Air, California, was presented with an OBE by the Queen for services to show business. No one could argue that the honour was not deserved. Since the first, blinding impact of *It's Not Unusual* Tom Jones has enjoyed chart success on more than thirty occasions, scoring hits in the sixties, seventies, eighties, nineties and, now, in the year 2000 the Jones Bandwagon continues to roll. In March, 2000 Tom Jones scooped the award for the Best British Male Solo Artist at the annual British awards bash in London, the first time he had received such an accolade. And still the awards keep on coming - in May, 2000 *Loaded* magazine awarded Tom the Carling Comeback of the Year Award.

PETER KARRIE

Compering *Wales in the West End*, the St. David's Day Cabaret broadcast on Saturday, February 28th, 1998, Victor Spinetti called Peter Karrie: "A revolutionary Che Guevara, a tortured Judas in *Jesus Christ Superstar* and a towering Jean Valjean in *Les Misérables*". The Cwm born star went on to say that "to the world he (Peter Karrie) is the Phantom of the Opera". And so he is, having played the part all over the world more than 2,000 times and also having been voted "the world's favourite Phantom".

Born in Bridgend, Peter Karrie was brought up in Llanmaes near Llantwit Major and Cardiff. His parents, Jean and Alan, ran pubs in Merthyr Tydfil, Bridgend and Cardiff. According to *Wales On Sunday* (February 23rd, 1997) Peter's real surname is Karagianis. He told the paper "My family are from Greece. My great grandfather got off a ship in Tiger Bay, fell in love with a girl in Bute Street and settled here. He ended up owning half of Bute Street". Peter first realised he could sing when he sang at a friend's birthday party aged nine. Later he started out singing in rock and pop groups and learned his trade on the road. In the 1960s his then band Peter and The Wolves shared the stage with The Rolling Stones and Tom Jones and he also featured in an Ely, Cardiff band called The Midnight Marauders.

A great raconteur who delights in regaling his audiences with tales of his theatrical experiences, Peter loves to tell the story of how he so nearly won fame at the game of rugby union. It happened in a Welsh Youth Trial when he had been selected to occupy the right wing position for the Probables XV. Before the game started the player who had been chosen to play on the left wing approached Peter and asked if he would change places with him as he could not kick very well with his left foot. Peter agreed and, in the event, had a 'stormer', scoring two tries and having a generally good all-round game. Imagine his surprise, therefore, when the man he changed places with was picked for the Welsh team! (Apparently, the selectors had picked the man who, or so they thought, had been playing on the right wing thinking they were selecting Peter Karrie! There appear to be more than a number of holes in this particular story but Peter still delights in telling it!) Other teams Peter played for were Newport Youth, (he had been playing rugby for Cardiff School when torn cartilages made him give up the game for two years. He then returned to the sport with Newport at about the time Welsh International outside half David Watkins was strutting his dazzling stuff for the Newport first team) Glamorgan Wanderers, Abertillery and Cardiff Athletic.

After games with Cardiff Athletic Peter Karrie would play pop songs at the piano. One night a producer heard him and got him a record contract with Decca. But his records got nowhere and his gigs were, by all accounts, dire and embarrassing. In desperation, he turned to busking on the London streets, sometimes sleeping on park benches. This new lifestyle soon began to take its toll. His energies deserted him and he became so drained, that he easily fell prey to a hereditary blood disease which caused him to take a break of two years in order to build up his strength again.

His health restored, he was a regular in the clubs for years before finding his way into the world of musical theatre in the 1970s. He was playing the Blue Angel club in Leeds at the time when the manager of Joe Brown and The Bruvvers took him aside and suggested he should audition for one of the big West End musicals. "Why?" asked Peter, such a move having never occurred to him before. "Why?" replied the manager, "Because there's a new musical *Fire Angel* being put on at Her Majesty's Theatre and I think you'd be just right for the part, that's why." At the time he auditioned Peter was thirty years old and scarcely realised what a life-changing decision it would turn out to be. As he said "It came late, it arrived on my doorstep late but, boy, did I let it in". But the road to success was still destined to be a long and hard one. It took another ten years of being an understudy and just missing out on the important parts until he could at last take centre stage. (Understudying the part of Che he got his 'big break' when the lead broke his ankle and he took over.) Then he made a name for himself in *Les Misérables* as Jean Valjean and then, of course, the role of his life came along, that of the Phantom, a role he has played in Toronto, Vancouver, New York, Singapore and Hong Kong.

Peter's love affair with the Welsh public, or at least one small section of it, has been dented somewhat since he branched out into pub ownership. He bought the *Red Fox Inn*, a pub in Penllyn in the Vale of Glamorgan in 1996 and, initially, it was run by his daughter and son-in-law and then by two of his nephews. It even had a themed restaurant called The Phantom's Lair. In June, 1999, he was still "more than happy with his pub" but, then, in April, 2000 the star of *The Phantom of the Opera* claimed it was running at a loss. He then aroused the ire of the locals by saying he wanted to turn it into a private dwelling with a view to perhaps selling it. He further claimed that he had put £200,000 of his own money into the pub and that not enough people were using it. At the time of writing, the pub's long-term future is still unresolved. (On July 23rd, 2000, *Wales on Sunday* reported that the pub, which no longer belonged to Peter, had re-opened after being closed for a month. Early in August, 2000 the pub was bought by the up and coming Welsh brewer, Tomos Watkins.)

Peter Karrie made his West End debut in 1977 and has been James Dean in *Dean*. He was Jean Valjean in *Les Misérables* for over three and a half years and toured Britain as Che in *Evita* in 1985. He also toured South Africa as Freddy Trumper in *Chess*. He first appeared in *The Phantom Of The Opera* on January 3rd, 1990. Since then he has sung the role all over the world and attracted 'legions' of women fans - in Toronto extra security men had to be laid on to protect the singer from over enthusiastic admirers - but he has never neglected his roots, appearing at the Swansea Grand, St. David's Hall, Cardiff, The Blackwood Miners' Institute and at Porthcawl's Grand Pavilion. (A patriotic Welshman - wherever he appears he ensures that his dressing room always has a Welsh flag - he sang *Impossible Dream* at the Cardiff Bay concert to celebrate the opening of the new National Assembly for Wales.)

He has co-written his own musical (yet to be produced) *Rasputin* with Jeff Guppy, and has had his own chat show broadcast on BBC Wales, *Peter Karrie Unmasked.*

Now living in Surrey, he has released scores of records, despite having no formal musical training, including the album *Peter Karrie Unmasked* which was released in November, 1998. *The Vancouver Sun* called his Phantom "definitive", a view shared by the The Phantom Of The Opera Appreciation Society which, in 1994 and 1995, voted him The World's Most Popular Phantom ahead of other competitors who had played the role such as Michael Crawford.

RONALD LEWIS

Described by Kenneth Williams as "attractively surly", he achieved fame when he appeared on stage with Vivien Leigh in 1956, in *The South Sea Bubble* by Noel Coward, but years later, when the fame and the money and the acting roles had run out, he took an overdose of drugs in his Pimlico boarding house and ended it all. Born in Port Talbot on December 11th, 1928, Ronald Lewis married Nora Gorsen and first made his mark in school plays. He trained at RADA with the likes of Joan Collins and enjoyed repertory experience, before making his first London stage appearance in Christopher Fry's *The Boy With A Cart*. Other stage roles included Peter Hall's *Mourning Becomes Elektra* (at the Arts Theatre), *Julius Caesar* and *Ghosts* (at the Old Vic), Jean Anouilh's *Poor Bitos*, *Lady Windermere's Fan* and *The Flip Side* by Hugh and Margaret Williams (all at the Royal Court). He played in Gwyn Thomas's *Jackie the Jumper* at the Royal Court in February, 1963. (He also provided the narration for the same author's Saint David's Day, 1964 ABC TV programme, *The Jagged Land.*)

Tall and dark-haired, and described by David Quinlan as "virile", Lewis made his film debut in 1953 as boxer Eddie Lloyd in the Ealing production *The Square Ring*, a role he had already created on stage at the Lyric Theatre, Hammersmith. (Years later, Bill Owen, Compo of *Last of the Summer Wine* fame was to write of this film, in which he also appeared: "Only one enthusiastic young actor, Ronald Lewis, declined the aid of a double" (in the fight scenes). Lewis then became contracted to Sir Alexander Korda's London Films and went on to play support roles in other British films of the '50s and '60s such as *The Prisoner, Storm Over The Nile* (as Peter Boroughs), *A Hill in Korea* (as Private Wyatt), *Robbery Under Arms* (as Dick Marston), *Sailor Beware* (as Albert Tufnell), *The Wind Cannot Read, Bachelor of Hearts, Billy Budd* (as Jenkins), *The Brigand of Kandahar* (as Lieutenant Case), *The Siege of the Saxons* (he played the outlaw Robert Marshall opposite Janette Scott in this 1963 film) and *Jigsaw*, but he will probably be best remembered for his role as the sinister chauffeur in the 1961 Hammer Horror film *Taste of Fear.*

When the more juicy film roles began to dry up he switched back to the stage, joining the Welsh National Theatre Company.

On TV Lewis took the part of Danny in Emlyn Williams's *Night Must*

Fall and also played in a sit-com series called *His and Hers*. In *The Rivals of Sherlock Holmes*, an ITV series broadcast in 1971 and 1973, he played the exotically named Dagobert Trostler in a one-off programme.

In all, Ronald Lewis made some twenty-seven films but, when the roles stopped coming, so did the money and, in 1980, he was declared bankrupt with debts amounting to £21,188. It all became too much and on January 11th, 1982, Ronald was found dead in his London boarding house. He was 53 years old. Two weeks later, on January 25th, 1982, a Westminster Coroner's Court found that the star had killed himself using an overdose of drugs. His brother told the court that Ronald had been "having financial difficulties and living on social security".

SAUNDERS LEWIS

The director of programme administration in Cardiff thought him "a very cantankerous man". Joseph Clancy, his translator, called him "the foremost

Saunders Lewis

dramatist to have written in Welsh". Julian Cayo Evans, the leader of The Free Wales Army in the 1960s said of him: "Saunders Lewis is the greatest man alive in Wales today. A man worthy of a better country and a prouder people". Born in Wallasey, Cheshire in 1893, the son of the minister at the town's Calvinistic Methodist Chapel, he attended Liscard High School for Boys and Liverpool University where he read English and French. In the First World War he was an officer and was wounded fighting in France with the South Wales Borderers. He worked in Glamorgan as a librarian for twelve months, before, in 1922, becoming a lecturer in the Welsh Department of Swansea University. In 1925, he co-founded the Welsh Nationalist Party or Plaid Cymru and, a year later, became its President. He became a Roman Catholic in 1932.

In 1936, he, together with D.J. Williams and Lewis Valentine, set fire to materials being used to build an RAF bombing school at Penyberth in the Lleyn peninsula. After the failure of a Welsh speaking jury to reach a verdict at Caernarfon, all three were convicted at the Old Bailey on January 9th,

1937 and sentenced to nine months imprisonment in Wormwood Scrubs, Lewis also losing his Swansea lecturer's job. On his release from prison he had to resort to journalism, farming, the odd piece of work as a school inspector and teaching to keep the wolf from the door. In 1943, he stood as Plaid Cymru candidate for the University of Wales seat but was beaten by the Liberal candidate, Professor W.J. Gruffydd.

In 1952, he became a Lecturer in the Welsh Department at Cardiff University, eventually rising to become Senior Lecturer. He retired in 1957 and his BBC Wales Radio Lecture on February 13th, 1962, *Tynged yr Iaith*, (The Fate of the Welsh Language) was the catalyst which led to the founding of *Cymdeithas yr Iaith Gymraeg* or The Welsh Language Society. (In 1956, he became the newly formed society's President but resigned after a row about pacifism some twenty years later.) He wrote some nineteen plays beginning with *The Eve of St. John* in 1921 and including *Blodeuwedd* (1948), *Gymerwch Chi Sigaret?* (Will You Have A Cigarette? - 1956), *Siwan* (1956) and *Brad* (Treason, 1958)

His Welsh language *Siwan* was broadcast by the BBC in an English translation on St. David's Day, 1960, starring Siân Phillips as the eponymous heroine, wife of Llywelyn, Prince of Wales, and her then husband, Peter O'Toole, as her lover, Gwilym de Breos. (Siân Phillips also played Iris in the first performance of *Gymerwch Chi Sigaret?*)

Saunders Lewis, who was twice nominated for the Nobel Literature Prize, was also a poet, a critic and a literary historian. *The Eve of St. John* is his only play in English. (He once wrote that "the Welsh are my audience, I have sought no other".) He died on Sunday, September 1st, 1985 at St. Winifred's Hospital, a nursing home in Cardiff. Two years previously, he had left his home in Penarth and, acting upon relatives' advice, moved into the hospital's geriatric ward with his wife Margaret. (Née Gilchrist, she died in 1984, aged 93.)

On Thursday, September 5th, 1985, a full one-and-a-half-hour Latin Requiem Mass was held in Cardiff's St. David's Cathedral Church. (Saunders Lewis had been made a Knight of the Order of St. Gregory by Pope Paul VI in 1975.) Three Welsh hymns were sung at the service - one of them, *O! Galon Crist* (O! The Heart of Christ) written by the playwright himself. Amongst those helping to carry the coffin were Dafydd Wigley the then leader of Plaid Cymru, Welsh political singer and Plaid Cymru activist Dafydd Iwan and the actor Meredith Evans. Saunders Lewis was then buried in Penarth cemetery beside his wife. He was survived by a daughter Mair.

ROGER LIVESEY

This gruff, husky/gravel-voiced actor made his first appearance on stage at the age of eleven. His grandfather, father and two brothers were all in the business and he often acted with his wife.

The young Livesey attended Westminster School and, afterwards, The Italia Conti Drama School and made his stage debut at the St. James

Theatre when still only seven years of age, the company including both his father Sam and Aubrey Smith. He continued to play boy parts around the West End theatres and toured South Africa and the West Indies. Roger Livesey made his New York debut in *The Country Wife* and it was in New York, in January, 1936, that he married Ursula Jeans.

Livesey's biggest film role was undoubtedly his part in the 1943 film *The Life and Death of Colonel Blimp* (he began in films in 1920, still only fourteen, with *The Old Curiosity Shop*). Other Livesey films were *Rembrandt* (1937), *Keep Smiling* and *The Drum* (both 1938), *I Know Where I'm Going* (1945) and *A Matter of Life and Death* (1946). He played in the 1947 film *Vice Versa* opposite Anthony Newley. He also gave a memorable performance as Billy Rice, the father of Archie Rice (Laurence Olivier), in *The Entertainer* (1960). He acted in films with the likes of Errol Flynn, Wendy Hiller and Richard Burton (*Green Grow the Rushes* was a film which starred both Welshmen but was not a critical success).

In a long theatrical career, he played such Shakespearian parts as Falstaff, Petruchio, Caliban, Sir Toby Belch, the Shavian roles of Shotover and Captain Brassbound, and Lord Caversham in Oscar Wilde's *An Ideal Husband* (a part he played for nearly a year). He shared the stage with the likes of Charles Laughton, Flora Robson, Robert Donat, John Gielgud, his brother Barry and father Sam (in William Congreve's *Love for Love*) and, of course, his wife, Ursula Jeans, appearing in Britain, America, Australia and New Zealand. No less an authority than Sir Tyrone Guthrie said of his performance in *Measure for Measure* when he played the Duke, "he is a most glittering and commanding actor".

His TV appearances included *The Man in the Iron Mask* (shown on the BBC, in 1968, he played Porthos, one of The Three Musketeers), *The Winslow Boy, All Our Yesterdays, The Master Builder, The Physicists* and the role of the Duke of St. Bungay in the BBC dramatisation of Trollope's *The Pallisers*.

Born in Barry's Holton Road, on June 25th, 1906, the third son of the actor Sam Livesey, he died on Wednesday, February 4th, 1976 in a Watford hospital. The trademark voice would be heard no more in live performance. He had been married for forty years to the actress Ursula Jeans who predeceased him in 1973.

DESMOND LLEWELYN

Will forever be known as 'Q', the man who provided James Bond with all his outlandish gadgets and weapons but, in a pre-Bond existence, he could be seen in many 1950s British films including: *The Lavender Hill Mob* (1951) and *Stryker of the Yard* (1953). It was with the 1964 *Goldfinger*, however, that his real rise to prominence began, but so identified has he become with the character of 'Q', that it became difficult for him to find directors willing to provide him with other roles - although he did appear in 1968's *Chitty, Chitty Bang Bang*, playing the part of Coggins.

Desmond Llewelyn signing copies of his biography at Newport not long before his fatal crash.
(South Wales Argus)

His Bond catch phrase was "Pay attention, Bond" and on Thursday, October 17th, 1997 he was awarded a Lifetime Achievement Award by the British Video Association. Having made his home in Bexhill-on-Sea, East Sussex, the Newport born actor (he first saw the light of day surrounded by servants in Blaen y Pant House - now a nursing home in the Malpas area of the town - and left Wales in the early 1930s) was James Bond's armourer, 'Q' in seventeen Bond films. He missed only two - the very first, *Doctor No* - and the one in which Roger Moore made his bow as Bond - *Live and Let Die*. Llewelyn cheerfully admitted to being typecast: "I've become so identified with this character that no one thinks of me for anything else. I've done two amateur films and it's jolly nice to do something that is not 'Q'." In one of these amateur films, a half-hour horror feature directed by an eighteen-year-old Wiltshire schoolboy, Edward Boase, Llewelyn played the part of a 'demonic' grandfather with an unhealthy interest in the occult. Boase actually rang up Llewelyn offering him the part in the film which he completed whilst still preparing for his 'A' Levels.

Llewelyn, who always supported Newport Rugby Football Club (and wore Malpas Cricket Club ties in the Bond films), was fond of telling how the director Terence Young wanted him to play 'Q' as a Welshman. But Llewelyn demurred, pointing out that he could not do an 'educated' Welsh accent, only a strong working-class one. When he heard what Llewelyn meant by this, Young quietly shelved the idea. In his pre-Bond days, Llewelyn worked in such films as the 1950 *They Were Not Divided* (when he played 77 Jones, a Welsh tank driver) and *The Amorous Adventures of Moll Flanders* (both directed by Terence Young), the 1953 *Valley of Song*, the 1958 film *A Night to Remember* and the 1962 *Only Two Can Play*. He was also seen in *Cleopatra*. His television credits include *Midsummer Night's Dream* in 1947, the *Ivanhoe* series with another James Bond, Roger Moore, occasional appearances in the 1970s TV show *Hazell* and *The Adventures of Black Beauty* (1972 to 1974), in which he played an eccentric Colonel, *Doomwatch* and *Follyfoot*. He is the only person to have starred with all five James Bonds. Other film appearances he has made are as: Mr. Brown in *Bunty Wins A Pup* (1953), Dr. Green in *The Silent Playground* (1963) and Professor Nixon in *The Golden Lady* (1979). He lived for years in Bexhill-on-Sea, near Hastings but always described himself as "a fervent Welshman". In November, 1999 he was told by Bond producer Michael Wilson he could stay in the part of 'Q' for as long as he liked. Typically, his reply was - "It's up to the Almighty how long that is".

Llewelyn made his bow as a professional actor at Porthcawl in 1935 with the Cardiff Repertory Theatre. He saw war service as a Second Lieutenant with the Royal Welch Fusiliers, being captured by the Germans at Dunkirk and forced to spend five years in five different prisoner-of-war camps. (During this time he attempted to learn Welsh - a noble failure, in his own words "I'm hopeless. I haven't got any rhythm". He also took part in prison camp plays.) The (November, 1999) Bond film *The World is Not Enough* starring Pierce Brosnan was 84-year-old Llewelyn's seventeenth outing in the role of 'Q'.

Desmond Wilkinson Llewelyn was born on September 12th, 1914. His family's roots in the mining industry went deep. His great grandfather - who was the landlord of a pub in Cwmbach/Aberdare - met his end in 1845 at the Llety Shenkin mine in Aberdare. His grandfather was not only a coal owner but also High Sheriff of Monmouthshire. His father, Ivor, was manager at Risca colliery whilst his mother, Mia, belonged to a mining family from Sunderland. Aged nine, the young Desmond was sent to a preparatory school. When he was seventeen his father died of angina and he was sent to Radley College, a public school near Oxford. Whilst at school he joined an Amateur Dramatic Society as a scene shifter. (He had been persuaded to take the plunge by his room-mate Dennis Price, of *Kind Hearts* and *Coronets* fame, and thus he caught the acting bug.) His mother was against him becoming an actor so he tried to become a policeman but, being rejected by the Wiltshire Constabulary, he worked for a time as an articled clerk. His mother relenting, he joined RADA in 1934 and studied there for the next two years. One of his first stage appearances was in Bexhill Weekly Rep in 1937 (he met his wife there) and he appeared in the stage version of *Rhondda Roundabout*. Whilst working in Rep he did a new play every week. His film debut was a walk-on part in the 1935 Gracie Fields vehicle *Look Up and Laugh* and he also appeared in Will Hay's 1938 *Ask A Policeman*. He had four lines in *Cleopatra* (according to Llewelyn "the most nerve-wracking moment" of his life). Curiously enough, the role he made his own and which made him world famous - that of 'Q' - went by the name of Major Boothroyd in the first two Bond films.

On Sunday, December 19th, 1999, at approximately 2 p.m. Desmond Llewelyn was involved in a head-on collision on the A27 not far from Firle in East Sussex. He had been returning from signing copies of his book in Newport, and was on his way to sign more books at Alfriston, not far from his Bexhill home. He was cut from the wreckage of his blue Renault Megane car and a police helicopter airlifted him to Eastbourne District General Hospital. (The driver of the other car - a Bronze Fiat Bravo Company car - a thirty-five-year-old London businessman was taken to the same hospital with serious injuries. His companion, a woman in her thirties, was not seriously injured.) Llewelyn, who had been alone in his car at the time of the crash, had suffered massive head injuries and never recovered consciousness. He died at 5.20 p.m. that same afternoon. His son Ivor was at his bedside.

He was survived by his wife, eighty-six-year-old Alzheimer's Disease sufferer Pamela (neé Pantlin), whom he married in 1938, at St. Mary The Virgin Church in Battle, and his two sons Ivor and Justin.

On Thursday, January 6th, 2000, at half past two in the afternoon, Desmond Llewelyn's funeral service was held at the same church in which he had married his wife some sixty years before. Among the mourners were actress Samantha Bond, the new Miss Moneypenny. Afterwards he was cremated at a private family ceremony at Hastings Crematorium. Following his death both *The Western Mail* and *The South Wales Argus* had devoted leading articles to him, a fitting tribute to a man universally regarded as a perfect gentleman and, in the words of *The Western Mail*, "a marvellous ambassador for Wales".

The Memorial Service to Desmond Llewelyn was held in St. Paul's Church, Knightsbridge on Monday, March 27th, 2000. Roger Moore paid tribute to his former colleague whilst Samantha Bond, the latest Miss Moneypenny, read *Peace* by Henry Vaughan and *Crossing the Bar* by Alfred Lord Tennyson. Members of the Welsh Regiment with whom Llewelyn had fought in France sang those Welsh stalwarts *Sospan Fach* and *Ar Hyd y Nos*. Among those present at the service were Christopher Lee and Goldfinger star Shirley Eaton.

On Tuesday, June 13th, 2000, at an inquest held in Eastbourne, the East Sussex coroner, Mr. Alan Craze, returned a verdict of accidental death, stating that, in his opinion, Desmond Llewelyn alone was responsible for the accident, his overtaking manoeuvre having taken place at an entirely inappropriate time.

ARTHUR MACHEN

The first time she met him Arthur Machen's second wife Purefoy remarked upon his "really beautiful speaking voice". Janet, his daughter, spoke of his "arresting appearance and superb voice". Oliver Stonor, his friend in later life, said that "his voice has an unmistakably Welsh cadence, pleasantly

Arthur Machen sitting in his garden in St. Johns Wood in the late 1920s.

modulated, and he reads excellently, as befits an old actor". Today, Machen is best remembered, if at all, as a writer, his books including *The Hill of Dreams*, *The Angel of Mons* - his First World War success - *The Great God Pan* and his autobiographical works, *Far Off Things* and *Things Near And Far*, but there was a time when Arthur Machen earned his living as an actor. In fact he spent eight years as an actor and another twelve as a journalist.

Arthur Llewellyn Jones-Machen was born in Caerleon on 3rd March, 1863, the only child of the Rev. John Edward Jones and Janet Robina

Machen, a native of Greenock in Scotland. Machen himself claimed to come from a long line of "Welsh priests and scholars" and, indeed, his grandfather had been vicar of Caerleon for some twenty-six years. The following year the Machens moved the few miles north to the village of Llanddewi Fach, and took up residence in the new rectory and it was there that the young Machen grew up.

Arthur was educated at Hereford Cathedral School from January, 1874 to April, 1880. In June, 1880 he visited London to enter his name for the preliminary examinations organised by the Royal College of Surgeons, but was unsuccessful when he sat those same exams some months later. Undaunted, he was back in the city the following year - this time to try his luck as a journalist.

By the end of 1885 his father had been declared bankrupt and his mother, who had long been ill, had died. On August 31st, 1887, Machen married Amelia (Amy) Hogg in Worthing parish church, his father having died some weeks previously. In 1899, he began writing for *The Globe* and *The St. James' Gazette*. In that same year, his wife Amelia died from cancer.

Machen decided to become an actor in January, 1901 when he joined the Frank Benson Company and embarked on a Shakespeare tour. He started with a walk-on part in *The Merchant of Venice*, then a one-line role in *As You Like It*, playing a Lord of the Forest. Some months later he was the Earl of Essex in *King John*. Other roles included a rioter in *Coriolanus* and the Clerk of the Court in the *Merchant of Venice* trial scene at the end of the tour. In the early 1900s he played Cardiff.

After the Shakespeare Tour was over Machen toured in the open air with veterans of the Benson company and then spent two weeks in the music halls of the East End. He then, variously, played a barber, doctor and solicitor in a play called *Silent Vengeance*, appeared in a comedy at Margate and spent two weeks touring in the West Country before returning to London.

In the summer of 1902, despite the difference in age - he was sixteen years older - Machen became engaged to Dorothie Purefoy (the name by which she was best known) Huddleston. They were married at Marylebone parish church on 25th June, 1903.

In the summer and autumn of 1902 Machen played in *If I Were King* at the St. James's Theatre and, in the spring of 1903, he was touring in *Old Heidelberg* directed by George Alexander. In the winter of that same year, Machen played in Benson's production of *A Midsummer Night's Dream* at Notting Hill Gate's Coronet Theatre. The Christmas season over, the company travelled to Stratford to prepare their English version of the Greek Aeschylean trilogy - *The Furies*, *Agamemnon* and *The Libation Bearers*, with Machen acting in the chorus.

In 1902, Machen had also had a small part as the servant, Carlo, in the Steven Phillips's play, *Paolo and Francesca*. Directed by George Alexander it opened at the St. James's Theatre. Machen also appeared with the Beerbohm Tree company - in 1905 he was in their production of *Mice and*

Men. In 1907 he had not acted for a year but then toured various country towns in Pinero's *His House in Order,* playing the role of Sir Daniel Ridgeley.

He made his last appearance on stage at Stratford in 1909 playing Bolingbroke in *Henry VI, Part II* (although, in 1922, he played the part of Dr. Samuel Johnson in a film about London - the old and the new - which, unfortunately, never saw the light of day).

In 1910 Machen became a journalist on *The Evening News* and remained on the staff of the paper until he left in 1921 around the time that his books began to enjoy success in America. On June 24th, 1929 he moved his family to Amersham in Buckinghamshire. Towards the end of his life Machen's sight began to fail him and, to make matters worse, Purefoy died on March 30th, 1947. His children, Janet and Hilary, then stepped in to take care of the by now frail and ageing Machen, but on 15th December, 1947 Arthur Machen died at the St. Joseph's Nursing Home in Beaconsfield, Buckinghamshire. He was 84 years old. He is buried in the cemetery at Old Amersham.

PHILIP MADOC

In his time, Philip Madoc has played Magua, the Huron Indian in *Last of the Mohicans,* Welsh politician David Lloyd George and the Russian Bolshevik Leon Trotsky, but the role he may well be best remembered for is that of the

Philip Madoc as Chief Inspector Noel Bain

captured U-Boat captain in *Dads' Army.* The latter role he was ideally suited to having studied German, French and Classics at the University of Wales, Cardiff and in Vienna where he became the first foreign student to be awarded the Diploma of the Interpreters' Institute. (Incidentally, the *Dad's Army* scene where Madoc learns Private Pike's true identity from Captain Mainwaring was voted Number One in a Comedy Top Ten by the readers of *Classic Television* magazine in a June, 1999 poll.)

Born in Merthyr Tydfil on July 5th, 1934, and educated at the town's Cyfarthfa Castle Grammar School, (where, in the early 1950s, he was plain Phillip Jones), Madoc then trained at RADA for three years before acting with the Royal Shakespeare Company in *Measure for Measure* and *The Blue Angel.*

On TV he has played the title role in *The Life and Times of David Lloyd George,* been Fison the newspaper tycoon in *A Very British Coup* and has also been seen in such popular programmes as *The Avengers, Target, The Saint, Randall and Hopkirk Deceased, Man in a Suitcase, The Persuaders, Porridge, The Sweeney, Manhunt, A Bouquet of Barbed Wire, First Born* and *Casualty.* In the 60s and 70s, he appeared in no less than four *Doctor Who* stories. In the early 1980s he played the coxswain in *Ennal's Point,* a BBC lifeboat station drama set in the Mumbles, Swansea. He also appeared in the seventh series of *Casualty,* episode twelve, playing an uncooperative, disabled old man.

A longtime member of Plaid Cymru/The Party of Wales, Madoc's film credits include *A High Wind in Jamaica, The Spy Who Came in from the Cold, Operation Crossbow* and *The Quiller Memorandum.* Formerly married to *Hi-de-Hi* star Ruth Madoc, he was glimpsed as a villainous bar manager in a 1966 episode of *The Saint* and played a petty criminal in a 1963 episode of *Maigret.*

In 1991, Madoc took on the role of Chief Inspector Noel Bain in the S4C thriller, *A Mind to Kill,* in which he co-starred with Hywel Bennett. Shot in Aberystwyth in both Welsh and English the film later led to a spin-off series featuring the Madoc character. This has been shown on satellite television and was being shown on Channel Five in 1997. Philip Madoc played the part of the vicar in *A Light In The Valley,* the Michael Bogdanov produced community film about present day life in the Rhondda shown on BBC1 Wales on Tuesday, December 8th, 1998.

THE MANIC STREET PREACHERS

Had things turned out differently, the biggest group to come out of Wales could have been called Blue Generation or even Betty Blue, their second stab at finding a name for themselves. As it is, a chance remark overheard by James Dean Bradfield about a man preaching in a street in Cardiff, brought the group a name with real clout and resonance - The Manic Street Preachers - a name that would ultimately serve them well.

It all started in Blackwood in Gwent's Western Valley. It was there that Nicky Wire (real name Nicholas Allen Jones - he got the Wire because he was so tall and skinny) was born on January 20th, 1969. Also brought up in the Blackwood area were James Dean Bradfield (born February 21st, 1969), Richey Edwards (born December 22nd, 1967) and Sean Moore (born July 30th, 1970). Nicky's father, Allen, was a builder, his mother was Irene. Richey's father and mother, Graham and Sherry, were both hairdressers. James was named after the Hollywood star James Dean. At school other pupils had another name for him - 'Crossfire' - a cruel reference to his slow eye. He sang in the school choir. Sean, James's cousin, went to live with him and his family in Pontllanfraith after his own parents split up. All four went to Oakdale Comprehensive School as did Miles Woodward, the group's first bass player. Sean and Richey attended the school between 1979 and 1984,

Nicky and James between 1980 and 1985.

After leaving school both Richey and Nicky went to Swansea University. When Nicky and James were not busking in Cardiff at the weekend, they, together with their friends, would make a beeline for Newport's Rockaway Records store. At the time they liked nothing better than wearing women's clothing and daubing their faces with eyeshadow and thick eyeliner, it all being part of their rebellious image. The Manics would frequent Blackwood's *Red Lion* in all their finery - make up, clothes etc. but apart from the odd remark on their sexuality, they were left alone. At first the line up was Nicky, James, Sean and Miles 'Flicker' Woodward.

In an interview he gave to the *Western Mail* in August, 1998, Woodward described how he had not seen the rest of the band for more than three years. Living with his parents in Blackwood and manning the picket line outside the Critchley Labels Factory in Oakdale, he recalled the band's early days when he bought himself a bass guitar, but had to be taught how to play the bass lines to the songs by James. At one gig they had been thrown out of the local rugby club because he had grabbed the microphone and told everyone else there to leave, although in rather less polite terms. At the time the group's first-ever manager was Mark Jones, another graduate of Oakdale Comprehensive. He had been approached by The Manics to take them on after they had seen what he had done for another local group, Funeral in Berlin. He agreed and their first ever gig was a joint one supporting Funeral in Berlin at the Crumlin Railway Hotel in 1986. Unfortunately, the two bands did not really mix, the Manics fans, being mostly punks, did not get on with those of Funeral in Berlin who tended to be mainly football supporters. At the second gig the bands shared, their respective fans clashed violently and the police had to be called. The place itself was covered in smashed glasses. When they played Blackwood's Little Theatre a grand piano was destroyed by fans throwing chairs. They also played at Ebbw Vale's *The Level*, now called *The Market Tafarn*.

Mark Jones managed The Manics from about the mid-80s until they recorded their first single *Suicide Alley* in 1988 at which time their business arrangement came to an end. The next thing he knew was that they had found themselves a new manager, "some big cheese in the record industry" and had got themselves a recording contract. As for 'Flicker' Woodward (fated perhaps to be the 'Pete Best' of the 1990s) he said he had left the band because the others were drifting more towards a 'poppy' sound rather than "the more hard-edged stuff" he himself espoused. Nicky took over on bass and 'Flicker' was replaced by Richard James 'Richey' Edwards a move which, with hindsight, also appears to have more than a little whiff of fate about it.

Suicide Alley, copies of which can now fetch from £300 upwards is said to be about a notorious back alley in Blackwood. The group recorded it in August, 1988, having scraped together enough money to hire Blackwood's SBS studios. The four track record with *Suicide Alley* as the single was their first. In all, three hundred copies were pressed and it was around this time that Miles Woodward and the others parted company. Besides selling it at Rockaway Records the group sent out copies of the record to anyone they thought might be of influence. Most of the copies they dispatched fell on stony ground except for the one received by Steven Wells, a reviewer for *The New Musical Express* who prophetically wrote, "They have more anger and intelligence than any band I have ever interviewed ... they will be the most important rock band in the world".

The band now made a conscious decision to leave South Wales behind and concentrate all their attentions on London. Wearing T-shirts emblazoned with such slogans as "Kill Yourself" and "Teenage Beat" they bombarded the capital's music press with anonymous letters full of bile and venom. Intrigued, the hacks soon realised from whom the letters were coming, and began to take notice of the Boys from Blackwood. At gigs the group made a point of 'earbashing' any journalist willing to listen as to their philosophies and musical aims. Their second E.P. which they brought out in June, 1990 featured the song *New Art Riot*. They sent the record to Philip Hall, who had managed The Stone Roses. He watched a rehearsal, liked what he saw and signed the band. Then, even though he had just got married, he asked them to sleep on the floor of his Shepherd's Bush flat. Richey would later tell reporters - "He was the first person that ever believed in our music". The Manics now signed to Heavenly Records and brought out the single *Motown Junk*. They followed this up with *You Love Us* and, in 1991, clinched a six-album deal with Columbia/Sony.

In an interview he did with producer Darren Brome at Swanseas's Marina Night Club just before The Manics signed for CBS early in 1991, Richey revealed that they realised that just doing local gigs was not enough for them so they made a tape and sent it to every place in London they could think of, and any groups they knew. Then they got a gig in a tiny upstairs room, in a London pub. For two weeks beforehand they had done nothing but phone up journalists. One actually came along, did a review and they were able to move on to better places to play. Richey also confessed that The Manics wanted "to be the biggest rock'n'roll band in the world". He was quoted as saying "We're the only band trying to articulate frustration and just total chronic boredom".

Sadly, Philip Hall died in December, 1993, his two year fight against cancer over. He had seen The Manics change from a raw punk-type band, playing at obscure venues in the South Wales Valleys, to audiences who were keener on fighting than listening to their music, to a tight outfit capable of putting together albums which could reach the Top Ten. His death was a keen blow but another, all-enveloping tragedy would soon befall The Manics.

Richey Edwards played his first gig with The Manics in 1989 playing rhythm guitar and singing. He was nicknamed 'Teddy' at primary school because he was like a cuddly bear. In a TV programme on The Manics broadcast on September 23rd, 1998 on BBC2 Wales, it was said of him "that the outsider chic never left Richey. He never had enough outside the band.

His life was The Manics". Known for his poetic and intellectual lyric writing and nihilistic world view, he became notorious when backstage, following a gig at the Norwich Arts Centre on May 15th, 1991, he confronted Steve Lamacq, a Radio One DJ and journalist, who had fiercely criticised the group and implied that they were, basically, only a creation of the media. The group spoke to Lamacq for an hour trying to convince him otherwise. Then, when he was about to leave, Richey called him back. Taking out a razor blade he proceeded to calmly etch the words "4 REAL" in his arm whilst a horrified Lamacq looked on. Richey later needed seventeen stitches for the cuts.

Richey Edwards was known to suffer from depression. He entered hospital in 1994 and was then sent to Roehampton for treatment at The Priory, a private rehabilitation clinic. He had been mutilating himself for two days and weighed a mere six stones. In October, 1994, he had recovered sufficiently well to play some British gigs but in December he was discovered beating his head repeatedly against a wall outside The Manics' Hamburg hotel. On December 21st, 1994, Richey played his last gig for The Manic Street Preachers at the London Astoria. At the close of the performance he smashed up his guitar just as he used to during the band's early days. (Ironically, Richey could hardly play the guitars he carried on stage.) In January, 1995 he disappeared for a few days but returned and appeared happy about the band's impending rehearsals. He also seemed to be at ease with himself. He had, however, shaved his head, telling a Japanese magazine he had become bored with the his hair and felt like a change.

In what now appears to have been his last ever interview he told the magazine he was in love with a girl but had never told her. He told the reporter that the worst thing he had ever done was try to be normal like other people, but all that had brought him was a stay in hospital. He went on to say that now when he woke up in the morning, he knew exactly what he wanted to do and that was write, the act of writing made him feel better in himself. Nine days later he left a box of presents to his secret love, with a note saying that he loved her, which was later found by hotel staff.

He left the London Embassy Hotel in Bayswater at 7 o'clock on the morning of February 1st, 1995 on the same day that he was supposed to be flying to America for a series of promotional TV interviews. But Richey never reached the airport. Instead he left room 516 and drove west to his flat in Cardiff. On February 16th, some two weeks later, his silver Vauxhall Cavalier car was discovered in a service station on the English side of the first Severn Bridge near a well known suicide spot. The police reported that the car had been slept in. Later the police found his passport at his home in Cardiff Bay together with some anti-depressants. They also found an unmade bed and some credit cards. Some believe that Richey jumped from the bridge into the cold waters of the Severn, but since the day of his disappearance his body has never been found (despite an extensive search of the Severn Estuary) and no one knows for sure whether he is alive or dead. In the meantime, royalties continue to pour into his bank accounts from his time with The Manics.

In 1998 it was reported that Richey had been sighted drinking in a bar on Fuerteventura in the Canary Islands by a British policeman and a woman tourist. When challenged, 'Richey', or whoever the man was, had run off. Desperate for news the real Richey's parents travelled to the island but all enquiries drew a blank - the mysterious stranger was never seen again. The missing Manic was also reported to have been seen in Goa, India, but again, nothing came of these reports.

When the news of Richey's disappearance broke the remaining Manics found themselves bathed in the harsh searchlight of publicity more than ever before. In the days that followed it emerged that he had taken large sums of money from his bank account. He was also said to have shown an inordinate interest in *The Fall and Rise of Reginald Perrin*, a TV show in which actor Leonard Rossiter played Perrin faking his own death. The effect of all this on the other members of the band was traumatic - "We were just frozen in disbelief" said Nicky Wire. James Dean Bradfield said "Richey was the most unintimidating sweet person" - and there was talk of the group giving up altogether. At the time, Nicky had married his girlfriend Rachel (they met in a disco when he was sixteen and she fifteen. They then went their separate ways but got back together again) and was living near Blackwood, James had a flat in London and Sean and his long-time girlfriend were living in Bristol. In May, 1995 the trio, their managers and Richey's parents held a meeting in which it was agreed that The Manic Street Preachers should carry on.

Richey had left a file of lyrics behind him and Nicky began to sift through them, seeing what could be done. The band also began to write new songs and to begin recording in a Normandy studio. Their first song to be written without Richey was called *A Design For Life*. Their new album, *Everything Must Go*, took its title from a play by Nicky's brother, the poet Patrick Jones. *Design for Life* made it to Number Two in the charts, the band's highest ever chart position.

Many feared that, with Richey gone, The Manics' acerbic edge would go, too, but they seem to have gone from strength to strength, even if they have alienated some of their original fans along the way. They did consider changing the group's name, but on reflection, thought that would only be right and proper once it was established beyond all doubt that Richey was dead. Meanwhile the Metropolitan Police, who were in charge of Richey's missing person case, insisted that his file was still open. Interestingly, in recent years the group have stated that, even if Richey were to reappear, he would be unlikely to regain his old place again.

Over the last few years the honours have piled up for The Manic Street Preachers. At the 1997 Brit Awards they won awards for Best British Group and Best British Album (for *Everything Must Go*). In August, 1998 their *If You Tolerate This Your Children Will Be Next* (a song about the Spanish Civil War) crashed straight into the Top of the Charts. It was their first ever Number One and they were the first Welsh entertainers to hit Number One since Shakin' Stevens did it with *Merry Christmas Everyone* in 1985. A 1998 readers poll in *The Melody Maker* put Nicky Wire at Number One spot in the Top Ten 'Sexiest Lads'. James Dean Bradfield was placed third and Sean Moore came fifth. (In a similar poll held the following year, *Melody Maker* readers again voted Wire into the Number One position and Bradfield was again third.) On Friday, October 30th, 1998 The *Q* Awards named The Manics as The Best Band In The World Today. In January, 1999 the group walked away with The Best Band, Best Single, Best Album and Best Video in the *New Musical Express* Premier Awards. In February, 1999 they won the award for the Best British Group and the Best Album (awarded for *This Is My Truth, Tell Me Yours*) at the Brit Awards held in the London Arena.

There have, however, as is to be expected, been a certain amount of setbacks. In September, 1998 a Welsh language poster advertising *This Is My Truth, Tell Me Yours* was criticised in certain quarters, amidst claims that the actual language used was substandard and incorrect Welsh. The band's spokeswoman countered this by saying they had been offered two translations - a North Walian and a South Walian one - and had chosen the southern version. Incidentally, the quotation This Is My Truth ... came from Welsh Labour politician Nye Bevan, the founder of the National Health Service.

More serious, perhaps, was their continued failure to 'crack' America. *Everything Must Go,* for example, sold only 30,000 copies in the States and the band's attempts to make an impression in that vast country have been dogged by bad luck. In 1995, Richey disappeared just before their promotional tour. Then, when The Manics toured the US in 1996 as the support band to Oasis, the tour was called off early because the Gallagher brothers had nearly come to blows following a spectacular 'bust-up'. The 1999 tour was postponed in July because James Dean Bradfield's mother was dying of cancer. When it finally got on the road a New York concert had to be postponed when James contracted a bout of laryngitis. When they did get to play they found themselves playing to crowds of hundreds instead of the thousands they were used to in Great Britain.

There is no doubt that The Manics have mellowed since their early days. Compared to The Sex Pistols when they first started out, they aimed to emulate The Clash, and made headlines more for their bad behaviour than for the quality of their music. Indeed, in the beginning, their capacity to outrage was rather greater than their musical accomplishment, and they deliberately cultivated a hellraising image. Richey was the band's spokesman and amongst their stated aims were putting an end to the monarchy, doing away with religion and burning down the House of Commons. They also proclaimed their intention to split up after making one best selling album of true brilliance. Nowadays, Nicky Wire contents himself with wearing skirts and skipping rope on stage. At home he owns three Dyson vacuum cleaners - one spare one, one for the downstairs rooms and one for upstairs. A self-confessed rugby fanatic, it was perhaps no accident that the band chose the Millennium Stadium to host their New Year's Eve 1999 concert. It was the first to be held at the show piece rugby theatre with its retractable roof and it was a sell-out with all 54,000 tickets being sold. (There had been talk of Catatonia and The Stereophonics joining The Manics on stage but nothing came of it. Catatonia's Owen Powell poured cold water on the project by declaring that a rugby stadium was the last place he would want to be on Millennium Eve.)

Nevertheless, the surviving Manics retained their anti-monarchist views and refused to play at the celebratory bash held in honour of The National Assembly of Wales because the Queen and the Duke of Edinburgh would be present. They also turned down a request by the Wales Labour Party to use *A Design For Life* during the elections for the Welsh Assembly. They preferred to stress their Welshness by flying the Welsh flag at all their concerts and supporting good Welsh causes such as The Owain Glyndŵr Society dedicated to the memory of the great Welsh guerrilla leader and statesman.

The Manics have come a long way since they pressed 300 copies of *Suicide Alley* all those years ago. Since then they have produced tracks such as *Motown Junk, You Love Us, Motorcycle Emptiness* and *Small Black Flowers That Grow In The Sky*. They have released five albums: *Generation Terrorists, Gold Against The Soul, The Holy Bible* (recorded at The Big Noise Studios in Cardiff Bay, the *NME* called this "a vile record" and many found its underlying themes to be too bleak and dark for their taste, but not everyone felt this way and the LP. got to Number 6 in the charts. It contained the stark power of Richey's lyrics, but to his dismay, he discovered that obsessive fans were trying to emulate him by not eating and mutilating themselves). Their fourth and fifth albums were *Everything Must Go* and *This Is My Truth Tell Me Yours*. The latter went triple platinum in Britain, platinum in Sweden and gold in Finland, Norway, Denmark and New Zealand as well as double platinum in Ireland.

RAY MILLAND

Ray Milland was born Reginald Alfred John Truscott-Jones in Neath on January 3rd, 1908. In his autobiography he claims to have been Welsh-speaking as a boy, and his paternal grandfather's mother came from Spain. (In later life, Milland would himself become a fluent Spanish speaker.)

Milland's early childhood was spent in Neath, (he was educated at the local Gnoll Hall primary school) but after his parents separated he went to live with his aunt for nearly six years, spending much of his later childhood in Pontypool, and then with his mother in Cardiff where he attended school at Radyr. Aged sixteen he went to King's College in the Welsh capital before getting a job as a junior clerk in the offices of a steel mill.

Six feet two inches in height and already a keen amateur horseman, he joined the Household Cavalry where he became a leading marksman and a crackshot winning service tournaments. After some three and a half years with the cavalry he left the army towards the end of 1928 and it was his sharp-shooting prowess which earned him a job as a marksman in the original version of *The Informer.*

He showed little interest in the theatre or, indeed, acting until he began socialising with a London 'showbiz set' and a chance encounter with the American film star Estelle Brody persuaded him that there was more to life than military matters.

When the name Reginald Truscott-Jones began to seem too unwieldy for the film world it was suggested he change it. Harking back to his childhood, he chose 'Milland' (from the Mill Land - a favourite boyhood haunt) whilst 'Raymond' was a studio suggestion. The picture chosen to feature the new star in the making was *The Flying Scotsman.* Seeking acting experience he got a part as the juvenile lead in *The Woman in Room 113* written by the Americans Sam Shipman and Max Marcin. The play opened in Southport, Lancashire, toured for five weeks and Milland was then sacked. Luckily for him the Vice President of MGM had seen The *Flying Scotsman* and offered him a contract to go to Hollywood. He left on *The Majestic* on August 17th, 1930 from Southampton.

In America he was given his first legitimate part in a film called *Bachelor Father,* starring Marion Davies and C. Aubrey Smith. After eight months courtship he married an American girl called Mal (Muriel Webber) in 1932 and this would prove to be one of the more longer-lasting Hollywood romances. Early in the same year he played in *Payment Deferred* with Charles Laughton but, two weeks after the film was completed, Milland was effectively sacked, MGM releasing his option, and he decided to return to Britain.

He made a couple of films there and then returned to America and his wife in August, 1933. Towards the end of 1933 he got a job with Paramount Studios in the film *Bolero* and stayed with them for the next twenty-one years. His first leading role in the U.S. was in *Jungle Princess* with Dorothy Lamour. He would finish one picture and start another three or four days after, playing cowboys, half-baked playboys and aviators and in one film he played the Devil and an eighteenth century procurer.

While in the army he had taken part in a boxing exhibition but his sporting prowess did not stop there. He learned to fly during his last year in the British army and then, when he moved to Los Angeles, took it up in his spare time before he became too valuable and the studio put a stop to it. By February, 1939, the studio had called 'time' on Ray's flying. In the summer of that same year he was in London making *French Without Tears.* He sailed back to America in the middle of August just in time to avoid the impending European war.

He won the Oscar for Best Actor (the first Welshman ever to do so) as the alcoholic writer in the 1946 film *Lost Weekend.* On a visit to Britain to promote the film he visited Cardiff and was given the keys to the city. He also visited London where he attended the Royal Command Performance for the film.

He directed six pictures (none of which lost any money) - the first being the 1955 Western film *A Man Alone* - and was seen a lot on TV in the 1970s. He played Bulldog Drummond in two pictures and some of his more well-known films included *The Glass Key* in 1935, *Beau Geste* in 1939, *French Without Tears* (also in 1939), *Ministry of Fear* in 1944, *Dial M for Murder* in 1954, *The Red Velvet Swing* in 1955 and *Love Story* in 1970.

'Suave', 'smooth' and 'debonair' are the words that come instantly to mind when speaking of Ray Milland. In a career spanning more than forty years in Hollywood and some 165 films, he won an Academy Award for Best Actor and played opposite such female stars as Paulette Goddard, Olivia de Havilland, Jean Arthur, Ginger Rogers, Barbara Stanwyck, Loretta Young, Carole Lombard, Claudette Colbert and Dorothy Lamour. He hobnobbed with the likes of Clark Gable and Gary Cooper and appeared on screen with such as James Cagney, George Raft, Charles Laughton and Bing Crosby. Not bad for someone who, in his own words, "was born on a mountainside called Cimla, high above Neath".

In March, 1981, his forty-one-year-old son, Daniel, committed suicide by shooting himself in the head with a shotgun. Thereafter, Milland made a point of spending time each March at the home of his relatives in New Inn, near Pontypool.

He died in hospital in Torrance, California on Monday, March 10th, 1986, aged seventy-eight. He had been suffering from cancer. Hours after his death in a Los Angeles hospital, Milland's body was cremated and his ashes scattered over the Pacific Ocean. There was no funeral or memorial service. Ray Milland had a son and a daughter. His wife Mal survived him. His last film was the 1984 *Sea Servant*. His TV roles included *Hart to Hart*, *Columbo* and *Charles and Diana - A Royal Romance*.

DIANA MORGAN

Described in *The Independent* after her death as being a character actress from Wales who normally only appeared in peripheral Welsh roles, Mary Diana Morgan was born in Radyr, Cardiff on May 29th, 1910, the only child of a bilingual Welsh/English family. Her father was Charles Morgan, a professor at the University of Wales, whilst her mother was a governor of Howell's School, Llandaff, an educational institution which Diana herself attended. She trained at the Central School of Speech Training and Dramatic Art in London. She made her professional acting debut at the Arts Theatre, Cambridge in *Cindelectra* which she herself wrote. In the late 1920s she toured with the Newcastle Rep Company, featuring in both the classics and in her own plays. By the early thirties she had reached the West End and was appearing in Noel Coward's *Cavalcade* at the Theatre Royal in Drury Lane. Amongst the successful plays she wrote before World War II are *The White Eagles*, *The House in the Square*, *Rain Before Seven*, *After My Fashion*, *Your Obedient Servant* and *The Dark Stranger*.

Together with her husband, Robert Macdermot Barbour, the first Head of TV Drama at the BBC, she created *The Gate Revues,* featuring Vincent Price, Hermione Baddeley, Peter Ustinov and Hermione Gingold amongst others.

Having started out as an actress she turned to writing for Ealing Studios where she helped to script the Clifford Evans-inspired *A Run For Your Money,* and also had a hand in the scenario of the 1943 film *Went The Day Well.* She collaborated on the scripts of *Dance Hall, Halfway House* (featuring Mervyn Johns), *The Foreman Went To France, Pink String and Sealing Wax* and *Fiddlers' Three.*

She scripted the 1949 film *Poet's Pub,* the 1957 film musical *Let's Be Happy,* starring Vera Ellen and Tony Martin and wrote the scenario for Philip Leacock's 1960 film, *Hand in Hand* for which she won more than a dozen international awards.

Diana Morgan was one of *Emergency Ward Ten's* first scriptwriters and also wrote plays for BBC Radio and American TV. Towards the end of her life she became almost completely blind. She died on Monday, December 9th, 1996 at Grenville Hall Retirement Home For Actors, Northwood, Middlesex.

JOHNNY MORRIS

Ernest John Morris first earned fame as The Hot Chestnut Man - whose job it was not just to sell chestnuts, but to tell children a weekly story. His fame grew "as a children's TV presenter who talked to animals" on his BBC TV

Johnny Morris

show *Animal Magic.* His gift for mimicry has seen him imitate all sorts of things from seagulls to squeaking signs and from steam engines to tiresome children. His gentle, whimsical humour was his trademark and his voice could still be heard on TV commercials long after his small screen heyday was over.

Born in Newport on June 20th, 1916 of Gloucestershire parents, Johnny Morris attended Eveswell Boys' School and Hatherleigh School. His family was a musical one - his parents and brother and sister all either sang or played a musical instrument. As a child he gained valuable experience performing as a boy soprano and a violin player. Aged about ten, he belonged to a children's concert party called The Kiddiwinks which travelled the South Wales Valleys playing the likes of miners' institutes and workhouses. He then went on to become part of a double act called The Two Johns, playing the violin, telling jokes, singing and tap dancing.

After leaving school he got a job as a junior clerk in a solicitor's office. He then moved to London to work on a building site in Hallam Street as a time-keeper before becoming the bailiff of a farm in Aldbourne, a Wiltshire village. Luckily for Johnny, another resident of the village was BBC man Desmond Hawkins (later to become Controller of the BBC's South and West region). Hawkins recognised Johnny's potential and offered him a few small acting parts on the Radio on the BBC Bristol service. Johnny's very first broadcasting talk took place on April 1st, 1946. It was called *Folly To Be Wise*, broadcast 'live' and Desmond Hawkins himself was responsible for compiling and producing it.

Having taken the plunge, Johnny proceeded to swim on. Talks about country life followed, there was a series called *The Plug in the Wall* and another series from the early 1950s entitled *Pass the Salt*. The latter which portrayed the jobs done by different people started out as a regional Home Service programme, but later switched to the Light Programme, and was broadcast nationally as *Johnny Comes to Town*. In it Johnny did over a hundred different jobs. It was heard right after the Sunday afternoon *Billy Cotton Band Show*, in those days a very good spot for anyone aspiring to radio stardom.

In June, 1957, *Johnny's Jaunts* took to the airwaves. In this programme, Morris travelled from the Bristol Channel to Cornwall and up as far as Lymington, walking, riding a bike and using a caravan. Further jaunts would take him to the Mediterranean and Istanbul and the programme moved to television.

In *Animal Magic* which was first broadcast in black and white in 1962, Johnny provided the words which came out of the animals' mouths. He also played the zoo keeper, actually feeding the animals and cleaning out their cages - mainly in Bristol Zoo but also in many other zoos both in Britain and Europe.

His first film part was in the late 1950s in a Thomas Hardy story called *The Secret Cave*. He featured in *Anything Goes*, a BBC West show co-written by and starring Benny Hill which was first broadcast on February 2nd, 1952. He visited the Scilly Isles, Mexico, Brazil and Fiji making TV programmes. He also wrote the scripts for Hans and Lotte Hass's underwater adventures and provided the British voices for the animals in the Canadian children's series *Tales of the Riverbank*.

His story *Delilah the Sensitive Cow* was first performed in 1959 at the Colston Hall in Bristol, having been put to music by Sidney Sager. Since then he has written a number of stories for children such as *Juanita the Spanish Lobster* and *Bouncer the Frog* all of which have been successfully set to music and in which he himself sang and narrated all the parts. He has also narrated

The Snowman to packed out concert halls.

He died, aged 82, in a nursing home on Thursday, May 6th, 1999. On Friday, May 14th, 1999, he was buried next to his wife Eileen in the garden of their Hungerford home in a simple, non-religious ceremony. After his death, the BBC broadcast a tribute programme - *Magic Morris*. Johnny Morris had no time for 90s-style animal programmes. Had he lived, he was scheduled to appear in a new ITV animal series, *Wild Thing* which would have made use of his old style animal conversations.

In November, 1999 it was revealed that Johnny had bequeathed his £210,000 house to his close friend Terry Nutkins who co-hosted *Animal Magic* with him. Even more controversially, he had cut his two stepsons, his four grandchildren and five great grandchildren out of his will altogether. (He had, however, left legacies to his housekeeper, gardener and builder.) Morris, who had been awarded the OBE in 1984, had received a severe blow in 1997 when his grandson Claud who had run the *Pelican Inn* in Froxfield, Berkshire went abroad after the pub went into receivership. Johnny Morris lost £500,000 of his own money on the deal. At the time of writing the Monro family had decided to contest the will and Nutkins to defend it.

TERRY NATION

Born in Cardiff on August 8th, 1930, Terry Nation will go down in history as the man who created The Daleks, those pepperpots of the fascist variety, as Kim Newman of *The Independent* memorably referred to them. Nation was asked to write for the *Doctor Who* series in 1963 and straightaway unleashed the mechanical monsters on an unsuspecting population. He got the idea for his immortal creation (the word 'Dalek' was later adopted by *The Oxford English Dictionary*) by going to a performance given by The Georgian State National Opera. The women dancers, in particular, impressed him as, dressed in their long skirts, they appeared not to move in the ordinary sense of the word, but to simply glide over the floor. In a pre-Dalek existence, Nation grew up in Llandaff, Cardiff and went to King's College School. He started out working as a salesman for his family's furniture manufacturing firm. Then, aged twenty-five he made the move to London. intending to become a comedian, but instead ended up writing radio scripts for established comedians such as Stanley Baxter, Eric Sykes, Frankie Howerd, Harry Worth, Terry Scott and Tony Hancock. He also provided material for the *Goon Show*. Together with Clive Exton, Nation wrote and produced the 1973 cinema film, *The House in Nightmare Park* starring Ray Milland and Frankie Howerd.

In 1979, he took his wife (he married Kate Gaunt in 1968) and two children with him to Hollywood where he worked for MGM, Columbia and Twentieth Century Fox, but found he could not repeat his British triumphs. He died in Los Angeles on Sunday, March 9th, 1997. He had been suffering from emphysema for some years.

Terry Nation had an impressive list of credits, having scripted *No*

Hiding Place with Inspector Lockhart. He wrote radio comedy scripts, together with John Junkin and Dave Freeman, and scripted *Floggit's* a vehicle in the mid-1950s for the sisters Elsie and Doris Waters. In 1961, together with John Junkin, he wrote *It's A Fair Cop*, a radio series starring Hattie Jacques and Eric Sykes.

The programmes Terry Nation wrote for read like a roll-call of sixties and seventies popular television entertainment history. He scripted *The Saint* and *The Avengers*, wrote for *The Champions*, *The Persuaders*, *Department S* and *The Protectors*, helped to create *The Baron* and had the original idea for the science fiction series *Blake's Seven*. For the BBC, he wrote *The Incredible Robert Baldick* as part of *Drama Playhouse*. But if he had never been involved with any of these programmes, he would still be remembered today as the man who invented the Daleks, those extra-terrestrial destroyers, who livened up Saturday tea-times for children and adults alike.

IVOR NOVELLO

Ivor Novello

Margaret Rutherford called him "the handsomest man in London"; fans besieged him at the stage door anxious to get a glimpse of his famous profile and his dark, gypsy looks; on tour in the provinces autograph hunters mobbed him; theatre and filmgoers alike queued to see his plays and films; he was that rare thing - a glittering phenomenon. Not only did he write hit songs, he starred in films and plays and musical comedies. More often than not, he wrote the plays and musical extravaganzas he starred in. Ivor Novello was a star in more ways than one. (Yet, according to his latest biographer - Paul Webb, speaking on BBC Radio Wales in October, 1999 - he never lost his Welsh accent: "if you listen to the recordings of him speaking, he had a very strong accent.")

He was born David Ivor Davies at a house called *Llwyn yr Eos* (The Nightingale's Grove) 11, Cowbridge Road, Cardiff, on January 15th, 1893, the son of Clara Novello Davies and David Davies and educated at Gloucester and Magdalen College Choir School, Oxford. (He would change his name by deed poll on January 15th, 1927 - his thirty-fourth birthday).

His films include *Call of the Blood* (1920), *The Rat* (1924) co-written with Constance Collier and in which he also starred; *The Triumph of the Rat* (1926), the 1926 thriller *The Lodger* directed by Alfred Hitchcock and *The Return of The Rat* (1929). In 1926, Novello came first in a readers' poll organised by the *Daily News* to determine which British film star was most popular. Two years later, he beat all other British and American opposition as the readers of *Picturegoer* judged him to be their favourite star, but by 1934, he had abandoned film making to concentrate on the theatre.

Ivor's famous batch of musicals include *Glamorous Night* (1935), *Careless Rapture* (1936), *Crest of the Wave* (1937) and *The Dancing Years* (1939) all of them produced at Drury Lane. This rich vein of musical successes continued during and after the war with such extravaganzas as *Arc de Triomphe* (1943), *Perchance to Dream* (1945), *King's Rhapsody* (1949) and *Gay's the Word* (1951).

Said to be a man of great personal charm with a pleasant speaking voice, he spent some time in Hollywood in the early 1930s, working on film scripts and playing minor parts in Hollywood films, before returning to Britain and the London stage. He played the title role in the Drury Lane production of *Henry V* in 1938, giving a splendid performance, but his fans, more used to seeing him in Ruritanian roles, could not really come to terms with their hero in such a vigorous, forthright part as the young King Harry and the production, directed by Lewis Casson, was by Ivor's standards, a comparative failure at the box office.

On April 24th, 1944, Ivor appeared in Bow Street Court accused of breaking the petrol rationing laws. Despite protestations of innocence - he had been misled by an ardent fan into thinking her firm would take over his Rolls Royce and allow him to use it at weekends to drive to his country home - he was sentenced to eight weeks in Wormwood Scrubs, a sentence which was later reduced to four weeks on appeal, but still came as a terrible shock to the 'golden boy' of British theatre. (It has since been alleged that Novello had the misfortune to come up against a theatre-hating homophobe of a judge.) In jail he mixed with the likes of the Kray Brothers' henchman, "Mad" Frankie Fraser whose mother, by all accounts, told her son to look out for and after the handsome Welshman. Despite this setback, on his release from prison he did his 'bit' for the British war effort - entertaining the troops in newly liberated France.

Ivor Novello died at his London home, in the top floor flat of the Strand Theatre at 11, Aldwych, a little after two o'clock on the morning of Tuesday, March 6th, 1951 of coronary thrombosis. (There are those who claim that his gaol sentence did nothing for his health - either mental or spiritual and, indeed, may have hastened his premature death.) He had returned home to his flat on Monday, March 5th but fell violently ill. His friend Bobby Andrews telephoned Olive Gilbert who lived in the flat below, had sung in many of Ivor's productions and, in many ways, acted as his unofficial housekeeper. Welsh-born Olive rushed upstairs, took in the situation at once and called the doctor. Whilst she was waiting for the medical man to come she gave Ivor some smelling salts, but they proved too weak, and she gave him some others which were extra strong. When the doctor arrived he examinined Ivor, and then Olive heard the composer give out a lengthy sigh, his last on this earth. He was gone.

On the day of the funeral which, incidentally, was organised by top London department store Harrods, on Monday, March 12th, 1951, vast crowds lined the route to the crematorium at Golders Green, and those who could not be present in person were able to follow events on the radio. When the hearse arrived the strains of *We'll Gather Lilacs*, one of Ivor's most famous songs could be heard through the open chapel door. His Memorial Service was held at St. Martin-in-the-Fields Church in London on Thursday, March 29th, 1951. Lyn Harding and Sir Lewis Casson read the Lessons and Carmarthen-born Olive Gilbert, who had appeared in many of his shows and was present when he died, sang *How Lovely Are Thy Dwellings*. (Ivor did not neglect Olive Gilbert or forget her for all her kindnesses - he left her his collection of rose quartz, amber and jade.) Welsh actor Roddy Hughes was amongst those who attended the service.

Ivor Novello was bisexual by nature and amongst his affairs was one with the First World War poet, Siegfried Sassoon. Multi-talented, Novello (surprisingly) could not sing or dance but this did not stop him from writing close on fifty songs between 1910 and 1951, not counting the songs he contributed to musical comedies and revues between 1916 and 1929. His most famous song is probably *Keep The Home Fires Burning* which he wrote during the First World War.

Ivor decided to give the song a trial-run and asked Welsh singer Sybil Vane, one of his mother's old pupils, to sing it in a concert she was giving at the Alhambra Theatre. Ivor accompanied Sybil on the piano and, as soon as the audience began to join in, he knew he was onto a winner. The audience liked the song so much that Ivor and Sybil played and sang it some six times in all. At the end, flushed with pride, Ivor embraced Sybil Vane who, in her turn, embraced the conductor of the band. It was immediately taken up by soldiers and civilian population alike and rapidly became a best seller.

Then there were Ivor's musicals: he wrote eight of these between 1935 and 1951. He also appeared in twenty-two films between 1920 and 1934 and acted in twenty plays between 1921 and 1944. Today Ivor Novello's plays are judged to be rather too old fashioned for modern tastes to be revived commercially, but his musical extravaganzas are still staged regularly by amateur societies. In the meantime, the famous profile (Noel Coward once said "There are two perfect things in this world - my mind and Ivor's profile".) lives on! - his ghost is said to haunt London's Palace Theatre where his musical *King's Rhapsody* was being staged when he died.

JOHN OGWEN

Wendy Hiller once famously said of him that he was an "All-Celtic sensation. There is nothing Anglo-Saxon in his make-up at all". George Melly, then the *Observer's* TV critic, went further, likening him to James Cagney. He was one of two twins born to Mary Griffiths on April 25th, 1944, but she felt unable

John Ogwen

to look after two children, so asked her sister Annie, who was living in Sling, a small village not far from Bangor, if they would be willing to bring up the child. She and her husband, who were both in their forties agreed, and John arrived in Sling, aged six weeks, in June, 1944. Educated at Ysgol Bodfeurig, as a boy he sang and competed in local *eisteddfodau* and sang with the Dyffryn Ogwen children's choir. He attended Ysgol Dyffryn Ogwen in Bethesda where he played football for his school and for the old county of Caernarfonshire. Scouts from Nottingham Forest and Sunderland took an interest in him, but his other love at school was acting in school plays, an interest which was fostered by his science

teacher, Gwenlyn Parry. (Gwenlyn Parry himself would later go on to carve out his own niche in the Welsh language theatrical and TV world.)

At Bangor University John studied Welsh and English. He played football for the University first team and then signed to play for Bethesda in the Welsh League. A member of the Welsh Drama Society he met his wife, Maureen, whilst acting in Welsh language plays at the College. (In one of them, he played Jimmy Porter in a Welsh translation of *Look Back in Anger.*) They married in the summer before his last year in College and their first son, Robin, was born in August. After getting his degree, Ogwen joined Cwmni Theatr Cymru.

His first professional performance took place at the Bala Eisteddfod in 1967 when he played Dewi in Saunders Lewis's *Cymru Fydd*. It was not an auspicious beginning. On the first night the set caught fire, the performance was abandoned and had to be repeated the next day. (Incidentally, in this play and in the Welsh language TV production *Pros Kairon* he acted under his given name of John Hughes, on joining Equity, however, he was told that he would have to change his name, so chose Ogwen after his native region.)

After leaving Cwmni Theatr Cymru, John Ogwen spent 1973 to 1976 working for HTV in Cardiff providing the voice and hand for the puppet dog Llewelyn in the Welsh language children's series *Miri Mawr*. He also played Meredith Edwards's son in the HTV networked series *The Inheritors*. Tiring of Cardiff, he returned to North Wales and a new post as Drama Lecturer at Bangor University on a two-year contract, but did not enjoy the experience and soon returned to acting.

His English-language television appearances include Emlyn Williams's *The Corn is Green* on BBC TV, St. David's Day, 1968 when he starred as Morgan opposite Wendy Hiller; *Triangles*, a Granada TV production with Ray Brooks and Anna Massey; playing a young tearaway in *Softly, Softly*; parts in *Doctor Who* and *District Nurse* and, most noticeably, Twm Siôn Cati in *Hawkmoor* in the summer of 1975. (Hawkmoor went out at the very popular time of five o'clock on a Sunday afternoon, the tea-time slot.)

He also had a one-line part in the Peter Sellers/Goldie Hawn film *There's A Girl In My Soup*. His radio work included a spell in *The Archers* as Gwyn Evans, son of Haydn Evans, the garage owner (played by Welsh actor and *Pobol y Cwm* stalwart Charles Williams). However, as Ogwen himself says in his autobiography, *Hogyn o Sling* (The Boy from Sling): "I knew full well that I wanted to be an actor working almost entirely in Welsh" (referring to his not wanting to spend two years in Stratford and London working for the RSC).

He prefers film to the theatre and, since the advent of S4C, has appeared in many of that channel's productions, including *Deryn* and *Minafon*, and the part of Uncle Dic in the North Wales based series *Cyw Haul*. Amongst his other achievements in the world of Welsh language drama are: adapting and taking the main part in Kate Roberts's *Twyll Heno* for an S4C production; appearing with his wife in the Gwenlyn Parry play *Y Twr* and translating Ted Whitehead's two-handed play *Alpha Beta* into Welsh and then acting in it with wife Maureen. He took the part of Owen Hales in *White Rocks*, a 1992 episode of the S4C detective series *Heliwr/A Mind to Kill*.

DENNIS O'NEILL

A tenor born in Pontarddulais, Dennis James O'Neill's Irish father (William P. O'Neill) was a doctor whilst his mother (Eva A. O'Neill, née Rees) was Welsh. Born February 25th, 1948, Welsh-speaking Dennis was the eldest of six children in a home full of music where all the children played the piano and sang in local *eisteddfodau*. Dennis himself won the male championship at Pontrhydfendigaid Eisteddfod. He has worked with the Welsh, Scottish and English National Opera Companies. O'Neill has sung some of the greatest roles in world opera including Alfredo in *La Traviata*, Rudolfo in *La Bohème* and the Duke in *Rigoletto*. He was awarded a CBE in the 2000 New Year's Honours List and sang the Welsh air *Cymru Fach* (Little Wales) at the London Millennium Dome on New Year's Eve, 1999.

First married to Ruth Collins in 1970 (they had one son and one daughter but the marriage was dissolved in 1987), he married his second wife, Norwegian Ellen Folkestad in 1988. Educated at Gowerton Boys Grammar School, Trinity College of Music and the Royal College of Music, Dennis's forte is Italian operas, particularly works by Verdi.

He has appeared all over the world in concerts and operas including the Royal Opera House, Covent Garden (debut, 1979), the Vienna State Opera (debut, 1981), Hamburg State Opera (debut, 1981), San Francisco Opera (debut, 1984), Chicago Lyric Opera (debut, 1985), Paris Opera (debut, 1986), Metropolitan Opera, New York (debut, 1986) and the Bayerische Staatsoper, Munich (debut, 1992). In July, 1997, he headlined the Welsh National Opera's third annual free concert at the Music Festival in Cardiff Bay. Famed for his performances of *Nessun Dorma*, (everywhere he goes, he is inevitably requested to sing it and always cheerfully obliges) Dennis toured with the Welsh National Opera in *Turandot* in February, 2000. Reviewing WNO's first night performance of *Turandot* at Cardiff's New Theatre on Monday, February 21st, 2000, David Barnes described Dennis O'Neill in *The South Wales Argus* as "fantastic", saying "O"Neill's rendition of *Nessun Dorma* was superb. Whenever I had heard it before it had conjured images of football. This performance banished such images forever." (Dennis performed *Nessun Dorma* at the 1999 Voices of A Nation Concert to celebrate the official opening of the National Assembly for Wales.)

Dennis O'Neill has given masterclasses on television. As a boy he was a soprano and in his younger days a frequent competitor in singing competitions. He won the tenor solo for the under-twenty-fives at the 1966 Aberafan National Eisteddfod. He sang Gustav in Verdi's *Un Ballo in Maschera* for the Welsh National Opera at the New Theatre, Cardiff in October, 1998. Known for his Neapolitan songs he has many times stood in for Luciano Pavarotti and was flown in especially from Munich to take the place of Bryn Terfel at the Euro Gala Concert held in Cardiff Castle on Saturday, June 13th, 1998. (He performed so well as a 'stand-in' that he had the audience all but forgetting Bryn and practically eating out of his hand.) He also sang at the musical celebrations to hail the inauguration of the new National Assembly for Wales.

In an article written by Michael Boon in the *Western Mail* (March 4th, 1998) Dennis told the paper's readers how he had started out singing with the chorus of the BBC Singers in London and stayed with them for a few months. In the meantime, he kept taking singing lessons and kept auditioning for all the parts he could find. His big break came when he joined a small company called Opera For All which toured church halls performing shortened versions of the classical operas to piano accompaniment. Sponsored by the Arts Council these tours proved to be a source of good experience to the struggling young tenor as he tried to make his way in his chosen profession.

Unlike many others, Dennis was not an overnight success. He had to work hard at his music, taking lessons wherever possible (he once spent two years studying voice training in Australia) and auditioning every chance he got, besides building up his repertoire. Now, through his masterclasses and the help he has given to young, emerging singers, he has returned with interest the joy and happiness he himself has derived from his musical career. Over the years Dennis feels his voice has matured and improved. He now spends his days preparing for his roles, endlessly rehearsing, accompanying himself on his own piano. "He laughs a lot and has a whimsical sense of humour" wrote Michael Boon of the man who is said to be "one of the best six tenors in the world".

TESSIE O'SHEA

Born in Plantagenet Street, Riverside, Cardiff on March 13th, 1913, Tessie O'Shea started out as a tap dancer at the age of three. Aged six she began taking piano and elocution lessons and, when seven years old, won a Cardiff clog dancing competition. At the age of eight, she and a Welsh choir were sharing first prize at a talent contest in Aberdare. By the age of nine she had made her first acquaintance with the ukulele which was to become her trademark and, one year later, was visiting hospitals, providing wounded Welsh soldiers with her own unique brand of entertainment.

Tessie O' Shea came from humble origins although there seems some doubt as to precisely what those origins were. Read *The Times* and you will learn that she was part Irish, part Lancastrian. Consult the *Western Mail* and you find that her mother hailed from Tyneside and her father was an American of Irish descent. The confusion may go some way to explaining her accent which was said to be part American, part North Country, combined with twangs of Cardiff. Whatever the truth of it, when she was twelve years old - an important age because now she could start working as a professional - young Tessie was offered a week's work at the Bristol Hippodrome by Sir Oswald Stoll.

Even at the age of twelve Tessie O'Shea was already a big girl wearing clothes coming in at size twenty-eight. As she herself said, "I was a big child, I was fat, so I had to become a comedienne". Big or not, the Bristol booking led to further outings in Stoll-owned theatres, clad in a curious costume of striped stockings, elastic-sided boots and a vast hat with a fur twined round her neck, an outfit she abandoned when she realised that the clothes were getting the laughs and not Tessie O'Shea.

Her big break came in 1934 when she did a twenty-week summer season on the North Pier at Blackpool. She subsequently did the rounds of the Moss Empires theatres with the Jack Hylton Show. This then opened at the London Palladium and, for the next five years, Tessie O'Shea's name was topping the bill in theatres all over Britain.

Tessie spent the war entertaining the troops, playing the West End and, together with Tommy Trinder, being invited to perform at a private Windsor Castle party for King George VI and Queen Elizabeth. Her voice was heard more and more on the radio and she made regular guest appearances on the *Happidrome* variety show. In April, 1946 she appeared at the London Palladium in Val Parnell's first revue *High Time* in which she made a spectacular entrance riding on the back of an elephant. Unfortunately for Tessie no one realised that the elephant - a female - was pregnant until the night she threw Miss O'Shea to the floor of the stage and put her out of commission for the next three months. But it took more than a pregnant elephant to stop Cardiff's finest and, by 1949, she was hosting her own radio show with the band-leader Billy Cotton.

Films were now on the agenda and in 1944 she appeared in the film *The Way Ahead*. This was followed by more films with the comedians Sid Field (*London Town*, 1946 which failed disastrously at the box office) and Frank Randle (two low budget films with the northern comic: *Holidays With Pay*, 1948 and *Somewhere in Politics*, 1949). Tessie also featured in cameo roles in the police drama *The Blue Lamp* and *The Shiralee* (1957). She was nominated for an Oscar for her role in the 1966 film, *The Russians Are Coming*.

Eventually her career reached a low ebb from which she was spectacularly rescued by Noel Coward who took her to America to play in his Broadway musical *The Girl Who Came To Supper* adapted from a play by Terence Rattigan, *The Sleeping Prince*. The show itself did rather poorly, but the American theatre-going public took Tessie to its heart, and her part of Ada Cockle, a cockney woman working in a fish and chip shop brought the house down and won her a Tony award. It also opened the doors to America's vaudeville houses where Tessie found herself billed as 'London's Own' (sic) and she was able to indulge in her trademark cartwheels come curtain-call.

America now opened up to Tessie. She appeared on the *Ed Sullivan Show* with the Beatles; was seen again on Broadway in *A Time For Singing*, a musical version of *How Green Was My Valley*; played the Nurse in *Romeo and Juliet* and was awarded an Emmy for her role in a television remake of *Dr. Jekyll and Mr. Hyde*.

Her American success had the effect of revitalising her career in Britain. She played the Blackpool Summer Opera House in 1968 with Ken Dodd and played a transport cafe cook in *As Good Cooks Go*, her first stab at a British TV comedy series.

In 1971 it was back to the States and a part in the Disney extravaganza *Bedknobs and Broomsticks*. Two years later she was starring at the Sands Hotel, Las Vegas in *London Revue*. She was now a permanent U.S. resident but continued to make the occasional appearance in Britain.

The words 'buxom blonde' could have been coined with Tessie O'Shea in mind. At one stage she weighed in at seventeen stones, although her sheer bulk does not appear to have affected her mobility on stage in any way, she could high kick it with the best of them as she delighted in proving to her audiences. 'Two Ton Tessie' they called her, the nickname coming from a song, *Two Ton Tessie from Tennessee*, she herself had made popular.

Tessie O'Shea's hobbies included cordon bleu cookery, writing poetry and painting in oils. She also liked her food. Breakfast would, more often than not, consist of six rashers of bacon accompanied by two eggs; desserts would include mountains of peaches and cream and large hunks of cheese.

The Times is adamant that she married David Rollo in 1940, their marriage was dissolved in 1950 and there were no children, but, read the *Western Mail* and you will learn that she never married. She died in Florida on Friday, April 21st, 1995, aged 82. Her last performance had been in Washington in 1985. After her death Dan O'Neill, a *South Wales Echo* feature writer, wrote "she was to Cardiff what Gracie Fields was to Lancashire".

JOHN ORMOND

John Ormond Thomas, to give him his full name, was born in Dunvant, now a western suburb of Swansea, on April 3rd, 1923, the son of a shoemaker. He was educated at Swansea Grammar School and at the city's university where he gained a degree in English and Philosophy. A conscientious objector during the war he worked on local papers in Essex and then for *Picture Post.* He returned to Swansea and was sub-editor on the city's local paper, *The South Wales Evening Post* from 1949 to 1955 before moving onto the BBC in Cardiff as a news assistant. Within two years he was appointed to take charge of a newly set-up television documentary unit. He retired in 1984 having made documentary films since 1957. In 1990, after suffering a stroke he was taken to the University Hospital of Wales, Heath, Cardiff where he died on Friday, May 4th, 1990.

A poet good enough to have his poems published by Penguin Modern Poets, and to win the 1975 Cholmondely Award for English Poetry, John Ormond's selected poems were published by Poetry Wales in 1987. He was also a documentary film maker of note. In the 27 years he worked for the BBC he made films on poets of the calibre of Alun Lewis, Vernon Watkins, W.B. Yeats, Dylan Thomas, Edward Thomas and R.S. Thomas. He shot films on such painters as Graham Sutherland, Josef Herman, Ceri Richards and Kyffin Williams.

The first full documentary feature he produced was the 1958 *A Sort of Welcome to Spring.* His *Borrowed Pasture* (1960) narrated by Richard Burton, told the story of two veterans of the Second World War Polish Army living in a derelict farm, trying to make a living from inhospitable terrain to the north of Carmarthen.

The 1961 *Once There Was a Time* had two pensioners from Treherbert in the Rhondda discussing the relative merits of Marxism and Christianity. His 1963 *From a Town in Tuscany* dealt with the Italian city of Arezzo. The *Desert and the Dream*, also from 1963, won the *Western Mail* Television

Production of the Year Award for its portrayal of the Patagonian Welsh and their struggle with their rugged homeland.

Visions out of Wales (1969) took as its subject the painters Ceri Richards (a fellow native of Dunvant) and the Englishman Graham Sutherland who was inspired by Pembrokeshire. *A Day Eleven Years Long* (1975) concentrated on Josef Herman the Polish artist who fled the Nazis, and discovered a kind of spiritual retreat in the Swansea Valley and its working miners. *In Land Against the Light* (1979) Ormond turned his camera lens on the Anglesey painter Kyffin Williams.

Bronze Mask (1969), with narration provided by Neath-born actor William Squire, was concerned with Dylan Thomas as was *Return to Swansea*. The 1982 *I Sing To You Strangers* was, again, dedicated to the life and works of Dylan whilst *Fortissimo Jones* approached the subject from another angle, concentrating on Daniel Jones the composer and boyhood friend of Dylan's. David Berry called this film "undoubtedly one of Ormond's finest, most deeply felt works".

Between 1958 and 1982 John Ormond made some thirty-odd films, all of them for the BBC. A consummate craftsman, his cameramen would later recall how he would personally insist "on lining up every single shot himself" before shooting. Having toyed with the idea of becoming a painter himself, it is little wonder that most of his films were about painters or poets. Indeed, just before he died he had been hard at work illustrating an edition of his own selected poems. His funeral, a private one, took place on May 11th, 1990 at the Thornhill Crematorium and a Memorial Service took place at Llandaff Cathedral fourteen days later.

JOHN OSBORNE

Described as "a Welsh-Fulham upstart" by one of his ex-wives (he has been married four times: to actress Pamela Lane, actress Mary Ure, *Observer* film critic Penelope Gilliatt and actress Jill Bennett), John James Osborne is the original 'angry young man'. He was born at 2, Crookham Road, Fulham, on December 12th, 1929, the son of Thomas Godfrey Osborne, a Newport-born copywriter working for a London advertising agency, and Nellie Beatrice Grove, a London barmaid. (His parents met in the *Essex* pub near the Strand where his mother was working. Coincidentally, his paternal grandmother, an avid reader of *The South Wales Argus*, had kept the *King's Arms* in Newport with her husband towards the beginning of the twentieth century. The family is also said to have provided a Mayor of Newport.)

He attended Finlay Road Infants School and Ewell Boys School. Because of his father's illness (he had had to give up working in the summer of 1938), the Osbornes moved to Ventnor, Isle of Wight where John went to St. Boniface's School. Osborne senior died in Ventnor on January 27th, 1940 and John and his mother returned to London where he attended a new school - Elmsleigh Road - for the next two years. In 1943 he went to St. Michael's Boarding School in North Devon, appearing in plays and sketches, but was asked to leave after hitting the headmaster.

He learnt shorthand and typing at Clark's College and, in January, 1947, got a job working for Benn Brothers on a paper called *The Gas World*, moving onto *The Miller*. Passed unfit for National Service he learned to dance and joined an amateur dramatic society in Leatherhead. His attempt to secure the lead role in *Blue Lagoon* having ended in failure, he got a job as Assistant Stage Manager with Barry O'Brien productions touring with a play called *No Room at the Inn*. On Sunday, January 18th, 1948 he travelled with the company by train to Cardiff. He now began a relationship with an actress called Stella Linden in a vegetarian hotel in Llandudno. The two set up home in a Brighton flat and Osborne got work over Christmas acting in *Treasure Island*, but was then forced to wash dishes in Brighton hotels to survive. Stella left him and he had to give up the Brighton flat.

A job as Assistant Stage Manager at the Royal Rep Company in Leicester did not last long but his first play, *The Devil Inside*, written together with Stella, was given a week's run at the Theatre Royal in Huddersfield, Easter, 1950. Osborne next took a job in Ilfracombe with the Saga Repertory Company - three men and three women - and moved with them to Hayling Island (where he played Hamlet). Osborne then joined the Bridgewater Company where he met Pamela Lane who became his first wife. Moving to London with Pamela he worked in Camberwell for the Harry Hanson company. He took three weeks work in Frinton-on-Sea and, in the summer of 1953 played in *Kidderminster*. He then worked in Derby with Pamela. and was Assistant Stage Manager on the Arts Council Tour of *Pygmalion* touring South Wales and the Rhondda in the autumn of 1954. He played Freddy Eynsford Hill in *Pygmalion* and appeared in *Seagulls over Sorrento* in Morecambe, 1955. Osborne began writing *Look Back in Anger* on Wednesday, May 4th, 1955 and finished it on Friday, June 3rd, 1955. After numerous rejections, The English Stage Company accepted the play and offered Osborne a job as understudy and play-reader. At the first night performance - at the Royal Court Theatre on May 8th, 1956 - Binkie Beaumont walked out and playwright Terence Rattigan had to be persuaded to stay. The first reviews of *Look Back* were mostly poor but *The Observer* and *The Sunday Times* loved it.

For the record: on December 14th, 1962 he was divorced from Mary Ure. On May 25th, 1963 he married Penelope Gilliatt, *The Observer* film critic. Mary Ure (who starred in the first production of *Look Back in Anger*) died in 1975. Osborne was married to the actress Jill Bennett between 1968 and 1977. She committed suicide on October 6th, 1990.

Apart from *Look Back in Anger* which made his name, the best-known of John Osborne's twenty or so plays are *The Entertainer, Luther, A Patriot For Me* and *Inadmissible Evidence. Look Back, The Entertainer* and *Luther* were all subsequently filmed. Osborne also wrote the script for Tony Richardson's film of Henry Fielding's *Tom Jones* - a big hit in the sixties - and himself played a villainous Tyneside gang boss in the violent Michael Caine crime thriller *Get*

Carter. After 1975 and his play *Watch It Come Down,* Osborne struck a fallow period, his next play to be performed on a British stage being *Déja Vu* in 1992.

ALUN OWEN

Alun Davies Owen wrote some of the most acclaimed radio and TV plays of the 1950s and 60s, but he may well go down in history as the man who wrote the screenplay for the Beatles' first film *A Hard Day's Night.* (His filmscript was nominated for an Oscar. In the British Film Institute's Top One Hundred British Films of the Twentieth Century it came in at Number Eighty-Eight.)

Born on November 24th, 1925, there appears to be some doubt over Alun Owen's birthplace. David Berry gives it as Menai Bridge on Anglesey, others state that he was born in Liverpool. It is a fact, however, that, as a child, he spoke only Welsh. (In fact, until he went to school, Alun Owen spoke only Welsh. When he was eight years old, his parents moved to Liverpool and, from then on, the dominant language in his life became English.) Educated at Cardigan County High School and Oulton High School in Liverpool, at the age of sixteen he married Mary O'Keeffe with whom he had two sons.

Owen wrote the screenplay for the 1960 Joseph Losey film *The Criminal* starring Stanley Baker but he also carved out a significant niche for himself in the field of TV drama. *No Trams to Lime Street, After The Funeral* and *Lena, Oh My Lena* (with Billy Whitelaw as Lena) formed a powerful Liverpool trilogy in the late 1950s and early 60s. His *Dare To Be A Daniel* was broadcast on BBC Wales in 1968. His 1964 musical *Maggie May* was written in collaboration with the composer Lionel Bart.

Owen had a variety of jobs: During the war he worked as a Bevin Boy down the pits of South Wales for two years and also saw service in the Merchant Navy. From 1942 to 1959 he was employed as a theatre actor and director. In 1942 he became Assistant Stage Manager with the Perth Repertory Company, moving on to the Morecambe and Southport Repertory Companies. After the War he joined the Birmingham Repertory Company. In 1951 he moved to London where he was directed by Tyrone Guthrie and acted with the likes of Donald Wolfit, Stanley Baker, Ronald Harwood and Harold Pinter. He also spent eight months waiting tables in Paris. Wearing his actor's hat, Owen appeared as Pritchard in the 1953 film comedy, *Valley of Song, The Dambusters, I'm All Right Jack* and in the 1959 *Jetstorm.* He could also be seen as the curate in the 1963 film *The Servant.* Other acting experience included working as a 'stooge' for the comedian Arthur Askey, *The Benny Hill Show,* appearing in *The Dick Lester Show* (one of ITV's first Christmas programmes in December, 1955), playing a pantomime dame and being seen on TV with the Grove family, Britain's first attempt at a soap opera. He acted in Shakespeare roles with the Birmingham Repertory Company, the Old Vic and the English Stage Company. His last serious acting role was opposite Siân Phillips in a 1959 TV production. The Guild of TV Producers and Directors honoured him with their best TV Playwright Award in 1960.

The Guinness Book of Classic British TV called him "this wonderful writer". In the 1960s he continued to write for the BBC: *The Stag, Making of Jericho, Shelter* and *Charlie*. In the 1960s TV plays flowed from his pen: *Progress in the Park, A Little Winter Love* and *The Old Fella*. In 1970 he wrote *Joan, Pal, Joy, Female of the Species, Giants and Ogres, Norma, Forget-Me-Not* and *Buttons*. In 1983 he came up with *Kisch, Kisch* and, in 1989, adapted *Unexplained Laughter*. On a more jovial note he scripted BBC TV's *Corrigan Blake* (1963) and also contributed to the *Ronnie Barker Playhouse*. Alun Owen died on Tuesday, December 6th, 1994.

JOSEPH PARRY

Paham mae'n dicter, o Myfanwy ... (Why is there anger, o Myfanwy ...). Thus begins one of the finest and most well known of all Welsh songs, a staple item for Welsh Male Voice Choirs ever since it was first written in about 1875, and,

Joseph Parry (Cyfarthfa Castle Museum and Art Gallery)

if its composer, Dr. Joseph Parry, had never written another note, that one tune, lilt or melody, call it what you will, would have been enough to ensure his place in the pantheon of Welsh music's finest. But he did go on to write other music - hymns, cantatas, operas and oratorios - and achieve great fame during his lifetime both in the land of his birth - Wales - and in his adopted homeland, America.

Joseph Parry died at 9.45 on the night of Tuesday, February 18th, 1903 in Cartref his house in Penarth, where he had lived for many years. His wife and two daughters were by his side. A few years before he had undergone an operation for gallstones but the problem had recently returned to plague him. A second operation had been performed ten days before his death and, at the time, had seemed to be a success, but as the *Western Mail* reporter put it, "a certain amount of poison was diffused through the blood" and it was this which caused the composer's death. Five days after the operation his condition had begun to deteriorate and he eventually became unconscious.

Those present estimated that more than seven thousand mourners attended Parry's funeral service on Saturday, February 22nd which took place at Penarth's Christchurch Congregational Chapel. So great was the crush that many of them were forced to stand outside. After the service the man from Merthyr was buried on the north side of St. Augustine's Churchyard.

The day after his death *The Western Mail* devoted a leading article to his memory. Having written of the "unaffected grief" Welshmen everywhere - both in Wales and in America (where whenever he visited, the writer pointed out "he never failed of an ovation") - would feel at the news of Dr. Parry's death, the leader writer concluded by saying, rather prophetically, that "there can be little doubt that his hymn tunes, notably *Aberystwyth*, will live longer than any of his other and more elaborate compositions, and will, indeed, probably be sung as long as there is a Welshman left to sing them".

Joseph Parry was born in either Number 4 or Number 2 (there appears to be some doubt, but, according to Dulais Rhys, it was probably Number 2), Chapel Row, Merthyr Tydfil on Friday, May 21st, 1841. One of five children, three sisters and two brothers, his father was Daniel Parry and his mother (neé Richards) Elizabeth. The family was a musical one and the young Parry showed signs of musical ability when still young, but his parents were so poor that he was forced to start working in the puddling furnaces when he was still only nine years of age. In 1853 his father left for America and, the following year, the family sailed to join him. They departed from Cardiff on the *Jane Anderson* in July, 1854.

Once they had arrived in the New World they settled amongst other Welsh immigrants in the town of Danville, Pennsylvania where Joseph found employment in the Rough and Ready Rolling Mills. In Danville Parry was taught the elements of musical composition by two local Welshmen on his free Sundays. At work he is said to have written the musical notation of compositions he was writing on the side of a truck, if he had no time to jot the notes down on paper. (He did not learn to read music until he was seventeen years old.) He worked in the rolling mill between 1854 and 1865, marrying his wife Jane Thomas, a native of Danville (and a non-Welsh speaker) in the town on his twenty-first birthday - May 21st, 1862.

Interestingly, the period between 1861 and 1865 was a time when the American Civil War was raging. Joseph's brother, Henry, joined the Union forces in the battle against the Confederates on August 8th, 1862, signing-up for the cause in the town of *Minerseville* in Schuykill County in the state of Pennsylvania, but Joseph declined to follow his brother's example. Indeed, he twice paid other men to take his place in the Union ranks when he was called-up on two occasions between 1863 and 1864.

The War over, during the next twenty-odd years Parry would spend much time travelling the Atlantic between the United States and Great Britain (an arduous voyage, the ship could take up to as long as five weeks to complete its journey). He competed and won prizes at the following *eisteddfodau*: Danville (1860), Llandudno (1862) and Swansea (1865). Mr. Brinley Richards, one of the musical adjudicators at the Swansea eisteddfod, was so impressed by what he heard that he promptly organised a fund to raise money for the young composer to enter the Royal Academy in London. By 1868 the fund had swelled sufficiently to enable Parry to attend the Academy where he studied under William Sterndale Bennett, Manuel Garcia (who taught him the art of composition) and Dr. Charles Steggall (who taught the organ). In 1870 he was awarded the Academy's Bronze Medal and, the following year, secured the Silver Medal. In 1871 he was awarded a Bachelor of Music Degree from the University of Cambridge. Whilst in London, Parry, a lifelong teetotaller, apparently did little except study and take part in the activities of the Welsh community. During his college holidays he could be found travelling the length and breadth of Wales, giving recitals and performances all over the country.

After London he returned to America and travelled through twelve different States in the North-east of the country, giving concerts and raising money to establish a musical college. The Danville Musical Institute opened around October, 1872 with Parry himself teaching the principles of composition, singing and the organ. The school began life with thirty pupils but greater things were in store and, from 1873 to 1879, he was Head of Music at the University College of Wales, Aberystwyth which had been founded in 1872. Unfortunately, his 'extra curricular' activities in Aberystwyth - composing, holding concerts, (frequently featuring his own music) during term-time and journeying all over Wales in the holidays - did not go down too well with the Council of the University and there were rumblings of discontent emanating from the college authorities all through his period of tenure. In 1878 he was awarded the title of Doctor of Music at Cambridge, but friction still remained, and Parry and the college had parted company by September, 1879.

The composer's riposte was to open The Aberystwyth School of Music on September 17th, 1879, but it failed to flourish and had to close in 1881. About the end of March, 1881, Parry moved to Swansea and was employed by the town's Ebenezer Independent Chapel as their organist for a yearly salary of £60. He also set up a private music school in Swansea which lasted from 1881 to 1888. In the summer of 1883, Parry applied for the post of Lecturer in Music at the University College of South Wales and Monmouthshire in Cardiff. There proved to be eleven applicants in all and the post was given to an Englishman, Clement Templeton. In 1888 Parry applied once again for the post of Lecturer in Cardiff and, this time, he was successful. He started work in October 1888 at an annual salary of £100 a year. He was also employed to play the organ in Ebenezer Chapel in Charles Street, Cardiff for £40 a year. From then on until his death he earned his bread lecturing in music in Cardiff.

During his lifetime Parry's compositions were very popular, both in Wales and the USA, and he enjoyed almost the status of a legend amongst his fellow Welsh musicians and pop star like acclamation amongst ordinary lovers of music. The vast majority of his work leans towards the choral and the dramatic although he did write some chamber and orchestral music. His *Blodwen* is said to be the first opera to be written in Welsh. Begun in February, 1876, the work was completed on Wednesday, February 7th, 1877, and first performed publicly on Tuesday, May 21st in the Temperance Hall at Aberystwyth to a packed audience on the composer's thirty-seventh birthday. It proved to be popular both in Wales and with Welsh-Americans, so much so that a brand of flour was named after it in the States. At the Cardiff Festival of 1892 Parry's *Saul of Tarsus* oratorio (with a libretto written in English) caused a great stir.

His operas are *Blodwen* (1878) (the first ever Welsh opera and the first ever opera with a Welsh libretto, it was performed nearly five hundred times between 1880 and 1896, and parts of it can still be heard regularly today), *Virginia* (1882), *Sylvia* (1889), *Aberdare, Arianwen, King Arthur,* the one-act opera *Ceridwen* and *The Maid of Cefn Ydfa. Blodwen* was performed at the Alexandra Palace in London and his oratorio *Emmanuel* was given a performance at the St. James's Hall in 1880.

Amongst Parry's many tunes - he wrote as many as six hundred titles – are *Merthyr Tydfil* and *Sirioldeb* (or 'Cheerfulness'). His *Aberystwyth* (written in 1876) was the first Welsh hymn tune to achieve universal acceptance throughout the British Isles and appear in hymn books everywhere.

The 1951 *Off to Philadelphia in the Morning* by Rhondda born author Jack Jones, which was subsequently made into a television film, is a fictionalised account of Parry's career and celebrates his eventful life. It was a life which was one constant round of singing, playing, conducting, composing and adjudicating and, of course, his paymasters expected him to do the occasional bout of teaching every now and again. It was a life which was not without its sorrows. His mother and brother died far from Wales in America (Henry survived the Civil War but died in Minersville on July 4th, 1892. Parry's mother died on June 11th, 1886 in the U.S. state of Maine) and he lost two of his sons, both of whom were musically gifted, when they were only in their twenties - his youngest son William Sterndale Parry died on April 5th, 1892, aged twenty and Joseph Haydn Parry died in 1894, aged twenty-nine.

Joseph Parry left behind a personal fortune of £440. He was survived by his wife and three of his five children - a son, Mendelssohn and two daughters, Dilys and Edna. His wife died in Penarth on September 25th, 1918, aged seventy-five and was buried next to her husband on September 30th.

In the second episode of *Wales - A Musical Nation?* shown on BBC1 Wales in May, 2000, Dr. Lyn Davies referred to Parry's "colourful life", calling him "the quintessential Welsh Victorian composer" and describing him as "a typical Celt, emotional, mercurial, also pragmatic and hugely loved for all his faults. When he died, he, together with Lloyd George, were probably the most famous Welshmen in the world".

His most recent biographer, Dulas Rhys, has called Dr. Joseph Parry the most important musician in Wales in the nineteenth century, but concludes that his music appealed mainly to his fellow countrymen in Wales, the Welsh exiles of America and Welsh people living in England. Rhys also stresses the parlous state of music in Wales before Parry's arrival on the scene. Little music was taught in the schools and Welsh musical expression found its main outlets in the chapel, the *Gymanfa Ganu*, the Sunday school and the eisteddfod. Nowhere in Wales were there any concert halls worthy of the name nor any opera houses such as were to be found in other European countries. What Welsh composers there were, were mainly self taught amateurs and, compared to these others, Parry stood out like a shining beacon.

Not that Parry was above criticism. According to Rhys, his music was sometimes less than original and, as a composer, he lacked the gift of self criticism and his style was heavily influenced by other composers. Interestingly, Rhys adds that none of the music Parry composed whilst living in America betrayed any American influences, certainly not in its style.

Be that as it may, there can be no denying that Parry, more than any other composer, spanned two worlds - the Old World of Wales and the New World of America - and rose from humble beginnings. What other composer, of whatever nationality has had such an underprivileged start in life, but Parry overcame all such disadvantages and through his inborn talent and sheer hard work rose to the top of his chosen tree. In the beginning Parry's vocal talents were as much to the fore as his composing gifts and he would often accompany himself on the harmonium. In fact as Dulais Rhys has pointed out, Parry's first ever instrument was his own voice. He began as an alto and then a tenor singing with choirs in his native Merthyr and his adopted home of Danville, before developing into a baritone. It was in America that he first learned to play the melodion, harmonium, piano and organ. He was accepted into the Gorsedd of Bards at the 1865 Aberystwyth National Eisteddfod and chose as his bardic title *Pencerdd America* (The Chief Musician of America), but he ceased competing at *eisteddfodau* after the 1866 National Eisteddfod. Today the ironworker's cottage where he grew up, just a half a mile west of the centre of Merthyr, has been sympathetically restored to give an idea of what it was like in the 1840s and there is a Joseph Parry exhibition occupying the first floor.

DONALD PEERS

In his book, *Cavalcade of Variety Acts*, Roy Hudd called Donald Peers "the unlikeliest heart-throb of them all" and in a sense he was. Known as 'The Cavalier of Song' and always immaculately decked out in evening dress, he seems to modern eyes more than ever a throwback to a bygone age, nothing like the teenage idols of today. Yet his place in popular music history is secure and, in his time, he brought a great deal of pleasure to millions of people. He was even making hit records in the Sixties and Seventies. He was born Donald Rhys Hubert Peers on July 10th, 1908 in a rented house, Bellamy Villa, 106, College Street, in the West Wales mining town of Ammanford. His father was an Englishman whose family came from Kent whilst his Welsh mother's maiden name was Rees. (Her father, Ebenezer Rees, had founded a weekly newspaper called *Llais Llafur,* or The Voice of Labour.) Donald's father came from Ash near Canterbury and met his mother, Mary, in Chicago. Both parents were members of the Plymouth Brethren (Donald's father had converted in 1894) and together they had five children (three sons - Elwyn, Howell and Donald and two daughters - Gwyneth and Janie.) Because of his strong religious beliefs, Donald's father, a miner, would never enter a theatre and never saw Donald perform on stage.

As a child, the young Donald suffered from rickets and, when he was aged about five, the family moved to the village of Bettws not far from Ammanford. He was educated at Bettws Council School and Amman Valley County School and took part in a number of school productions. Donald Peers was supposed to have been earmarked for a teaching career but the young Peers had other ideas. The day before his sixteenth birthday he left Ammanford. He quickly found work as a painter at Guadeloupe Barracks, Bordon, near Aldershot where he stayed for four months and then moved on to York and Edinburgh. Whilst in Edinburgh, in 1925, he heard Sybil Vane, "the famous Welsh soprano" sing. She was married to Lee Donn, an American, who accompanied her on the piano. During his first stint as a painter Peers took part in a talent contest organised by Fred Karno at Catterick Camp, and sang with a dance band.

Still restless, Donald went to sea as a mess-room steward on *The British Earl* on Tuesday, January 4th, 1927. The ship sailed from Swansea and travelled to Port Said, the Suez Canal, the Red Sea and Abadan in the Persian Gulf before returning to Swansea. Peers now returned to painting and his job took him to Lowestoft. Here he joined a concert party called Tons of Fun in 1927. His first professional performance took place at Lowestoft's New Theatre on September 20th, 1927. Then on Saturday, December, 17th, 1927 came his first broadcast for the BBC singing *By A Babbling Brook* to his own ukulele accompaniment (but it was to be another twenty years before he would have a radio series). He spent 1928 touring with Clifton Shaw's Concert party under the name of 'Smiling Donald Peers and his Ukulele'. At Christmas time he sang in the chorus and understudied Randolph Sutton's principal boy in *Babes in the Wood* at Plymouth's Grand Theatre. Peers made his London debut at the Bedford Theatre, Camden Town in August, 1929 as part of Sutton's touring revue, *Spare Time.* Thus began a slow but steady climb up through the ranks of show business. In 1930, however, Peers took time off to marry Mary Musgrave. The two had first met when the Welshman was working as a painter in Richmond, Yorkshire and their wedding took place on June 7th in Harrogate.

After the wedding the young singer continued to do the rounds of the music halls and the theatres, learning his trade. 1933 saw him step up the ladder with his name featured on good bills at good theatres. His big break came in April, 1933 when John Sharman signed him up for his radio programme *Music Hall*. Writing in *The Daily Express* the critic Collie Knox gave Peers an enthusiastic review which did him no harm at all, and was instrumental in HMV bringing out his first record. Soon after the outbreak of war Donald joined the Royal Army Service Corps but continued to entertain. He received his discharge from the Services on D-Day, June 6th, 1944.

Then in an amazing turn of events Peers found himself propelled to fame in the late 40s and early 50s becoming Britain's first heart-throb and wowing mainly female audiences who screamed and swooned at him, foretelling the advent of Beatle-mania years later. It all started when his radio show *The Cavalier of Song* was broadcast live from London's Kilburn Empire theatre in 1949. It immediately made him Number One in the popularity stakes. 'Peers-mania' broke out all over the place and he topped the bill everywhere, taking the entire country by storm. Apart from his signature tune *By A Babbling Brook*, hits from this period included *Lavender Blue, Far Away Places, Powder Your Face With Sunshine, Dear Hearts And Gentle People, If I Knew You Were Coming, I'd've Baked A Cake* and the Ammanford warbler sold over ten million records in Great Britain alone. (Compilation albums of his hits continued to be released in the 70s and 80s.) He also had his own TV series *Donald Peers* and featured in several films including *Sing Along With Me*.

At the height of his fame he was earning £600 a week and receiving 3,000 fan letters a week. At one stage a throat ailment threatened to rob Donald of his greatest asset, his voice, but following treatment, it recovered. He topped the bill at the Royal Albert Hall in 1949 with his one-man show and also starred at the London Palladium. On February 8th, 1950, he was back on the radio and, in the same year, headlined at the Palladium and took part in the Royal Variety Performance. He left his wife, Mary, a Roman Catholic in 1953, but had to wait twenty years before he could get a divorce. His companion ever since the split was Kay O'Dwyer, a music publisher.

At the height of his success he was taking home £50,000 a year but the adulation did not last and, at one stage, it seemed as if his career would be washed away by a tidal wave called Rock 'n Roll. But Peers refused to fade away and in the late '50s spent a lot of time in Australia, South Africa and India. On his return to Britain he had to fight to re-establish himself and chose to build up his reputation again by playing the clubs in the North of England. In 1969, he recorded a comeback song called *Please Don't Go*, which got to Number Four in the Charts. Then, on a tour of Australia in 1971 he suffered horrendous injuries to his back in a freak accident. Incredibly, he fell through a hole on a Sydney stage and broke his back. He had to be strapped into a steel harness, losing two inches in height in the progress but he showed great resilience and courage in learning to walk again. He even brought out another record in 1972, the appropriately titled *Give Me One More Chance* which brought him back to prominence again.

Sadly the comeback was not to last. In the summer of 1973 he had to leave his home in Hove and go into a Brighton nursing home. He spent five weeks in the home but this time there was to be no fightback. He died in the home on Thursday, August 9th, 1973.

It can safely be said that Donald Peers was a Welsh-speaking Welshman. Nowhere in his autobiography, *Pathway*, published in 1951, does Peers say he can speak Welsh but he gives the game away when he says that he understood what the two men were saying in Welsh on Neath station on the day he left home. His most famous song *By A Babbling Brook* with which he will always be associated was, in reality, entitled *In A Shady Nook* and "By a Babbling Brook" actually belonged to the second line.

Not everyone, however, fell under the Peers spell. In his 1998 book, *Grace, Beauty and Banjos*, Michael Kilgariff carefully enumerated the names by which Peers had been known on the halls: "The (Laughing) Cavalier of Song; England's (sic) Greatest Chorus singer; Radio's Cavalier of Song - originally known as smiling Donald Peers and his Ukulele" and then he went for the jugular: "We find his singing voice scratchy and his manner over-weeningly schmaltzy".

SIÂN PHILLIPS

Husky-voiced, Welsh-speaking Siân has been married and divorced three times. Her first husband was Don, a postgraduate student she met during her time at Cardiff University. Her second husband, to whom she was married for twenty years and by whom she had two daughters, was the Irish actor, Peter O'Toole. (They married in 1959 and the marriage was dissolved in 1979.) She was married to her third husband Robin Sachs, an actor sixteen years younger than herself, for twelve years, but their marriage ended in divorce in 1992 since which time she has lived alone in her West London flat.

An only child, Siân was born on May 14th, 1934 at Ty Mawr farm, Betws, a mountain farm high above Gwaun-Cae-Gurwen, famed for being the home village of rugby immortal, Gareth Edwards. She grew up (she has been quoted as saying that the people who brought her up were nearly all women) being able to read music and play the piano and was educated at Pontardawe Grammar School, the University College of Wales, Cardiff and RADA (where she won the Bancroft Gold Medal). Originally known as Jane - her Welsh teacher at school, Eic Davies (the same man who would later teach the singer Mary Hopkin), called her Siân - she was aged eleven when she won the National Eisteddfod for the first time and never stopped working after that. In 1955, she began work as a BBC Wales newsreader and announcer and was a member of the BBC Repertory Company.

Since then she has appeared in many TV productions including *How Green Was My Valley* (where she played the part of Beth Morgan), *Off to*

Siân Phillips (Mike Martin)

Philadelphia in the Morning, Warrior Queen (she played Queen Boudicca in the 1978 Thames TV production), *Tinker, Tailor, Soldier, Spy,* Lady Churchill in *Winston Churchill - The Wilderness Years, Smiley's People* and *The Borrowers.* She has acted a lot of Chekov in Welsh (she spoke no other language before the age of ten).

Siân has made a number of films, among them: *Becket, Young Cassidy, Laughter in the Dark, Goodbye, Mr. Chips, Murphy's War, Under Milk Wood, Clash of The Titans, How Many Miles to Babylon, A Painful Case, Dune, Return to Endor, Beyond all Reason, Valmont, Dark River, The Doctor and the Devils* and *Age of Innocence.* She undertook her first professional singing role when she appeared in *Pal Joey* in London's West End in 1981.

In 1994, Siân appeared in *Ghosts* at the Sherman Theatre, Cardiff. In 1995, she played in *An Inspector Calls* on Broadway. Currently Siân has been wowing West End audiences with her show *Marlene: A Tribute to Dietrich* where she sings fifteen songs. Written by Pam Gems, *Marlene* was first performed for two nights only in front of an invited audience at the National Theatre. Siân later went on to take the show to Broadway. Siân has written articles for *Radio Times, Cosmopolitan* and *Vogue* as well as a book, *Siân Phillip's Needlepoint.*

One of Siân's best-known TV roles was as the scheming Livia, Augustus's wife in the 1976 BBC production of *I, Claudius* for which she won a BAFTA award. Other BAFTAs were given for best actress in *How Green Was My Valley* and for *The Borrowers* in 1992. Her role as Mrs. Driver in the latter made her for a while "the most hated woman in the U.K.", Siân would claim later. She also appeared as the Red Queen in the Channel 4 Christmas 1998 production of *Through the Looking Glass.* She published the first part of her autobiography *Private Faces* in October, 1999. In November, 1999 she starred as the reclusive Meg Lewis in BBC1's *The Magician's House.* In June, 2000, Siân was awarded a CBE in the Queen's Birthday Honour's List.

JONATHAN PRYCE

Born Holywell, North-East Wales on June 1st, 1947, the son of a Welsh speaking shopkeeper. Educated at Holywell Grammar, his schooldays were not particularly pleasant: most of his time was spent hanging around outside the headmaster's room. He was not asked to return to the Sixth Form. Surprisingly, after his own experiences in school, he trained to be a teacher at Ormskirk where he took a drama course and then applied for RADA, but no Welsh local authority was prepared to give him a grant. It was only when RADA agreed to waive the fees, and his family offered him financial support, that he was able to go.

After leaving RADA one of his first roles was playing in 1975 in the Nottingham Old Vic in *The Comedians.* Since then, he has played Macbeth for the RSC, Hamlet at the Royal Court, appeared with the Royal Shakespeare Company in *Anthony and Cleopatra* and *Measure for Measure* and starred in *The Comedians* in both London and New York. His 1985 performance in Chekhov's *The Seagull* earned him critical acclaim as did his role as the

Jonathan Pryce

country doctor in the 1988 performance of the same playwright's *Uncle Vanya* at the Vaudeville.

He enjoyed great success singing on Broadway in the hit musical *Miss Saigon* after his initial triumph with the same show at the Theatre Royal, Drury Lane. His other musicals include *Oliver* where he played Fagin and, on the big screen, *Evita*, playing President Juan Peron with Madonna as Mrs. Peron, the Argentine phenomenon.

His well-stocked awards cupboard includes Tony Awards for *Comedians* in 1977 and the 1990/91 Broadway performance of *Miss Saigon;* a Laurence Olivier award for his 1980 role as Hamlet and Laurence Olivier, Variety Club Awards for his 1989 appearances in *Miss Saigon* and Best Actor Prize at Cannes in 1995 for his role as Lytton Strachey in the film *Carrington*.

His small screen appearances include *Timon of Athens, The Caretaker,* the 1993 BBC Wales film *Thicker Than Water* (the first time he had worked in Wales), *Mr. Wroe's Virgins, Selling Hitler, Roger Doesn't Live Here Anymore* and *Martin Luther.*

His first cinema film was the 1982 Disney vehicle, *Something Wicked This Way Comes.* He has also been seen to good effect in the cinema in *The Ploughman's Lunch* (1983), *Brazil* (1985), *The Doctor and The Devils* (1986), *The Adventures of Baron Munchhausen* and *Jumping Jack Flash.* His '90s films include *Glengarry Glen Ross, Tomorrow Never Dies* (the 1997 James Bond film in which he played the villain, media mogul Elliot Carver) and *Regeneration,* the first world war drama which caused the film critics to fall over themselves in their search for superlatives to describe Pryce. He was in the film *The Testament of Taliesin Jones* and also in the Sara Sugarman directed *Pavarotti in Dad's Room.* Since 1974 he has been married to Kate Fahy.

ANGHARAD REES

Angharad Rees was born in Cardiff in 1949. She was ten when her father, Linford Rees, moved the family to London after becoming professor of psychiatry at St. Bartholomew's Hospital. Aged sixteen, she trained to be a teacher at the Sorbonne in Paris and actually taught English at a psychiatric unit in Madrid for a time. Her stage appearances include *The Winter's Tale,*

Hamlet and *Romeo and Juliet*, but she is probably most famous for her role as the Cornish temptress Demelza in the TV series *Poldark*. Other TV programmes she has appeared in include: *The Way We Live Now, As You Like It* (as part of the BBC Television Shakespeare broadcast on BBC2, December 17th, 1978), *Armchair Theatre, The Persuaders, The Piano Player, Butterfly, The Protectors, Play for Today, Joe's Ark, Thriller, The Gathering Storm, The Avengers, Dear Brutus* and *Close to Home*.

She has appeared in such films as *Hands of the Ripper, Under Milk Wood, To Catch A Spy, Bedevilled, It's A Two-Feet-Six-Inches-Above-The-Ground World, Moments* and *The Curse of King Tut's Tomb*. Angharad gave up acting in the mid-80's for ten years in order to raise her two children, Linford and Rhys. She returned to television in the ITV comedy series *Close to Home* starring with Paul Nicholas.

In the 1977 *Morecambe & Wise Christmas Special* her first name proved too much for Eric Morecambe who resorted to calling her "Handgrenade" and she was made to sing at the end of the show. She was in Joe Orton's *What The Butler Saw* together with Philip Madoc, Ray Smith and Gareth Thomas, in a production directed by Hywel Bennett. Her first acting role was as a maid in a TV production of *Man and Superman*. In Dennis Potter's 1974 *Joe's Ark* she played a girl at Oxford University who had contracted cancer. Married to actor Christopher Cazenove in 1973, the couple had two sons, but divorced in 1992. Her elder son Linford, named after his grandfather, was killed in a motorway crash on the M11 on Friday, September 10th, 1999.

MATTHEW RHYS

Matthew Rhys Evans (he dropped the 'Evans' on joining Equity and discovering that there was already an actor called Matthew Evans) hails from the Whitchurch area of Cardiff. The son of a Welsh headmaster, he attended Glantaf Welsh School (where he took part in two school musicals) and, aged sixteen, was part of the National Youth Theatre of Wales. Two years later he moved to London and trained at RADA. In March 1996, he interrupted his studies to film *House of America* as Boyo. After leaving RADA in the summer of 1996 he appeared in Alan Ayckbourn's *Chorus of Disapproval* and then in the BBC1 series *Backup* playing the part of P.C. Stevie 'Hiccup' Higson.

A fluent Welsh speaker, he starred in the S4C film *Be Brave*, playing a gay teenager from the South Wales valleys, struggling to come to terms with the nature of his sexuality. He also played a gay character in *Cardiff East*, first at the National Theatre, South Bank, London in the spring of 1997 and then at Cardiff's New Theatre. He took part in the Old Vic production of *Gracenote*. He played the minor role of Saskia Reeves's son in the film *Heart* released in the autumn of 1997. Other films he has been involved with include *Elizabeth* and *Whatever Happened to Harold Smith*. In December, 1997, he was in *Stranger's House* at the Ambassadors Theatre in a Royal Court production.

He won the BAFTA Cymru Award, Sunday, March 22nd, 1998 for Best Actor for his role in *Bydd yn Wrol/Be Brave*. He also appeared with Sir Anthony Hopkins in the 1999 film version of *Titus Andronicus* as Demetrius. He was in the film *The Testament of Taliesin Jones* and also in the Sara Sugarman directed *Pavarotti in Dad's Room*. He shares a flat in London with Ioan Gruffudd (Both actors attended Ysgol Glantaf before going on to RADA.) His first leading role was playing Carl in the thriller *Sorted*, which he began filming in October, 1999. In April, 2000 he played the part of Benjamin Braddock in a West End stage version of *The Graduate* (at the Gielgud Theatre), with Hollywood actress Kathleen Turner taking the Mrs. Robinson role. This aroused great interest in the theatre-going public the more so when it was learnt that the forty-five-year-old Miss Turner, veteran of such films as *War of the Roses*, *Jewel of the Nile* and *Romancing the Stone* in which she co-starred with Zeta Jones love Michael Douglas, would be appearing naked in one of the scenes.

As news of her impending nude scene spread (in reality it was tastefully done and took up a mere fraction of the play's running-time), tickets for the show began to sell like the proverbial hot cakes, some forty thousand of them being sold. Turner, who was making her West End debut, said of her Welsh co-star "He can really act. With acting it's like dancing, where one leads and the other follows, and then they change over. Well, he can dance." On the play's first night – April 5th, 2000 such luminaries as Cilla Black, Barbara Windsor and Hugh Grant turned up. The *Blind Date* presenter Cilla Black thought Rhys's performance "incredible" and *The Times* was impressed with the way he partnered Turner. Susannah Clapp in *The Observer Review* (April 9th, 2000) was another theatre critic who had nothing but good to say about Matthew's performance. Such exposure can have done Rhys's burgeoning career no harm.

Matthew himself took a leaf out of Kathleen Turner's book when he appeared naked (and semi-naked) in *Metropolis,* a steamy, six-part thriller shown on the ITV network in May, 2000. Playing the cannabis smoking university graduate, also called Matthew, the young Welshman is filmed pacing his flat, naked as the day he was born, and also caught on camera baking a cake with only an apron to cover his private parts. The quality papers' TV critics were suitably impressed with Rhys's riveting performance.

ALAN RICKMAN

Famous for his "laconic drawl", Alan Sidney Rickman was born on February 21st, 1946 at 24, Lynton Road in the London suburb of Acton. His father, Bernard Rickman was an Irishman, a painter and decorator by trade, whilst his mother, Margaret Doreen Rose Bartlett, came from Treforest, near Pontypridd. Alan was the couple's second son. When he was eight his father died from cancer leaving his mother to bring up her four children alone, relying on the money she earned from her job at the Post Office.

Rickman was educated at West Acton First School and Latymer Upper a private school in Hammersmith to which he won a scholarship aged eleven, and where he took part in many school productions. Leaving school, in 1965 he began a three-year art and design course at the Chelsea College of Art following this up with a one-year graphic design course at the Royal College of Art. His studies over, he was instrumental in founding a freesheet newspaper - *The Notting Hill Herald* - and Graphiti, a graphic design company but the lure of acting proved too strong and, aged 26, he applied for and was given a place at RADA.

The fact that he was born with the speech defect of a tight jaw has not prevented him making his mark in the acting profession. At RADA he won both the Bancroft Gold Medal and the Forbes Robertson prize. On leaving RADA he became Assistant Stage Manager at the Manchester Library Theatre. He then joined the two Leicester Theatres run by Michael Bogdanov – the Haymarket and the Phoenix. In 1978 he joined the RSC but, unhappy with the way things were developing, left a year later. He rejoined the RSC in 1985 and made his name playing the part of the Vicomte de Valmont in Christopher Hampton's *Les Liaisons Dangereuses*, subsequently playing the role in the West End and on Broadway.

He made his film debut in *Die Hard* when he was aged forty-two, playing Hans Gruber, the German terrorist leader thwarted by Bruce Willis. Other film roles include the Sheriff of Nottingham in the 1991 film *Robin Hood: Prince of Thieves,* Jamie, Juliet Stevenson's ghostly lover in 1991's *Truly Madly Deeply,* P.L. O'Hara, the tormented actor in *An Awfully Big Adventure* (1994) and Colonel Brandon in Emma Thompson's 1995 film version of Jane Austen's *Sense and Sensibility.* He has also been seen as Eamon de Valera in *Michael Collins* (1995), *Rasputin* (1995) for which he won a Golden Globe and an Emmy and the 1991 film *Close My Eyes* in which he played a husband cuckolded by his own brother-in-law.

On January 26th, 1992 Rickman won the *Evening Standard* Drama Award for Best Actor for his performances in the films *Close My Eyes, Truly Madly Deeply* and *Robin Hood: Prince of Thieves* (in this last film his bravura performance completely stole the show from Kevin Costner who was playing the nominal hero Robin Hood). The 1992 BAFTAS made him Best Supporting Actor. In the 1994 Montreal Film Festival he was proclaimed Best Actor for his role in the film *Mesmer.* Rickman was forty-six years old before he played Hamlet for the first time on the professional stage at the Riverside studios in London in the autumn of 1992.

His television triumphs include: Vidal in the 1979 dramatisation of Zola's *Thérèse Raquin* and Obadiah Slope in the BBC's 1982 production of *Barchester Towers.* He has been heard in numerous radio productions. Lately he has begun to branch into directing: he directed Sharman Macdonald's *The Winter Guest,* both on stage and now, 1997, on film. (He also co-wrote the screenplay for the film version). He played Metatron in the 2000 film *Dogma* directed by American writer Kevin Smith. In August, 2000 it was announced that he had been lined-up to play the part of Professor Snape in the film version of *Harry Potter and the Sorcerer's Stone.*

RACHEL ROBERTS

Known to her friends as Ray, cat loving Rachel Roberts was born in Llanelli on September 20th, 1927 of Welsh-speaking parents. As a child she was shy and asthmatic. Aged ten she played Scrooge in a primary school production of *A Christmas Carol.* She was educated at the University of Wales, Aberystwyth in 1946 and then went on to audition for both RADA and the Central School of Speech and Drama. She was accepted at both but, in 1948, decided to go to RADA where she won awards for her comic gifts but did not complete her course. Whilst at RADA she won two student prizes.

In 1950 she was part of the repertory company put together by Clifford Evans which included Richard Burton and Kenneth Williams, and was based at the Swansea Grand Theatre. After a year she had moved on to Stratford-upon-Avon and the Shakespeare Memorial Theatre. Here she understudied Sybil Burton but, after one season, was not retained on the company's books, and packed her bags for London, where she worked in some of the capital's small theatres, before getting the call to work with the Old Vic company.

In 1955, she married actor Alan Dobie at York Place Baptist Church, Swansea. Her father, the Rev. Rees Roberts, a Welsh Baptist minister, officiated at the ceremony but, by her own admission, she proved to be less than faithful to her new husband. This first marriage lasted until 1961, her second, to Rex Harrison, whom she met whilst playing opposite him in the Royal Court Theatre's 1960 production of Chekov's *Platonov*, from 1962 to 1971. They were married in Genoa City Hall on March 21st, 1962, but separated in the late sixties and, in February, 1971, Rachel took out divorce proceedings against Rex Harrison in the Santa Monica Courts, although she remained obsessed with him till the end of her life. (Incidentally, Harrison's real name was Reginald Carey Harrison and Rachel always called him 'Reg'.)

During her marriage to Harrison, Rachel became increasingly disillusioned with all the trappings associated with Hollywood film-making, and became prone to bouts of depression often verging on the suicidal. She would also drink too much and often howl like a bassett hound and, even stab Harrison's hands with a knife while they were eating in public. In an effort to save their marriage the couple worked together on a John Mortimer adaptation of Georges Feydeau's *A Flea In Her Ear* in November, 1968, but the differences between them had now become too marked for the relationship to continue.

The death of her father, Rees Roberts, in June, 1965 at the age of seventy-one (her mother was to die in 1974) cannot have helped matters, and the 'cries for help' became ever more frequent. She tried to kill herself in Rome when Harrison was filming *The Honeypot.* When Harrison was filming *Dr. Dolittle*, Rachel said she would throw herself off a rock. At Christmas, 1969, she had to have her stomach pumped out at St. George's Hospital after swallowing, so she claimed, fifty aspirin tablets.

Yet as an actress in her own right, she was herself a star and more than capable of holding her own. She made her film debut playing 'Bessie the Milk' in *Valley of Song* and went on to give powerful performances as Brenda in *Saturday Night and Sunday Morning* (1960) (a part previously declined by Diana Dors), the repressed Mrs. Hammond in *This Sporting Life* (1963) and as Mrs. Appleyard in the 1976 film from Australia, *Picnic at Hanging Rock*, directed by Peter Weir. Other films she featured in were *Our Man in Havana* (1959), *The Reckoning* (1970) and *O Lucky Man* (1973).

She won British Academy Awards for both *Saturday Night and Sunday Morning* (she was named as Best Actress in April, 1961) and *This Sporting Life* and, as well, a Best Supporting Actress Award for the film *Yanks*. She also won the Clarence Denvent Award for Best Supporting Actress for her performance as Anna Petrovna in the Royal Court Theatre's production of *Platonov*.

Darren Ramirez, a Mexican almost twenty years younger than Rachel now came on the scene and would share the last ten years of her life. She met him in a bar in California at the beginning of 1970. He was to provide her with some, but ultimately not enough, comfort.

In January, 1972 she appeared with Albert Finney at the Royal Court in *Alpha Beta*. Her role as his wife won her the *Evening Standard* Award for Best Actress at the end of 1972 and the play was later shown on television. She next played Claire Zachanassian in *The Visit* and Francine in *Chemin de Fer* on Broadway in November, 1973 and was nominated for Tony Awards in both roles (although she did not win). Whilst the plays were on she left Darren to take up with one of the stage managers, Val Mayer.

In the early part of 1975 she appeared with Jill Bennett at Greenwich in *The End of Me Old Cigar* written by John Osborne. At this time she was still together with Val Mayer. In the autumn of 1975 she toured in *Habeas Corpus* by Alan Bennett, starting at the Martin Beck Theatre in New York. After *Habeas Corpus*, she appeared in *The Tony Randall Show*, an American sit-com, for two years, playing Tony Randall's English (sic) housekeeper. At the same time she took up with Darren Ramirez again.

In March, 1979 Roberts returned to Los Angeles after visiting the Far East and, soon afterwards, became a member of her local branch of Alcoholics Anonymous, but did not attend meetings very often and then, allegedly, only to "meet men". Rows with Darren now became more and more frequent as Rachel's nerves began to fray. She confided in her diaries: "I live each moment in a jumble of past, present and future". At about this time she began to learn to drive, although she needed two instructors working simultaneously to teach her.

Now began a morbid fear of not being able to remember her lines. She would drink and then be unable to remember what had happened. She began rehearsing for her part of Mother Peter in *Once A Catholic* by Mary O'Malley. The play toured for a few weeks in August, 1979 and Rachel received good reviews but the play moved to New York. Here she felt so alone she found solace in the Bronx with a paroled ex-convict called 'Knuckles', or John, whom she had met at an Alcoholics Anonymous meeting. 'Knuckles' had done time for armed robbery and, like the Black hustler she had earlier taken up with in L.A., was typical of Rachel's tendency to link up with 'undesirables'. The same week that it opened on Broadway *Once A Catholic* closed. Rachel now began to see doctors and analysts.

In January, 1980, Rachel arranged a lecturing job, teaching drama, including *King Lear*, at Yale University, a move she came to regret. The campus was a lonely place in the depths of winter and the situation was not improved when the South African playwright, Athol Fugard, arrived on the scene. He wanted Rachel to play the part of Gladys in his new play, *A Lesson from Aloes* which he intended to produce at Yale. But instead of helping her, the role of Gladys only mirrored Rachel's own fears and anxieties and this, coupled with the growing deterioration in her own lectures, caused her to leave the play and then Yale altogether. On her time at Yale she wrote in her Journals: "I remained in the grip of melancholia - a dummy without a ventriloquist. That's what I am."

About the end of March or the beginning of April, 1980, she returned to California. Roberts had been hired to work in a Hollywood film comedy called *Charlie Chan and the Curse of the Dragon Queen*. It was to be directed by Clive Donner, with Peter Ustinov as the Chinese detective. Unfortunately, Rachel decided to take an overdose of sleeping tablets. This nearly put paid to her part in the film, but she did complete it although suffering agonies.

In July and August, 1980 she found herself in three different hospitals in England. In October, 1980 she was at Galsworthy House, trying to break the hold alcohol had on her.

Rachel Roberts died on November 26th, 1980 at 2620, Hutton Drive, Los Angeles, the house that Darren Ramirez had bought whilst she was acting in *Habeas Corpus*. At first it was thought that Rachel had died from a heart attack but, on Saturday, November 29th, the Los Angeles county coroner stated that she had committed suicide. The autopsy found that she had died from swallowing a caustic substance, variously described as an alkali, a lye or some sort of "deadly acid". In addition, she had taken a massive dose of barbiturates. The day she died she had been due to fly to New York to audition for the role of Lolita's mother, in the musical version of *Lolita* adapted by Edward Albee.

The only person present when her body was cremated was the faithful Darren Ramirez. In her will she stated that her ashes were not to be brought back to Wales nor kept in a chapel. She wanted them scattered over water. Not knowing what to do with them, Darren eventually gave the ashes to Lindsay Anderson to look after in his flat in North London.

Loyal, generous, humorous and impulsive, Rachel Roberts could often be arrogant and rude. She was also outrageous and self destructive and, when drunk, would happily insult anyone. Drink affected her – one glass of wine would be enough to set her off. When drunk she would howl like a dog, crawl under the table and bite guests on their ankles. Nevertheless, she was a consummate professional when she was working, as she proved with her stunning performances in some seminal sixties films.

She played Mrs. Dai Bread Two in the original 1954 radio production of *Under Milk Wood*. In 1956 she took over from Wendy Hiller the part of Emilia in *Othello* at the Old Vic. In September, 1968, she appeared in an Emlyn Williams scripted monologue *A Blue Movie of My Own True Love* on BBC2. Always very proud of her Welshness, she appeared in two dramas for HTV, *Back of Beyond* and *Graceless Go I* (1976) in which she played opposite Stanley Baker. She was versatile, too. In September, 1964, she was offered the leading role in *Maggie May*, the new London musical by Lionel Bart and continued to play the part until February, 1965.

But, in the end, all this counted for nothing. Rachel Roberts, her many and varied talents notwithstanding, died far from home, a depressed alcoholic still hopelessly obsessed with her former husband, Rex Harrison.

SIR HARRY SECOMBE

Harry Secombe was born at Dan-y-Graig Terrace, Swansea on September 8th, 1921, the son of a commercial traveller, and attended St. Thomas School and Dynevor School in the town. After leaving school at sixteen, he started his working life as a junior pay clerk at the Colliery Department of the steel firm Richard, Thomas and Baldwin Ltd. in Swansea. When war broke out he became a Lance-Bombardier in the Royal Artillery, fighting in Tunisia in 1942 and from there on into Italy, but soon graduated to taking part in shows entertaining the troops. Whilst still in the army he met Spike Milligan in the summer of 1945. The following April he was demobbed and auditioned successfully at London's Windmill Theatre where he was put on the pay roll at £20 a week. At this time his comedy routine involved various ways of shaving and a penchant for blowing raspberries in his performances. Then came another audition, this time for *Variety Bandbox*, one of the most popular radio shows of the time and, by the end of 1947, Harry found himself playing the Dame in *Dick Whittington*.

On February 19th, 1948, Harry married Myra Atherton, a Swansea girl, at St. Barnabas's Church in Sketty. They are still together. On May 13th, 1949 Harry journeyed to Cardiff to record an edition of *Welsh Rarebit* the long running radio variety show. Listeners heard him sing *Falling in Love* without any funny overtones and he soon became a regular on the programme. The show's theme song, *We'll Keep A Welcome* now became an integral part of his stage act. In his biography, Harry recalls that the shows took place in the Corey Hall in Cardiff. This provided excellent acoustics but the backstage toilet facilities were not so grand - being limited to a bucket strategically placed in one corner of the dressing room!

Meanwhile Harry's radio career continued to thrive. He was one of the ventriloquist dummy Archie Andrews' tutors in the 1950s radio series *Educating Archie*. He also stood in for Tony Hancock when the comedian was absent from a few episodes of *'Ancock's 'Alf 'Our* on the wireless.

All this time he would be meeting Spike Milligan, Peter Sellers and Michael Bentine socially. Gathering together at Jimmy Grafton's London pub, the four would bounce ideas off one another and gradually develop a team spirit. For three years Grafton bombarded the BBC with recordings of the group's efforts but they were all rejected as being "too way-out". Finally, on 28th May, 1951 the Home Service broadcast *The Junior Crazy Gang*, starring those crazy people, The Goons. An option for a further six programmes was taken up, then another and, in the summer of 1951, Secombe found himself leaving Blackpool (where he was doing a summer show) very early in the morning to drive down to London for recording what was now called *Crazy People* at the Aeolian Hall in Bond Street.

A founder member of the Goons where his main role was that of the larger-than-life Neddie Seagoon, his place in the history of British radio comedy is secure. Besides his wit and humour, Secombe had one other weapon in his armoury: his voice (he has recorded over seventy albums) which brought him musical stardom in such shows as *Pickwick* – in which he performed the title role, both in the West End and on Broadway.

A frequent performer at Royal Variety Performances - some eleven in all - he enjoyed five variety seasons topping the bill at the London Palladium. He has been in a number of films, amongst them *Helter Skelter* (1949), *Fake's Progress* (1950), *Oliver!* (1968) and *Song of Norway* (1970), none of which, however, achieved for him any real critical acclaim. He has been seen on TV in a variety of different shows (he was for many years a regular on Yorkshire TV's *Stars on Sunday*) built around his musical and comic talents, but is probably now best associated with the religious Sunday evening programme, *Highway*, having presented the show since 1983. Awarded the CBE in 1963, Harry Secombe received a knighthood in 1981. He has recently presented the BBC's *Songs of Praise*. He was diagnosed as suffering from prostrate cancer in September, 1998. He suffered what was described as a "mild" stroke on Saturday, January 30th, 1999 and was taken to the Royal Surrey County Hospital. He was then moved to the private Nuffield Hospital in Guildford to recover. At one time paralysed down the right hand side of his body he had recovered sufficiently well to be able to fly out to his holiday home in Majorca in December, 1999.

MICHAEL SHEEN

Born in Newport on February 5th, 1969, Michael Sheen attended the town's Malpas Court Primary School. His first appearance on stage was as a crying baby in a Newport Operatic Society amateur production in which his parents, Irene and Meyrick, were taking part. He was only a few days old. His family comes from Port Talbot where he grew up (the Sheens moved from Newport when Michael was eight) and where he went to the local Glanafan comprehensive school. At school he did school plays such as *The Wizard of Oz* and entered the West Glamorgan Youth Theatre when he was fourteen years old. His great grandfather used to play in Shakespearian tragedies, whilst his great-great-grandmother could claim to have been one of the first female lion tamers with Barnum and Bailey. As a youngster he was a talented enough footballer to be asked to play with the Arsenal Junior Team. He was in the National Youth Theatre of Wales. He won the 1990 Laurence Olivier Award for the most promising drama student of the year. In 1991 he was seconded from RADA (he was offered places at all the other theatre training schools in London, but chose RADA), to play a young Greek pianist with Vanessa Redgrave in the West End production of *When She Danced.* (At the Globe Theatre – since renamed the Gielgud.)

His TV credits include *Maigret* and *Gallowglass* with fellow Welsh actor Paul Rhys. His cinema films include *Mary Reilly* with Julia Roberts and *Othello* with Lawrence Fishburne and Kenneth Branagh. He played Robbie Ross, Oscar Wilde's faithful friend, in the 1997 film, *Wilde.*

In the theatre he has played Peer Gynt at the Barbican, Romeo at the Royal Exchange in Manchester, Lenny in *The Homecoming* at the National Theatre, Norman in *The Dresser* and Jimmy Porter in *Look Back In Anger.* Susannah Clapp, writing in the *Observer,* September 4th, 1997, on the RSC Stratford production of *Henry V,* was full of praise for Michael Sheen's convincing performance as the young king, complimenting him on his ability to speak verse and on the ease with which he played his part.

Michael Sheen is a founder member of the theatre company Thin Language (set up to do plays about Wales with Welsh actors and writers in London) and directed them in *Badfinger* at the Donmar Warehouse in Covent Garden, a production which Lyn Gardener in *The Guardian* was well pleased with. (She had already described Sheen himself in the same paper on Tuesday, September 2nd, 1997 as being like an elf in his stage presence.)

He has also founded a production company called The Foundry to encourage especially the work of newer writers. He met his girlfriend, Kate Beckinsale, (the daughter of the late *Porridge* star Richard Beckinsale) when they were both touring in a production of Chekov's *The Seagull.* (In 1999 she gave birth to a daughter, Lily Mo.) Michael played Mozart in the new Peter Hall production of Peter Shaffer's *Amadeus,* and Jimmy Porter in the National Theatre production of *Look Back In Anger* in July, 1999. He was heard on Radio 3 as Hamlet on September 12th, 1999. In December, 1999 Sheen received rave reviews from the New York critics for his first night performances on Broadway as Mozart in *Amadeus.*

SARAH SIDDONS

The ghost of Sarah Siddons is said to haunt the Theatre Royal in Drury Lane where she celebrated many of her greatest triumphs. She was seen, dressed in eighteenth century dress and cloak, by Elizabeth Larner who at the time, 1960, was playing in *Camelot*. Returning to her dressing room during the interval she was surprised to find a tall, stately-looking lady occupying her armchair. At first she thought a new dresser had arrived, but when the 'dresser' rose from her seat only to vanish through the wall, she began to realise that something out of the ordinary was afoot. She later discovered that the apparition's description fitted the portrait of Mrs. Siddons in the National Gallery. (Mrs. Siddons is also said to haunt the Bristol Old Vic.)

Sarah Siddons was born at an inn called the *Shoulder of Mutton* (later known as the *Siddons Wine Vaults* – this has since been updated to the *Sarah Siddons Inn*) in Brecon on July 5th, 1755, the daughter of Sally and Roger Kemble, the manager of a company of strolling players. (Curiously, nearly two centuries later the English actor/actor manager Owen Nares died in the very same room Sarah Siddons was born in. Born in 1888, he had been touring camps in Wales for several weeks entertaining the troops when he took time out to visit the birthplace of the famous actress. Nares had been in good health all that week - swimming and rowing - but on Saturday, July 31st, 1943 he collapsed in the room where Siddons had been born and, an hour and a half later, he was dead.) Little is known of Siddons' early life other than that she appeared in various performances with her parent's troupe, but it was already clear that hers was a rich talent. On November 25th, 1773, she married William Siddons, eleven years her senior, at Trinity Church, Coventry. He had been an actor in her parent's company, but far from this endearing him to them, they were violently opposed to the love match, even going so far as to send Sarah to Guy's Cliffe in Warwickshire to attend Lady Mary Greatheed and her family, but eventually the lovers were re-united.

Word of Mrs. Siddons' acting potential reached the great David Garrick in London and he eventually offered her a position. On December 29th, 1775, she made her Drury Lane debut as Portia in *The Merchant of Venice*, giving a nervous first performance followed by nondescript performances in several other other plays - some opposite Garrick - but after new management took over from Garrick, her services were no longer required. She turned to the provincial theatre - Birmingham, Bath, Liverpool, Manchester - where she played Hamlet - and York. It was on October 24th, 1778 that she made her debut at the Theatre Royal in Bath and she quickly became a great favourite, playing four seasons in the town, before Drury Lane re-engaged her and she began her London career again in September, 1782.

Women fainted and men wept when they saw Mrs. Siddons. Hazlitt said that she "was Tragedy personified" and that to have seen her "was an event in everyone's life". Portrait painters vied with each other to immortalise her likeness. The possessor of a "deep melodious voice", she was said to be "reserved", "solemn", and "shy" with "black eyes".

Among her many roles were Imogen in *Cymbeline*, Katherine of Aragon in Shakespeare's *King Henry VIII*, Volumnia in *Coriolanus* and Juliet in *Romeo and Juliet*. She played Desdemona and Cordelia to her brother's Lear. (On the downside, like many an actress before and since, she also acted in many indifferent and now long forgotten plays.)

June 29th, 1812 saw her farewell performance in *Macbeth* at Covent Garden and, such was the emotion on the night, the audience insisted that the play end with the sleep walking scene and go no further. After this final triumph she confined herself to one-woman shows where she would read from Shakespeare and Milton. An avid snuff-taker her suppliers provided her with a quarter of an ounce of the stuff weekly. As she grew older so she began to lose her remarkably slim figure and, increasingly, to put on weight. A family trait, it did not endear her to long suffering sedan chairmen who objected to having to carry her anywhere.

Described by one biographer, Yvonne French, as a "sensible, matter-of-fact woman", Mrs. Siddons became the most famous actress of her age, and her Lady Macbeth a legend in the theatre. In her "first great London season" the box office takings broke all previous records. She died on June 8th, 1831 at the age of seventy-six, having given birth to seven children, and was buried in her former church of St. Mary's in Paddington. Five thousand people attended the funeral and sixteen mourning coaches and four followed the hearse.

DELIA SMITH

The Sunday Mirror has called her "the matron saint of English cooking". Her Welsh-speaking mother Etty Lewis was born in Twyn but lived in Llwyngwril on the Gwynedd coast between Tywyn and Barmouth until the age of sixteen when she moved to London. Her father, Harold, came from the north-east of England and was a printer who served in the RAF in the Second World War as a wireless operator. Delia's first television series was broadcast in 1974. A committed Norwich City supporter for more than twenty years, she is a director of and a shareholder in the football club. She has also played a 'hands-on' role at Carrow Road, having a hand in everything from launching the Canaries' new playing kit to assessing the diets of the players. (Since 1997, she and her husband have owned sixty per cent of Norwich City's shares.) Delia is famous for her many cookery programmes on the television. Her latest was *Delia's How to Cook, Series 2* in January, 1999. She was awarded the OBE in 1994. Her mere recommendation of an ingredient is bound to see that item disappear from the supermarket shelves. Her endorsement of omelette pans, cranberries and eggs in previous programmes saw sales soar. The process continued in the year 2000 when her liking for brands of rice noodles, sea salt and fish sauce once again worked its magic, leaving the supermarkets rubbing their hands with glee. She is married to a Welshman, Michael Wynn Jones.

Delia in the kitchen (Miki Duisterhof)

The broadsheet Sunday newspapers have sometimes been less than flattering in their reviews of her TV programmes, but Delia should worry, at the last count she was said to be sitting on a fortune somewhere in the region of £24 to £30 million. She herself has been quoted as saying "I am not a mega or multi-millionaire, just an ordinary one". (In a recent top One Thousand British Rich List, Delia was placed 932nd.)

Delia Ann Smith was born on June 18th, 1941 in Woking, Surrey (at the Wynberg Emergency Maternity Hospital) and was raised in Kent, one of two children (the other being her younger brother, Glyn). She attended Upland Infant School, Bexleyheath, but failed her eleven plus and, aged sixteen, left Bexleyheath Secondary Modern School for Girls without an O-Level to her name. Starting out in hairdressing, she then became a shop assistant and worked in a travel agency before joining The Singing Chef, a very small restaurant in Paddington, London, working first as a dishwasher and then as a waitress, paying particular attention to the chef's cooking methods. In her spare time she read English cookery books in the British Museum Reading Room in an effort to discover why the quality of English food was so poor. The recipes she found she tried out on a Harley Street doctor's family with whom she was then staying.

Her big break came when a photographer friend of hers introduced her to literary agent Debbie Owen, the wife of SDP politician David Owen. In 1969 Owen got her a cookery column with the *Daily Mirror's* new magazine where her editor was none other than her husband-to-be Michael Wynn Jones. Delia's first book *How To Cheat At Cooking* hit the stands in 1971. The following year she began a column for the London *Evening Standard* which was to last for twelve years. (Her first recipe appeared in the paper in March, 1972.) She later wrote a column for *The Radio Times* until 1986. Then came the BBC and television - her first programme entitled *Family Fare* was broadcast from 1973 till 1975 (her first ever appearance was on September 12th, 1973) - and a long line of cookery programmes, the latest of which was broadcast in January, 2000.

Meanwhile, other books followed including the phenomenally successful Cookery Course series which have consistently topped the best seller lists. (*Delia Smith's Christmas*, the book of the TV series, alone has sold an astonishing 1,300,000 copies. Another of her books - *Delia Smith's Summer Collection*, first published in May 1993, to accompany a 10-part television series on BBC2 has sold 1,600,000 copies to date and continues to sell. In fact all of Delia's cookery books have now sold over Fourteen Million copies in just the United Kingdom.)

What is the secret of Delia's success? As a TV cook she eschews the gimmicks employed by the multitude of other chefs who now fill our screens. She exudes reliability. What you see is what you get with Delia. A converted Catholic, she was baptised in the Church of England, went to a Methodist Sunday School, and was in, first, a Congregationalist Brownie group and then a Church of England youth group. She decided to join the Catholic Church at the age of twenty-two. She has also written a number of religious books, including *A Feast For Lent* and *A Feast For Advent* both of which contain reflections and reading on these seasons. *A Journey Into God* is a full-length book on prayer. She attends mass daily and lives in a converted cottage in the village of Combs near Stowmarket in Suffolk. She and her husband, whom she married on September 11th, 1971 in Delia's parish Church of Our Lady in Stowmarket, have no children.

RAY SMITH

This deep-voiced, fourteen stone actor was well equipped to play mining roles. Most of his family had earned their living working underground. His own father was killed in a mining accident when he was a mere three years old and his grandfather succumbed to that occupational hazard of miners the world over – coal dust disease. Fortunately for the world of theatre and television, however, Smith showed an interest in matters theatrical from his earliest days in the Rhondda and chose not to follow his forbears down the pit.

Born in Trealaw, Rhondda on May 1st, 1936, he left school and got work as a labourer but soon found a job with a stage company from Cardiff, gaining experience through acting in such plays as *Pygmalion, Woyzeck, Hamlet* and *What The Butler Saw.* Whilst doing his national service he started his own drama group.

Often on TV from the 60s onwards, he became known for playing 'heavies'. Among his roles were Dai Bando, the punch-drunk boxer in the 1976 version of *How Green Was My Valley;* George Barrowclough, the miner from the North of England in *Sam,* and Detective Inspector Firbank, Frank Marker's partner in the *Public Eye* series. He also played the severe father, Albert Mundy, in *We'll Meet Again* and Chief Superintendent Gordon Spikings, Dempsey and Makepeace's "bawling boss" in the series of the same name. He featured in *Z-Cars, A Family at War, Callan, Gideon's Way, Rogue Male, The Sailor's Return* and *Masada.* Smith played the miller in the BBC production of *Mill on the Floss.* He appeared as a chapel deacon working in the docks in the BBC Wales play *Before the Flood.* On film Smith appeared as Mr. Waldo in the 1971 version of *Under Milk Wood* when Richard Burton took the part of First Voice and Guide.

Ray Smith fell ill soon after finishing BBC Wales's 1992 television adaptation of Kingsley Amis's *The Old Devils.* (It would be his last screen appearance.) He died of meningitis in Llandough hospital, not far from Cardiff, on Sunday, December 15th, 1991, at the age of fifty-five. In his *Western Mail* tribute, Mario Basini described Ray Smith as probably the best actor Wales had produced since the days of Richard Burton, but he was also a great Welsh patriot – in the early 1960s he worked as an organiser for Plaid Cymru in South Wales and actively canvassed for the party's candidates at election time. His interest in Welsh affairs extended to his long efforts to establish a National Theatre in Wales.

In 1986, Smith won the Sony Award for Best Actor. At one time prone to drinking, (O'Toole and Burton were just two of his drinking partners), carousing, chasing women and the odd bout of fisticuffs, he gave up these 'interests' after meeting his second wife, the singer Siân Hopkins. (His first wife to whom he had been married for seventeen years, and by whom he had two children, was the former actress Gale Richardson. They divorced in 1981.)

As a boy Smith was already interested in the theatre and his first acting break came shortly after he had left school. John Smith who ran the Swansea Grand gave his namesake Ray his first paid acting job. Then the lure of the big city drew him to London where he spent a difficult year, trying to find theatre work with no acting money coming in, and being forced to rely on the dole. His big break came when he was given a part in a play about the 1956 Hungarian Uprising and this started him on the road to fame and fortune.

Pugnacious and with a sonorous voice, he would often spend part of the night in bars, and the rest of it behind bars, as the police were called to arrest him after he had instigated or been caught up in a drunken brawl somewhere. But Ray showed he held no grudges against the men in blue, often treating them to an an impromptu poetry concert, as he contemplated the error of his ways. It was no surprise, really, that he excelled in radio plays and poetry readings.

VICTOR SPINETTI

Victor Spinetti

Born in Cwm, Ebbw Vale on September 2nd, 1932, the son of Italian parents Guiseppe and Lilian, and educated at Monmouth Boys School, Victor Spinetti's greatest claim to fame may be that he has appeared in all three Beatle films: *A Hard Day's Night, Help* and *The Magical Mystery Tour,* the only person apart from the group themselves to have done so. The Beatle connection goes further: Spinetti co-wrote with John Lennon *In His Own Write* and himself directed the play at the Royal National Theatre. He has appeared in two versions of *Under Milk Wood,* the first, in 1971, with Richard Burton and Elizabeth Taylor (with whom he also appeared in *Taming of the Shrew* playing Hortensio) and in a second, later version with Sir Anthony Hopkins. He also enjoyed a cameo appearance in *Return of the Pink Panther.*

Spinetti appeared in amateur dramatics with the Ebbw Vale Playgoers Society. Trained at the Welsh College of Music and Drama in Cardiff, he first set foot on the West End stage in *Expresso Bongo* and *Candide* and subsequently spent six years with Joan Littlewood's Theatre Workshop. He was rewarded with a Tony Award in New York for his performance in *Oh! What A Lovely War*. He has toured with such productions as *Peter Pan*, where he took the role of Captain Hook, *Oliver*, in which he played Fagin, and *The Pirates of Penzance*. His was the voice of Texas Pete in the S4C children's programme *Superted*.

His one-man show *A Very Private Diary*, telling of his experiences with Richard Burton, Elizabeth Taylor, John Lennon et al, played in London, Sydney, New York and, nearer to home, at the Borough Theatre, Abergavenny in 1990. He played Lord Foppington in the 1996 RSC production of *The Relapse* and took the part of the Narrator in the *Rocky Horror Show* Silver Jubilee Tour.

Growing up in the tiny village of Cwm with sport, music and drama all around him, Victor Spinetti originally wanted to be a teacher but he joined his local amateur dramatic society and secured a grant to go to college. Working in a factory in London, he auditioned for *South Pacific*, got the part of an understudy and took over when the man he was 'shadowing' broke his leg. He then, as they say, 'never looked back'.

DOROTHY SQUIRES

Quick-witted and with an effervescent sense of humour; volatile, passionate, quick-tempered, cantankerous, temperamental and with a fierce intelligence – Dorothy Squires was all of these. The girl who would go from nothing to the top of her profession was born Edna May Squires in a field in Pontyberem, near Llanelli in the year 1915 in the back of a travelling van. In the mid-1930s she performed at the Ritz ballroom in Llanelli as a dance band singer. After leaving school she worked at the local Woolworths.

She arrived in London when she was eighteen and, for a time, worked as a nurse at Croydon Hospital. She made her West End cabaret debut at the Burlington Club where the pianist Charlie Kunz heard her play. He booked her for his Casani club and then, in 1936, she made her first broadcast for the BBC. Then a performance with Billy Reid and his Accordion Band changed her life completely. The partnership gelled and success followed. Reid wrote the songs and Dot sang them. At the height of her fame in the 40s and 50s she, together with Reid, filled the theatres throughout Great Britain, was often heard on the radio and sold records by the million.

The two finally split in 1950 following a scene in the bar of the Llanelli Theatre (which Billy Reid had bought). Dorothy's father Archie tried to intervene and pull the quarrelling twosome apart but only received a fist in his face for his trouble. Dorothy now decided it was time to begin a solo career, but then fate took a hand, and she met the love of her life. At the

Dorothy Squires

time she met Roger Moore - twelve years her junior - at one of her parties in 1951, he was a struggling, unknown actor. The future James Bond was then married to the skater Doorn van Steyn but he divorced her in 1953 and immediately married Dorothy in New Jersey. She wasted no time in using her connections to advance his acting career, putting her own 'on hold' to help his.

But in 1961 Moore flew to Zagreb to film *The Rape of the Sabines* and promptly fell in love with the Italian actress, Luisa Mattioli. It was the beginning of the end for the Moores. The marriage fell apart when Dorothy discovered some letters sent to Roger by Luisa and the couple were divorced in 1969. (Moore would later divorce Mattioli in 1996.) Their separation, however, was far from amicable. At one stage Dorothy attempted to legally force Roger to return to the marriage bed. The court granted her request and ordered the errant husband to go back to her within twenty-eight days. When he refused she was heartbroken. (Dorothy continued to love Moore long after he had left her and continued to style herself Edna May Moore. In *The Slate* programme devoted to her on BBC Wales TV she revealed that he had been one of the "two great loves of her life", the other being Billy Reid.)

Unable to get her records played on the radio and unwanted by the TV stations Dot took the bold and brave step of hiring the London Palladium. She made a comeback at the theatre on Sunday, December 5th, 1970 paying £5,000 of her own money to finance the show, but the gamble paid off. She received a fifteen-minute standing ovation and her rendition of *My Way* (a song that was surely made for her) hit the charts. Once again she filled concert halls all over Great Britain. She went on to sing at Carnegie Hall the following year, and her fan club made history by hiring a jet to fly to New York and see her, but the good times were not about to last.

In 1974 her mansion in Bexley burnt down, nearly taking her with it, but she survived clutching her jewel box in one hand and, in the other, another box containing four hundred of Roger Moore's love letters. She was acclaimed by her fans but the adulation did not last and she had to rely on the generosity of friends for a place to live, finally arriving at Esme Cole's house at five o'clock on a June 1995 morning scarcely able to walk. The owner of a fish and chip shop in Trebanog, Rhondda, Esme had, after hearing about her tribulations, offered Dorothy the loan of a house. The detached house had four bedrooms and a conservatory but it was still a far cry from the mansion by the Thames with its swimming pool and thirty-four rooms Dorothy had ruled over at the height of her success. But there were consolations, Esme not only let the singer live rent-free, she cleaned, washed and shopped for her as well. It was to be Dorothy's final home where she lived alone with her black and brown cat, Good Girl.

In 1996 Dorothy had a cancerous tumour removed in Cardiff's BUPA hospital in an operation paid for by Roger Moore and said to have cost thousands of pounds. In 1998 she was preparing to sue a record company for, as she claimed, releasing a CD of her songs without permission – she had, it seems, lost none of her old taste for litigation. In the event, the case would never reach the courts.

Dorothy Squires died of lung cancer on Tuesday, April 14th, 1998 at five past two in the morning in a private room just off Ynyscynon Ward, Llwynypia Hospital in the Rhondda. She had been registered as a National Health Service patient under her married name of Edna May Moore. Her funeral service took place in Port Talbot a week later. One hundred and fifty people crowded into St. Mary's Church to hear comedian Stan Stennett and actor Siôn Probert pay tribute to the dead star and members of her family were present, among them her niece Emily Jayne. However, 61-year-old Esme Coles did not attend and Roger Moore did not send flowers. Stan Stennett called Dorothy "a real star, someone who had what it took to be great". The coffin entered the church to the sound of *Song of the Valley* which Dorothy had written and sung herself. Siôn Probert read the Dylan Thomas poem *And Death Shall Have No Dominion*. Stephen Barnes, the vicar holding the service, thanked Esme for her help for Dorothy and, at the end of the service, asked those present to rise and give Dorothy one last, final standing ovation. The fans, who had come from as far away as Birmingham and London to pay homage to the woman they called Dot, rose as one to stand in tribute.

Dorothy Squires was buried in Streatham, South London on Friday, April 24th, 1998. Over two hundred people attended the funeral but, again, they did not include Esme Coles or Roger Moore although both sent flowers, Roger Moore's message reading "I've Said It With Flowers", a poignant reference to one of her most famous songs. She was buried in the same grave as her brother, Captain Frederick Squires, not far from where their parents were buried.

Even after her death controversy continued to rage around the singer and her memory. Esme Coles was unhappy that the remembrance service took place in Port Talbot and not in Trebanog. There were also problems as to who exactly owned the Trebanog house – Emily Jayne Squires, the niece claiming that she had not been allowed into the Rhondda house to select a dress for the singer to be buried in. In August, 1998 a play about her life *Dorothy Squires – A One Woman Show*, written by Mark Ryan and starring Gerry Smith, was staged at the Edinburgh fringe festival. The play was promptly attacked by Esme Coles and Dorothy's niece, Emily Jayne, the latter objecting to the phrase "road to hell" which was used in the official fringe brochure to describe the singer's life.

During the 1970s Dorothy was involved in libel battles and fighting Roger Moore for maintenance. Litigious to a fault, one of those she took to court was the actor Kenneth More who had made the mistake of calling Luisa Mattioli Roger Moore's wife when Dot was still married to him. She lost the case and, to make matters worse, received a fine for driving carelessly. She did, however, successfully sue *The News of the World* in 1971. Also in 1971, she swore never to sing on Welsh soil again after only selling half the tickets for two performances at Cardiff's Capitol Theatre. In 1972, Dorothy Squires found herself in court once more charged with kicking a taxi driver in the head. Even then, the case had a showbiz touch – the taxi driver in question turning out to be none other than *Carry On* star Bernard Bresslaw's brother. In 1973 Dorothy still had money. She owned, for example, two horses, Esban and Norwegian Flag, which put her amongst the top twelve leading National Hunt owners, just one place behind Queen Elizabeth the Queen Mother but, eight years later, in 1981, she was declared bankrupt and her constant legal battles earned her the title of 'vexatious litigant' in 1987. (In other words she could not begin legal action without permission from The High Court.) In 1989 she was again declared bankrupt and evicted from her Thames-side mansion home which with its seventeen bedrooms had once belonged to the famous actress Lily Langtry.

Almost at once she began a long legal struggle over an £80,000 cottage in West Yorkshire she was renting from a friend. She had shared the house in Ackworth with her friend Doris Joyce but when Doris died of cancer in April, 1993, Dorothy was forced to leave, her hopes that Roger Moore would buy the house for her, shattered when the Bond star offered only £5,000 and not the £80,000 she needed to buy the house. She was eventually forced out and came back to Wales and Trebanog where she practically lived as a recluse – only emerging from the house once a week to see the doctor. She paid the bills and, until arthritis hit home, was able to walk upstairs but when the arthritis became too much for her she was forced to live downstairs. In January, 1989 'Nenna', as, according to the *Daily Telegraph* obituary, Dorothy always called herself, paid a visit to Swansea's Grand Theatre, aiming to put on a one-night show there that spring. The theatre duly sent her a contract but she failed to return it and the performance did not go ahead.

In 1990 the Trustees in Bankruptcy sold the contents of her former house. In 1996 she had two bladder tumours removed and, the following year, the University Hospital of Wales declared her to be free of cancer. On

March 30th, 1997, *Wales on Sunday* reported that Dorothy was said to owe Rhondda Cynon Taff County Borough Council £525-65 in unpaid council tax on the Trebanog house. There was even talk of her being sent to gaol for three months if she did not pay up. Trying to raise money she had her jewellery (including some items Roger Moore had bought her) auctioned at Sothebys the week before, hoping the sale would bring in some £15,000 but the jewels only went for £6,000.

In February, 1998 Dorothy suffered a stroke and collapsed in the bathroom of the Trebanog house. She broke her hip in the fall and several hours went by before a neighbour found her, dazed and confused, firmly believing that she had spent the last few days in the garden. She was taken to East Glamorgan Hospital in Church Village, Pontypridd and diagnosed as suffering from lung cancer. It was to be the beginning of the end.

The Dorothy Squires story is one of tremendous highs and terrific lows. Life with Dot was an emotional roller-coaster, a tempestuous Big Dipper, a soap opera to beat all soap operas. She wasted her not inconsiderable energies and thousands of pounds trying to win court cases she had no hope of winning yet she effortlessly won the praise of her contemporaries. Norman Newell, her record producer, called her "a marvellous singer"; Russ Conway who used to accompany her and played piano on her big hit *Say It With Flowers* said "she was show business – a one-off colossus"; he added that he "learnt more stagecraft by playing for two artistes than for anyone else in the business, one was Dorothy Squires, and the other – Gracie Fields". David Howard, the man who produced the February, 1998 programme *The Slate* knew her as "a fighter" and "a survivor". *Dad's Army* star Bill Pertwee said of her she was "a bit of a handful at times with some fruity language but with a heart of gold".

Joan Collins was rather less complimentary. In her autobiography she recalled an encounter her father, an agent, had with Squires. Agent and singer were standing toe to toe, screaming at each other at the tops of their voices. Now Joan's father could bellow as well as the next man but, according to Joan, Dorothy bowed to no one when it came to shouting and bawling. As for her voice – that was so shrill it could easily have shattered any unfortunate glass that happened to be in the way. When the shouting match was over, Joan's father confided to her that he had just signed Dorothy up for a tour. She had demanded this, that, and then the other. She was always, lamented Joan's father, asking for the moon. And that, for a time at least, was what she got.

According to John Lloyd, the Hon. Sec. of the Dorothy Squires Fan Club, she launched *Say It With Flowers* at Billy Smart's Circus in a cage with six tigers. A worried Bruce Forsythe said to Roger Moore, "Have you taken out insurance?" at which Moore paused, raised one eyebrow and said, "Yes – on the tigers". John Lloyd also recalls that Elvis Presley went to her Moulin Rouge show in Hollywood every night and asked to hear *Mother's Day*. Sinatra (Frank) said she "was Britain's only female singer with balls". Sinatra

(Nancy), on hearing Dot sing *My Way* said "What a wow of an interpretation of that anthem. I think my father was half asleep when he recorded it!"

Dorothy Squires was the first British Female Artist to break the U.S. monopoly at The Talk of the Town when she was booked in there for four weeks. She once appeared in pantomime (*Jack and the Beanstalk*) playing the Principal Boy (*The Times* obituary referred to her magnificent pair of legs) to husband Roger Moore's King. Her hits included *My Way, Say It With Flowers, Till, For Once In My Life* and *I'm Walking Behind You* (written by Billy Reid). Her one and only film (in which she sang four songs) was the 1956 *Stars In Your Eyes*, a tribute to the personalities of what was, even then, a fast fading music hall scene.

THE STEREOPHONICS

According to Kai Jones writing in the *Mono* supplement of the *South Wales Argus* (Friday, March 12th, 1999), The Stereophonics "are the bastard sons of rock 'n' roll, possessed with the demon swagger of Dylan, Hendrix and Angus Young". Praise indeed and, as if this was not enough, Jones went on to say that the group "write brilliant songs ... they're the people's band ... they're our band". Nick Horton of the *Western Mail* obviously agreed. Some months, previously (Saturday, June 20th, 1998) he had written of the dynamic trio that "they combine meat and potatoes rock 'n' roll with an acute ear for a soaring tune, a rare lyrical adventurism and a superb, charismatic frontman in Kelly Jones".

The men who had such lavish praise heaped upon them came from a small, ex-mining village called Cwmaman high up in the Cynon Valley, a stone's throw from the town of Aberdare. Their names are Kelly Jones, guitar, vocalist and chief lyric writer, Richard Jones, bass guitar and Stuart Cable, drums. Originally called The Tragic Love Company, they changed their name when they discovered that there was an English group with the same name. They then toyed with the idea of calling themselves The Somethings but finally settled on The Stereophonics after the radiogram which belonged to Stuart Cable's father. They have known each other since they were infants.

Kelly is the youngest of three brothers. His mother Beryl married his father Arwyn Jones, a professional singer himself for nigh on thirty years, and better known in some quarters as 'Oscar' – he once appeared on the same bill as 'The Big O', Roy Orbison. Like the other two, Kelly went to Blaengwawr Comprehensive School in Aberdare, but none of the three could really be described as 'academic'.

Richard Jones – the fifth of six children, his mother Mairwen had four boys and two girls - lived in Park View just over the other side of the park from Kelly. (Both the Jones boys are approximately the same age whilst Stuart is four years older.) Stuart who lived in the same street as Kelly was born in May, 1970 and has an older brother. His father died when he was only ten and his mother, Mabel, brought up her two children alone. As a boy Stuart was a strong swimmer and a good snooker player, good enough for the landlord of his local pub to link his name with the Wales Youth snooker team. He used to practise his drumming at home. Given a drum kit as a present he used it so much the constant drumming and pedal pressure eventually wore a hole in the carpet in Mabel Cable's spare room. The boys were lucky – the neighbours did not mind them practising as long as they were done by 9.30 p.m. Otherwise they used to practise in Cwmaman's Community Hall – the Canolfan.

When he left school Kelly Jones worked on a fruit and vegetable stall in Aberdare's indoor market on the weekend. When the work got too monotonous (he was paid £16 a shift) he would pause to scribble down any lyrics that came into his head using the stall's brown paper bags as a notebook. When not selling fruit Kelly led another life studying graphic design and animation at the Mid Glamorgan Centre of Art and Design. He also turned his hand to scriptwriting. Stuart sold double glazing, while Richard delivered school dinners for a living and also worked for his father's scaffolding company.

Their first ever gig took place in 1986 at the Cwmaman Social and Working Men's Club (Kelly's dad had booked them) and from then on it was a case of working their way up to the top, sometimes, at the beginning, playing to very indifferent audiences indeed. One of their great heroes when they were first starting out was the American group Creedence Clearwater Revival. The boys' big break came when Richard Branson, the proprietor of Virgin, phoned them from his private holiday island of Necker in the Caribbean and offered to sign them to his record label for £265,000. The contract he offered was, initially, for two albums with an option for five others. Kelly - in the time-honoured tradition of such occasions - at first thought the call was a joke. They signed on the dotted line on August 1st, 1996 and, the following year, proceeded to play more than one hundred gigs all over the country, building up an enthusiastic fanbase.

According to Kelly the band's first album *Word Gets Around* was "about where we come from, how we saw ourselves and the world at a certain point. We only knew about Cwmaman when we wrote the first album, but now the world's got bigger". Many of Kelly's songs on the album were based on real life incidents or stories he had heard. Their second album *Performance and Cocktails* went straight to Number One in the U.K. and, four months after being released, had notched up sales of some 600,000 copies.

Their third single *Local Boy In The Photograph* got to Number 51 in early 1997. *More Life In A Tramp's Vest* reached Number 33 in May, 1997. *The Bartender and the Thief did better.* It hit the Top Five in November, 1998 and *Just Looking* occupied the Number 4 spot in March, 1999. Released on Monday, February 22nd it formed part of the soundtrack to *This Year's Love* a British film starring Kathy Burke and Jennifer Ehle.

Members of the band have been struck by misfortune on more than one occasion. When they first started out their instruments were stolen. Luckily, The Prince's Trust came to the rescue and gave them a grant to buy some new instruments and also bought them a computer to help Kelly with his lyrics. In June, 1999, drummer Stuart Cable broke his ankle whilst playing football in Cwmaman but still made it to the Glastonbury Festival where he had to hobble around in the clinging Glastonbury mud. More seriously, it was reported in July, 1999 that Richard Jones had been the victim of a vicious attack seconds after leaving *The Rock* public house at Aberaman with his girlfriend, Donna Jones. He had been celebrating with the rest of the band after finishing the Japanese stage of their world tour. As Richard and Donna passed salesman Robert Baker's house, Baker, who until then had been leaning out of the window, charged out and subjected the Phonics' bassist to a "prolonged and brutal" assault, kicking and punching the defenceless musician. Baker, who claimed that Jones had spat on his mother's car, broke Richard's nose, finger and ribs during his frenzied onslaught. Jones was taken to hospital after the attack but insisted on taking part in the band's T In The Park concert in Scotland the weekend following the assault. A rugby player, married, and with an eighteen-month-old daughter, Baker pleaded guilty to causing Richard Jones grievous bodily harm and was sent to prison for a year.

More upliftingly, and encouragingly, the band have now started to win their fair share of awards and accolades. On Tuesday, August 25th, 1998, *Kerrang!* magazine voted them The Best New British Band. On Monday, February 9th, 1998 at the London Arena they won The Brit Award for The Best Newcomer a prize which got Kelly into a little 'hot water' on the night. After receiving the award he used just three little words he should not have, namely that it was "about f... time" the Stereophonics had gained some recognition. (A pointed reference to their being previously ignored by most of the music papers and also getting very little air-time on Radio One compared to other bands.) He did, however, later apologise for his ill-chosen words. The incident did him no permanent harm, however, as later that year, in November, 1999, *Q Magazine* named them as the Best Live Act of the Year. Two other awards garnered by Kelly came in the 1998 and 1999 *Melody Maker* readers' poll when he was twice voted Number Two in the Top Ten 'Sexiest Lads'. In May, 2000, Kelly was voted Number 6 in *Company* magazine's Top One Hundred Men.

Since their rise to fame the lads from Cwmaman have also begun to play bigger venues. On June 12th, 1998 a Cardiff Castle gig pulled in 10,000 fans, the first time the castle walls had echoed to the sound of a rock concert since Queen last played there in 1978. The concert was billed as 'Cwmaman Feel The Noise'. In July, 1999 they played the Morfa Stadium in Swansea in front of 50,000 appreciative fans. Their latest single success came in May, 2000 when they backed Tom Jones in a cover version of the old Three Dog Night hit *Mama Told Me Not To Come*.

On March 20th, 1999 Stuart Cable married his longstanding girlfriend, Nicola, who worked as a therapist for Cynon Valley's social services department. They tied the knot at Aberkenfig's Court Colman Hotel, a few drumbeats away from their Cwmaman home. Meanwhile, the awards keep rolling in. In May, 2000 *Loaded* magazine named the Stereos as the Band of the Year.

THE SUPER FURRY ANIMALS

Writing in the Cardiff-based monthly magazine *Buzz* in April 1999, Jennie Allen had this to say about The Super Furry Animals: "The Furries' music is truly unique: neither Britpop, breakbeat, or Welsh guitar pop. Who else has sung about blood-sucking bats, Che Guevara, and Albert Einstein's parents on the same album: or driven around Reading festival in a tank pumping out music?" Kai Jones of the *South Wales Argus's* weekly supplement *Mono* (Friday, June 11th, 1999) was also rather taken with the band. He enthused that "Super Furry Animals are a black hole at the end of the bright universe that was the twentieth century, breaking everything down into tiny little atoms and fusing it together like beautifully warped Lego bricks laced with smiles and eyes on the other side". Christopher Rees in *The Western Mail* (Thursday, April 29th, 1999) was rather more restrained, although still impressed, finding that "Their catchy songwriting and innovative musicianship set them apart from everyone else".

The men responsible for all these outpourings - Andrew Smith in *The Sunday Times* could not resist comparing the band to the Kinks in their eccentricity and listed *The Swirling Demons* as one of his singles of 1997 - are Gruff Rhys, vocals, Huw 'Bunf' Bunford, guitar, Guto Pryce, bass, Cian Ciaran, keyboards and Daf Ieuan, drums. As a group they have been together since 1994 but they have known one another for ten years. Amazingly, Gruff and Bunf first met each other on the top of a train in North Wales! Both of them had decided to go up on to the roof of the train, as one does, it being a hot and sunny day, but the rail company did not appreciate their enterprise and threw them both off the train, leaving them to walk the last three miles to Bala and giving them a chance to get to know each other better. Bunf and Guto had both attended the same school in Cardiff but only knew each other slightly as one was several years older than the other. They did, however, play together in a group before the Super Furry era. (The nucleus of SFA was a Welsh language band called *Ffa Coffi Pawb* which means Everybody's Coffee Beans in English.)

Super Furry Animals really took off in 1995 when Gruff Rhys, the front man, guitarist and songwriter (he was born in Pembrokeshire where he lived until he was three) moved down to Cardiff from his home in Bethesda, where he had been the lead singer with *Ffa Coffi Pawb*. At the time Guto and Bunf had been playing with another Welsh language band called U-Thant. The three joined forces to play and were soon joined by Daf (the ex-Catatonia drummer) and then by his younger brother, Cian, who added his keyboard and sampling skills to the emerging group. They brought out two EPs, *Llanfair PG* and *Moog Drwg* on the Ankst Welsh record label before switching to Creation Records.

Their first album *Fuzzy Logic* seems to throw everything at the listener, not excluding the legendary kitchen sink, with hints of sixties psychedelia ever present. This same first album was covered with non-genuine passport photographs of the notorious convicted drug smuggler Howard Marks who appears to have formed an unlikely (?) friendship with the members of the band – the photos are a reference to Marks's early 80s convictions for possessing false passports. (One of the tracks on the CD is even called *Hangin' With Howard Marks*, a tribute to the man from Kenfig Hill who was incarcerated in an American jail.)

Nor is their originality confined purely to their music, they have been known to hoist giant, forty-feet high inflatable pandas at their concerts, sponsor Cardiff City Football Club, be occasionally accompanied by two macho men trumpeters wearing traditional Welsh women's costumes and, once, at the Cardiff International Arena gig, have an Austrian girl with a fit of the giggles back them with her Alpine Horn.

Daniel Borth reviewing a Super Furries concert in London for the *Melody Maker* on November 30th, 1996 was wary of the "drug-soaked 'spaciness' " associated with the band but concluded that "Super Furry Animals are our best new band of 1996. Love them, or love no one". Continuing his somewhat schizophrenic theme he found the Furries' lyrics "cabbage-brained nonsense" but, nevertheless, they were "easily the most lovable group around at the moment" and *Fuzzy Logic* was "a marvellous album".

Their first single reached Number 42, their second got to 29, their third climbed higher to Number 18, their fourth - the E.P. *Ice Hockey Hair* released in 1998 (which featured lyrics on Dutch football star Johann Cruyff) - did even better getting to Number 12 whilst their fifth – the catchy *Northern Lights* went in at Number Eleven.

Their first album was *Fuzzy Logic* (released in 1996), their second *Radiator*, their third *Outspace* was a collection of B-sides and not so well known early material from their time with the Welsh label Ankst and their fourth, *Guerrilla*, was released on June 13th, 1999. Deprived of the services of their usual producer, the boys produced this one themselves. Reviewing it on June 6th, 1999 *The Observer* found that *Guerrilla* was a far messier album, but showed much more ambition, than their two previous offerings, *Fuzzy Logic* or *Radiator* from 1997.

The Furries are big in Japan, have toured Australia and have dipped their toe into the American waters, having signed with Flydaddy, a small, independent American record company. (In 1999 they toured America, playing in such cities as Boston, New York, Washington, Chicago and Philadelphia with an additional concert in Toronto.)

There is no doubt that the Super Furries are proud of their Welsh background. Like Richard Burton, from whom they took the idea, when they signed for the Creation record label they insisted on a clause being written into their contract that they would not be obliged to work on March 1st, St.

David's Day. Writing about The Furries in *The Observer* on May 2nd, 1999, Sam Taylor revealed that the band now wanted to be known as SFA. Despite their eclectic mix of influences, and their ability to write a good pop tune, he considered that they continued, basically, to be a cult band, and, by their very nature, were still far removed from the prevailing currents of modern music.

Speaking for the band Guto Pryce has told the newspapers that the group are not interested in the cult of celebrity but they do want their music to be heard by as many listeners as possible. He is on record as saying that the band were in no way inward looking but also had no intention of disowning their native country, Wales. He went on to say: "We go around the world talking about Wales, raising the country's profile. Although this album (*Guerrilla*) is all in English because we decided that we wanted to keep it coherent. Rather than include a token song or two in Welsh, we are going to release a whole album".

And he was as good as his word. Following the unfortunate demise of their previous record company Creation, their all-Welsh album *Mwng* (Mane – as in lion's mane, horse's mane in Welsh) was released on Monday, May 15th, 2000, on their own record label, Placid Casual. It was a bold and brave step with no guarantee that the band's large, monoglot English-speaking following would take to the idea or buy the record. Speaking to Christopher Rees in the *Western Mail* (Saturday, May 13th, 2000), Gruff Rhys had this to say: "Maybe everyone is sick of Wales now and a Welsh language album is probably the last thing people want, but that's not why we did it. We did it for the art of music and a deep need to make this music".

But as the reviews came in, it appeared that the Furries had little to worry about, at least as far as the critics were concerned. Kai Jones of the *Argus* was completely won over. In *Mono*, he wrote (Friday, May 12th, 2000) "*Mwng* is a very moody album ... it's by far SFA's most downbeat album to date ... *Mwng*...is SFA's most perfect album so far. Not their best, but the most perfect ... Pure. And Perfect". *Buzz* agreed. In their May, 2000 edition they wrote that "Whether you understand Welsh or not is largely immaterial as here SFA are simply doing what they have always done so well; writing fantastic songs that cheerfully ignore the conventions of 'proper' pop composition. This record deserves to be a hit. Make it happen". Over the border in England, Neil Spencer in *The Observer*, May 14th, 2000, did not even mention the Welsh language but contented himself with remarking on the band's eccentricity and commenting favourably that the new CD was better than the Furries' work for Creation. It looked as if the gamble to release an all Welsh-language record might succeed after all. *Mwng* took two weeks to make and was recorded in Anglesey, Bath and Cardiff. It cost only £6,000 to produce. On May 21st, 2000, *Mwng* crashed into the Album Top Twenty at Number Eleven, the first Welsh-language album to do so.

BRYN TERFEL

With his powerful physique - he stands six feet three inches tall and weighs in at 240 pounds - bass baritone Bryn Terfel is a fine figure of a man. Some have drawn comparisons between his burly looks and those of heavy metal star Meatloaf but there the similarities end. Bryn has shared the stage with the likes of Placido Domingo, Jose Carreras and Luciano Pavarotti. The list of places he has performed at reads like an A to Z of the world's finest opera venues. He has appeared on stage at La Scala in Milan, the Staatsoper in Vienna, the Metropolitan Opera House in New York, the Sydney Opera House, Covent Garden's Royal Opera House, The Hollywood Bowl and the Chatelet in Paris. He has also performed in Berlin, Tokyo, Edinburgh, Florence, and Munich, not to mention Caernarfon Castle in August, 1998. His roles include Falstaff, Scarpia, Figaro, Dr. Miracle, Balstrode, Scarpia and Leporello.

Bryn Terfel (John Stoddart)

Bryn's commitment to Wales and its language is in no doubt. A native Welsh speaker, in 1997 he became a 'roving ambassador' for The Welsh Language Board and delighted the Albert Hall crowd at the Last Night of the Proms in 1994 by donning a Welsh rugby shirt to sing *Rule Britannia*. That delight was further increased when he chose to sing the last but one verse of the quintessential Proms anthem in Welsh.

Later, still wearing a Welsh rugby shirt, Bryn would perform with Shirley Bassey at the opening ceremony of the 1999 Rugby World Cup in Cardiff. (The choice of a Welsh rugby shirt is no accident. A passionate rugby supporter Bryn broke his nose playing the game seven times, before bowing to the inevitable and giving it up for the sake of his singing.) Nowadays, his sporting endeavours are confined to the golf course. Other Welsh celebrities he has appeared with are Tom Jones - they sang *The Green Green Grass of Home* together in a Christmas TV special - and Catherine Zeta Jones. He appeared with the Swansea star in concert when she was just seventeen. They sang songs from the musicals (at the time Zeta was starring in *Forty-Second Street*).

Bryn's verdict on his fellow Welsh icon - "She has a superb singing voice".

Bryn himself is no dour, stick-in-the-mud opera buff and has several times made forays into the world of popular musicals. Apart from his regular stream of classical recordings (ranging from *Salome*, a duet album with Cecilia Bartoli, English songs and Schubert Lieder, Handel arias through to Beethoven's Ninth Symphony and *Le Nozze di Figaro*) in 1996 he recorded an album of Rodgers and Hammerstein standards which earned him a silver disc, and he has also recorded an album of Alan Jay Lerner songs called *If Ever I Should Leave You*.

Bryn was born in 1965. His father Hefin and mother Nest Jones raised him in the little hamlet of Pantglas not far from the historic town of Caernarfon in North Wales. Bryn Terfel Jones (he only became Bryn Terfel later in life when it was learnt that there was already another singer called Bryn Jones in existence) went to the local primary school in Pantglas where, incidentally, he met his future wife-to-be, Lesley Halliday, at the age of eight. He then went on to secondary school at Penygroes. When he could Bryn helped out on his father's farm, and earned extra pocket money working behind the bar of the local pub - *The Goat Inn* - washing glasses. Meanwhile he honed his singing skills perfoming locally. Then the Guildhall School of Music and Drama in London beckoned. Terfel auditioned for the School in 1983 but, at the time, he did not know any classical pieces so instead sang a Welsh folksong. It did the trick and he even got a grant for the next few years. Whilst at the Guildhall he won the 1988 Kathleen Ferrier Scholarship and the 1989 Gold Medal Award. In 1989 Bryn won the Prize for singing Lieder in the Cardiff Singer of the World Contest. The magazine *Gramophone* made him Young Singer of the Year in 1992 and in 1993 he received the International Classical Music Award. (There was even talk at one time of Bryn becoming a 'king'. In August, 1999, the Trustees of Bardsey Island off the North Wales coast were actively reported to be considering offering Bryn the title of King of Bardsey Island, but, in the end, nothing came of the idea. A pity, really, King Bryn of Bardsey has a certain ring to it.)

He was only nineteen when he made his professional debut with the Welsh National Opera in *Cosi Fan Tutte* but it was his 1991 performance in Mozart's Figaro that really put him on the map as far as the world of opera was concerned. Easter 1992 saw his debut at the Salzburg Festspiele as Jochanaan in *Salome*. He made his debut at the Metropolitan Opera House in New York in 1994 in a performance of *Figaro*.

During 1998 Bryn was forced, on several occasions, to cancel performances (including a June appearance at Cardiff Castle) owing to attacks of laryngitis – experts blamed the "dry atmosphere" of the planes he continually travelled in, and too much singing in the open air. In April of that same year it was reported that Bryn's managers - Harlequin Agency - had joined forces with IMG Arts and Entertainments to bring order into the singer's crowded performance schedule and reduce the pressures on him.

In February, 2000 Bryn was unable to appear in four performances of *Tales of Hoffmann* at the New York Metropolitan Opera House owing to an attack of sciatica which forced him to stay at home in Bontnewydd, Caernarfon, his doctors telling him to rest for a week. Then, in March of the same year, he was unable to fulfil an engagement singing in Richard Wagner's *The Flying Dutchman* on March 21st at the Royal Opera House in London because of problems with his back. Happily, his back had recovered sufficiently for him to receive an award later that year. On Saturday, May 6th, 2000, at the Royal Albert Hall at the holding of the first ever Brit Classical Awards, Bryn was presented with the Best Male Artist Award.

Writing in *The Western Mail* - the national newspaper of Wales - Rian Evans has called Bryn "by far the biggest singing star to have emerged from Wales" and Pwyll ap Siôn referred to his "awesome physical and vocal presence". Bryn himself has been rather more modest in his pronouncements, he is quoted as saying "There's many times I've forgotten the words".

Meanwhile, Bryn continues to fly the flag for Wales. His record company, Deutsche Grammophon, plans to release a CD of him singing songs in the Welsh language in August, 2000 and, in the same month, he will launch his three-day Faenol Festival at the Faenol estate near Bangor which he hopes will become an annual event.

DYLAN THOMAS

He was primarily known as a poet but generations of Welsh actors should be grateful to Dylan Marlais Thomas for providing them with gainful employment. Had his *Under Milk Wood* never seen the light of day, one lucrative avenue, at least, would have been closed to aspiring Welsh actors and actresses. Since the original radio version broadcast by the BBC on January 25th, 1954, there have been countless stage performances, records, numerous TV versions and even a cinema film. (Even so, some, at least, in Thomas's home country were originally not so sure - the initial reaction of the BBC in Wales (after the play had received its first production) was to refuse to give it air time, claiming "that it was too lewd and lascivious for Welsh ears".

Dylan Marlais Thomas was born at 5, Cwmdonkin Drive, Uplands, Swansea on October 27th, 1914, the son of Welsh-speaking parents (although Dylan himself would grow up speaking only English). His mother, Florence Thomas, was the daughter of a deacon. His father, David John Thomas, was the Senior English Master at Swansea Grammar School. Dylan himself attended Swansea Grammar School from September 1925 to July 1931 and, after leaving in July, 1931, began working as a reporter for the *South Wales Daily Post*. In March, 1933 *The New English Weekly* published his poem *And Death Shall Have No Dominion*, the first time one of his poems had been published in a London magazine.

Dylan Thomas

In November, 1934 Dylan moved to London and, a month later, his first book of eighteen poems was published. In April, 1936 he met his future wife, Caitlin Macnamara, and thus began what was to prove, to say the very least, a tempestuous relationship. In September, 1936 his second book of twenty-five poems hit the bookstores. In April, 1937 he made his first radio broadcast. In July of that same year, Dylan and Caitlin married and, in May, 1938, they moved to Laugharne. Llewellyn, their first child, was born in January, 1939. Dylan's third book *The Map of Love* came out in August, 1939.

During World War II he wrote radio scripts and gave talks and readings over the air. From 1942 to 1945 he was employed by the London based Strand films as a scriptwriter. One of his screenplays *The Doctor and The Devils* was later made into a 1986 film starring Jonathan Pryce, Siân Phillips and Timothy Dalton as Dr. Rock.

December, 1939 marked Thomas's first appearance in the USA. (In all, he would make four American tours: February, 1950; January, 1952; April, 1953 and October, 1953. On the second of those tours he was accompanied by Caitlin and the pair brawled and quarrelled their way through America.) In the autumn of 1942, he brought Caitlin to live in London where he was a member of the Savage Club. In March, 1943, their daughter Aeronwy was born. In May, 1949 the Thomas family moved to the Boathouse in Laugharne, Carmarthenshire. In July, 1949, their second son, Colm, was born. In 1950, Thomas was part of a theatrical curiosity, taking on the job of Stage Manager in the London production of the only play ever written by the Spanish painter, Pablo Picasso.

In the immediate post-war years, Dylan wrote a number of film scripts for Gainsborough films, but none of them were ever filmed. According to Paul Ferris's biography, his fellow studio writers respected him as a writer but the studio bosses were not so keen. Again, according to Ferris, Thomas's talents lay in writing dialogue, when it came to constructing plots, he was not so sure of himself.

After the war Dylan also landed some acting parts with the BBC. The Corporation had launched the new Third Programme in 1946 and he played the Second Brother in John Milton's *Comus*, the new station's first drama production. He also played Aristophanes in a play written by the poet Louis MacNeice. Then in November, 1946 he played Private Dai Evans in a radio production of David Jones's *In Parenthesis*. (Interestingly, Richard Burton, who was then still in the RAF, played a Bombing Officer in the same production. He went on to appear with Dylan in a number of other radio plays.) Thomas also appeared on the Third Programme as Satan in an eight-episode version of Milton's *Paradise Lost* and, on the Home Service, he read from the Newport poet W.H. Davies's *Autobiography of a Super Tramp* for fifteen Sundays in a row.

In his 1950s reading tours Thomas spent many months in America visiting such places as San Francisco, Florida, Washington, North Carolina, Boston, Detroit and Los Angeles. (In Hollywood he met actress Shelley

Winters, who rejected his sexual advances in no uncertain manner, and the comedian Charlie Chaplin.) Thomas toured the universities giving readings of his poetry and that of other well known poets, and recorded his poems at the Library of Congress in Washington. The universities he read at included Chicago, Illinois, Iowa, Harvard, Princeton, Cornell and Columbia. He was feted and lorded by his hosts and mixed with such well known people as William Faulkner, Thornton Wilder, Dwight D. Eisenhower and Gore Vidal and was, at one point, interviewed for *Time* magazine by the daughter of the composer Irving Berlin. (Unfortunately, the poet talked such unmitigated rubbish at the interview that it was never published.)

His readings and appearances earned him thousands of dollars, but unhappily, a hopelessness with money and an inability to hold onto it, meant that there was very little left over at the end of each lecture tour. John Malcolm Brinnin, who organised Thomas's lecture tours, has chronicled these American days and the picture he gives is of a feckless, womanising, light-fingered, unreliable, irresponsible Thomas, capable of being very charming but also very obnoxious, who - coughing his way across America - was steadily drinking and smoking himself to death. Nevertheless, despite all his many faults, Brinnin shows conclusively that Dylan Thomas was capable of inspiring great love and loyalty amongst those who knew him – a loyalty which persisted right up to the very end.

Just before leaving London for his final visit to the United States, Thomas had spent an evening with Richard Burton's mentor, Philip Burton on October 13th, 1953 and spoken to him about his plans for a new play provisionally entitled *Two Streets*, but, as was usual with Dylan, the exact details of his new project were somewhat vague. (Burton had produced the radio broadcast of Thomas's *Return Journey*.) While in Burton's flat, Thomas phoned Richard Burton asking the actor to lend him £200, to help him educate his children, but the man from Port Talbot refused. Undaunted, Dylan tried again. This time he offered Burton the carrot of the rights to his new play, *Two Streets* but Richard Burton was not falling for this one either and Thomas got no money out of him.

According to Rob Gittins, Dylan's original, handwritten manuscript of *Under Milk Wood* was lost, some might say typically, on the weekend before he was to make his final journey to the United States. It was eventually retrieved from the *Helvetia* pub in Soho's Old Compton Street and fetched £2,000 when it was sold in 1961.

On his very last journey to America, Dylan brought the manuscript of *Under Milk Wood* (originally entitled *Llareggub Hill*) with him. Unfinished, it was constantly being revised, often between visits to the pub, and the poet was still working on it the very first night it was performed. He had at first thought that only Welsh actors with Welsh accents would be able to do the play justice, but was pleasantly surprised to find how well the chosen American actors coped. Dylan Thomas gave the first ever solo performance of *Under Milk Wood* at Harvard's theatre on July 12th, 1953 and, eleven days later, performed it in New York with the help of other actors – Nancy Wickwire, Sada Stewart, Roy Poole, Al Collins and Dion Allen. His sonorous, resonant voice was acclaimed by many (others, not so sure, found it contrived and somewhat affected. In a letter to John Malcolm Brinnin, Thomas himself referred to it as "his Welsh-English voice".) Undoubtedly his voice helped to give the play's early performances the necessary gravitas. The opening night was a triumph. At first uncertain, but then realising that, in Brinnin's words, "this story of a village was as funny as it was loving and solemn" the American audience soon began to laugh. At the end they showed their appreciation, cheering and clapping, and bringing the cast back for fifteen curtain calls in all with the author, who had played the part of the First Voice plus three other parts, taking the last of these by himself.

The audience were not alone in appreciating Dylan's talents. His fellow actors were also mightily impressed and, according to Brinnin, they "not only held him in warm affection as a person but ... showed an almost awed respect for his ingenuity as a man of the theatre". (Dylan appears not to have been without acting ability of his own, the author of *Gentlemen Prefer Blondes*, Anita Loos, saw him at one of his New York readings and broached the idea of him taking the lead role in a forthcoming Broadway comedy. Dylan even wrote home to his parents in Laugharne - but never posted the letter - referring to the proposal but, in the end, the offer remained just that, a proposal and nothing more came of the idea.)

Perhaps this is not so surprising. After all as a schoolboy Dylan had taken part in a number of school productions. He had also joined the Mumbles based Little Theatre, a Swansea amateur theatre group, after reviewing one of their plays for his newspaper. Paul Ferris, in his biography of Dylan, says that "he seems to have flung himself into parts and achieved his effects by over-acting". One of his fellow actors, Malcolm Graham, who later turned professional, said of him that "the more fantastic the part, the better Dylan was".

In 1932, Thomas played Simon in *Hay Fever* by Noel Coward and he also appeared in the Little Theatre's January, 1934 production of William Congreve's *The Way of the World*. Disaster struck though when he was scheduled to play the prominent role of a newspaperman in the Little Theatre's production of Jean-Jacques Bernard's *Martine*. There was a scene over Dylan's drunken behaviour at rehearsals and the part was given to Malcolm Graham. Nevertheless, after his New York triumph, the theatre may well have been the way forward for Dylan, had he lived. There was talk - at one time serious talk - of his providing the libretto for a new opera by the Russian composer Igor Stravinsky and Thomas did have plans for other plays which, sadly, were destined to come to nothing.

Dylan Thomas's last ever performance in *Under Milk Wood* took place on Sunday, October 25th, 1953 and he was never to see Wales again. He died in a New York hospital - St. Vincent's - on Monday, November 9th, 1953, his reputation as a hard drinking hell raiser undimmed. He had spent much time frequenting the bars of America and, when not drinking American beer, imbibing strongly of the American whisky during his lecture tours (Dylan's favourite New York 'watering hole' was *The White Horse Tavern* in Hudson Street where he would often hold court to a crowd of friends and 'hangers-on' and he also spent much time in the Greenwich Village district of the city.) According to *The Western Mail* report of the time the cause of death was said to be "a brain disease of unknown origin". Thomas had collapsed at his hotel the previous Wednesday and gone into a coma from which he never recovered. His widow Caitlin flew out to New York and it was decided to bring the dead poet's body back to Wales by ship.

On Sunday, November 15th, 1953 a Memorial Service was held at St. Luke's Protestant Episcopal Church in New York. On Tuesday, November 17th, the liner *United States* set sail for Southampton, bearing Dylan's body. When the *United States* arrived in the southern English port on the night of Sunday, November 22nd, eight Welshmen carried the body down the gangway. It had originally been planned to take the body to Wales overnight, but these plans were shelved and it was kept in a local mortuary. The next day it was brought back to Dylan's mother's home – Pelican House in Laugharne.

On Tuesday, November 24th, 1953, a private service was conducted at Pelican House by the Vicar of Laugharne, Chancellor S.B. Williams. At the graveside the mourners included the poet Louis Macneice, Vernon Watkins, Dylan's fellow Swansea poet and close friend, and the poet and film maker, John Ormond Thomas. Another of Dylan's Swansea circle, the painter Alfred James, was also present. The mourners crowded into the packed eleventh century parish church and, subsequently, Dylan was laid to rest in Laugharne churchyard. Following her own death, his wife is now beside him. Recent research has resurrected the controversy surrounding Thomas' death with claims that he was an undiagnosed diabetic, and that the treatment prescribed by his American doctor was unhelpful, to say the least.

GWYN THOMAS

Schoolmaster, member of the *Brains Trust*, novelist, wit, raconteur, TV personality, newspaper critic, contributor to *Punch* and *The Times Literary Supplement* – Gwyn Thomas was all of these. He was also an accomplished dramatist.

He was born at 196, High Street, Cymmer in the Rhondda on July 6th, 1913. His parents Walter Morgan Thomas and Ziphorah Thomas (née Davies) had twelve children in all - four girls and eight boys - and Gwyn was the last of these. Ziphorah died in 1913 when Gwyn was only six. After her death, her eighteen-year-old daughter, Hannah (known as Nana), took over from her and began running the family. (Both Walter and Ziphorah were Welsh speakers; and Welsh was the language they passed on to their first six children, but the last six were brought up speaking English only, including Gwyn.)

Gwyn passed the entrance exam to the Porth County School where he soon acquired a reading knowledge of both French and Spanish. He was accepted at St. Edmund Hall, Oxford University to read the two languages but hated the three years he spent there. He left Oxford with a Second Class Degree and, at first, was unemployed for some twelve months. It took him a year to write a novel *Sorrow For Thy Sons* which he sent to Gollancz the publishers in the first few months of 1937. After some time it was rejected. He took up various part-time jobs lecturing to the unemployed in the depression years and married Eiluned (Lyn) Thomas at the Registry Office in Pontypridd on January 5th, 1938. Gollancz did, however, encourage him, saying they were certain he had a future as a novelist. Meanwhile, he continued to write and found work teaching the unemployed at centres in Norfolk and Mansfield. He was then appointed Education Officer working for the National Council for Social Services for the Manchester region.

In the late summer of 1940, Gwyn was appointed to the staff of the Languages Department at the County School, Cardigan, a Welsh-speaking area, although neither Gwyn nor his wife Lyn had the slightest interest in Welsh. In October, 1942, he was appointed as French and Spanish teacher at the Boys' County School, Barry, a post he would occupy for twenty years to come. Terry Breverton, who was taught both languages by Thomas, remembers that the boys at the school gave Gwyn the nickname of 'Killer', because he used to 'kill' them with laughter.

He had four books published in the late 1940s. He wrote his last novel, *The Love Man*, in 1958. He made his first appearance in *The Brains Trust* in January, 1956 and appeared on radio and television versions of the programme for the next five years.

In August, 1960, Thomas's play *The Keep* (about a family living in the South Wales Valleys in the 1950s) was given a single performance try-out. (Glyn Houston, Dudley Jones and Jessie Evans took the leading roles) In November, 1961, it was staged at the Royal Court Theatre in London. It was also shown on TV and J.C. Trewin published it as one of his Plays of the Year. It also proved to be one of Gwyn's most successful dramas. The play was translated into German and performed in Hamburg. In the autumn of 1962 it was performed in such places as Swansea, Salisbury and Scunthorpe, Birmingham and Lincoln, Derby and Guildford and even staged in South Africa.

In October, 1962, another of his plays *Loud Organs* was performed at Blackpool but failed to set Lancashire alight. It moved to Cardiff where it opened on October 29th. Despite having a cast including Glyn Houston and Gerald James, it was hampered by the accompanying music and the choreography, neither of which were to the playwright's liking. It did not survive long after Cardiff.

In the summer of 1962, Gwyn retired from his teaching post to devote himself to TV work and writing plays. He also became a regular member of the *Any Questions* team after 1963. On February 1st, 1963, Gwyn's new play, *Jackie the Jumper*, which deals with the 1831 Merthyr Uprising, opened at the Royal Court. It was directed by John Dexter and the music for it was written by Welsh composer Alun Hodinott. Starring Ronald Lewis and Dudley Jones, the play received mixed reviews and, despite being included in his plays of the year by J.C.Trewin, by the end of the month it was gone.

In the spring of 1964, after spending twenty-two years in Barry, Gwyn and Lyn moved to 5, Sea View, Ogmore by Sea, and a new bungalow. But at the end of January, 1965, they moved house again to another bungalow, this time in the village of Peterston-super-Ely, about five miles from Cardiff. Their new home was called Cherry Trees and, although he did not know it, it was to be Gwyn's last.

Towards the end of 1965 he began to suffer from diabetes. For some time now the overweight playwright had also begun to drink heavily and the combination of heavy drinking and diabetes weighed heavily on his health. In January, 1966, Gwyn appeared in *10.42 and All That*, a programme which he himself scripted and which featured both himself and the actor Ray Smith. Gwyn was somewhat typecast as the talkative and occasionally rather argumentative pub drinker whilst Ray played the landlord of the pub Gwyn frequented.

In November, 1974, *Sap* was performed in Cardiff by an all Welsh cast. It was set against a World War I background and backed by music from the period. In November, 1977, *The Breakers* was performed at the Sherman Theatre in Cardiff. Bernard Levin gave it a good review but it failed with the public: its cause had not been helped by the controversy surrounding it. On the day before its opening, Ray Smith, its leading actor had walked out, alleging that "the production had been skimped". He was persuaded to return for the play's first night, but by then, perhaps, the damage had already been done.

In January, 1979, *Theatr yr Ymylon* put on *Testimonials* at the Sherman. It had been adapted from Gwyn's 1966 radio play, *The Alderman*, but the playwright himself was too ill to see the new production and no more new works flowed from his pen.

As far back as 1969, Gwyn's health had begun to fail. Now, early in 1981, he collapsed and was taken to the University Hospital at the Heath in Cardiff. At four a.m. on April 13th he was found dead by nurses making their morning rounds. Had he lived another three months he would have celebrated his sixty-eighth birthday. They scattered his ashes on the mountainside at Llanwonno, the last resting place of Guto Nyth Bran, the legendary Rhondda runner, and a favourite haunt of Gwyn's.

Gwyn Thomas was a novelist, a raconteur, a dramatist and a broadcaster: His TV plays included *The Ship*, broadcast on BBC1 on October 14th, 1963, and *The Dig* broadcast on the same channel on October 24th, 1963. Among his plays for radio were *The Walk Out*, broadcast on The Third Programme on March 7th, 1963, and featuring Kenneth Griffith as the headmaster who lets power get the better of him. Five years previously, his radio play about the Rhondda running legend, *Guto Nyth Bran* was broadcast on the BBC's Home Service (July 17th, 1958). He presented many TV programmes on Wales which he himself scripted.

Although himself the son of Welsh speakers, he had no time for the Welsh-speaking lobby. His was the English language voice of the South Wales Valleys. His stance towards the Welsh language often brought him into conflict with the advocates of Welsh. Famed for the gusto and power of his dialogue, his most famous play *The Keep* won the *Evening Standard* drama award and was translated into German, Dutch, Italian, Rumanian, Russian, Polish, Swedish and Norwegian.

MADOLINE THOMAS

"Strong" and "indomitable", *The Times* obituarist called her and, no wonder. After her husband died, leaving her financially the worse for wear, she embarked on a professional career in acting at the age of fifty-two. At the age of 87, she was playing a "merrily murderous grandmother" in *Tales from the Vienna Woods* produced by Maximilian Schell when she was knocked down by a motorbike in Regent Street and broke her hip. She insisted on carrying on till the end of the run. When she was rehearsing Uncle Vanya at the National Theatre in London in 1982 - at which time she was 92 years of age - she would regularly walk the two miles between her home and the theatre until the director, Sir Peter Hall, got to hear about it and ensured there was a taxi waiting each day to take her to rehearsals.

She was born Madoline Mary Price in Abergavenny on January 2nd, 1890, the daughter of a draper. She received a private education in Bristol and trained to be an organist, pianist and singer. She took part in amateur stage performances in Barry and Penarth and her voice was heard in radio plays which the BBC broadcast from Cardiff. In 1919 she married John William Halliday Thomas, a schoolmaster from Barry. When he died, she took to the professional stage to earn a living. It was Emlyn Williams who gave her her first chance on tour. Known to the profession as Maddy she made her West End bow at the Prince's Theatre in March, 1945 as Mrs. Evan Evans in *Three Waltzes*. She then appeared in *Fly Away Peter* in 1947 and was Mrs Boyle in *The Mousetrap*. She joined the RSC in 1963 and spent six seasons at Stratford-upon-Avon, playing such roles as Emilia in *Comedy of Errors*, Katherina in *The Jew of Malta*, Lady Northumberland in *Henry IV*, Queen Isabel of France in *Henry V* and Margery Jourdain, the Witch, in *Henry VI*. She spent a further five years at the National Theatre appearing in such productions as *Tales from the Vienna Woods*, *The Three Sisters* and *Uncle Vanya*.

She made her last appearance, aged 97, with Emlyn Williams in the 1986 BBC film *Caring*. She died on Saturday, December 30th, 1989 in Weston-super-Mare General Hospital. Her death came a week after she had suffered a fall in the Weston nursing home where she had lived for the last three years. The fall broke her other hip. She died just three days before her hundredth birthday and was survived by her son.

Madoline Thomas had parts in two Ealing films, Mrs. Stoner in *Painted Boats* (1945) and Mrs. Lloyd in *The Square Ring* (1953). She also played in such 'Welsh' films as *Valley of Song* (she was Aunt Mary), *The Last Days of Dolwyn* (in which she played Mrs. Thomas Shop) and the 1949 mining film *Blue Scar* directed by Jill Craigie, the woman who was later to become Michael Foot's wife. In this film, Madoline took the part of the cantankerous old grandmother whose life revolved around the football pools. She was also to be seen in the film *Champagne Charlie* with the comedian Tommy Trinder.

RACHEL THOMAS

Black haired, pale skinned and with strong features, Rachel Thomas will always be remembered as the "archetypal Welsh Mam".

Born in Pontardawe on February 10th, 1905, (according to *The Times*; *The Western Mail* claims her birthplace was Alltwen in the Swansea Valley) her maiden name was Rachel Roberts, the very name another Welsh actress would go on to make famous. Educated at Ystalyfera County School in the Swansea Valley she had a short career as a teacher, marrying a headmaster called Howell J. Thomas, before becoming an actress.

Although she came from a family with no acting tradition, her father - a miner who had his fair share of trouble with the mineowners because of his strong support for the union - encouraged his young daughter to sing and recite poetry at the local *eisteddfodau*, often carrying the young Rachel to them aloft upon his shoulders. From her childhood on she spent her leisure hours learning great chunks of poetry off by heart.

Her first big break came in the 1930s when she was heard on the radio reading a lesson from her local church. As a result of this broadcast the BBC was inundated with hundreds of callers all wanting to know more about the woman who had read so sensitively and Rachel was offered an audition.

She appeared in such films as the 1940 *Proud Valley*, *The Captive Heart* in 1946, *Blue Scar*, *David* and *Undercover*. She was in the 1959 film *Tiger Bay*. Thomas appeared with Richard Burton and Elizabeth Taylor in the 1971 film of *Under Milk Wood* and was in *Valley of Song*. She played Beth Morgan in the 1959/1960 production of *How Green Was My Valley*.

A Welsh-speaking Welshwoman (she loved Wales and the Welsh language passionately), her TV work included *How Green Was My Valley* (1968), *Owen MD* (1971) and the Welsh-language soap opera, *Pobol y Cwm* where she played Bella, an old woman resident in a nursing home (from 1974 to 1992). She was also in the early eighties *Ennal's Point*, a BBC lifeboat station drama set in the Mumbles, Swansea, playing a coxswain's widow.

On the London stage she played the part of Mrs. Pearce in *Pygmalion* and was seen in *Arsenic and Old Lace* at the Swansea Grand Theatre. Her final performance was playing opposite Philip Madoc as Sarah, the shotgun-toting grannie prepared to defend her farm to the last cartridge, in the BBC Wales Playhouse drama, *Whistling Boy*.

Rachel Thomas (S4C)

Awards showered over her: in 1968 she was awarded the OBE for services to Wales; in 1990 she was created a member of the Gorsedd of Bards at the National Eisteddfod; a year later she was given the BAFTA Cymru Lifetime Achievement Award.

A longtime resident of the Cardiff suburb of Rhiwbina, she died in the city on Wednesday, February 11th, 1995. Falling awkwardly she had damaged her hip and had had to go into hospital. Her husband died in 1964. On her own death, she was survived by a daughter, Delyth.

WYNFORD VAUGHAN THOMAS

The writer and broadcaster Lewis John Wynford Vaughan Thomas was born in Swansea on August 15th, 1908 one of three sons born to the musician, Dr. David Vaughan Thomas, and his wife Morfydd. He was educated at Swansea Grammar School where he first became friendly with the poet Dylan

Thomas. He attended Exeter College, Oxford and, after university, worked for a time as a Keeper of Manuscripts and Records at the National Library of Wales in Aberystwyth before switching to a job as Area Officer of the South Wales Council of Social Services. He then began working for the BBC on October 9th, 1936 as an outside broadcasts assistant in Cardiff and, in this capacity, reported on the Coronation of King George VI (this was his first broadcast and took place on May 12th, 1937). By November, 1937 he was helping out in the BBC's Swansea studios.

Wynford Vaughan Thomas (S4C)

But it was as a war reporter that he first really came to prominence (he received the *Croix de Guerre* from the French government in 1945). He was appointed to Head Office's Outside Broadcast Unit in April, 1940 and amongst his daring exploits were accompanying the crew of a Lancaster bomber in a raid over Berlin on September 3rd, 1943. (Broadcast on the radio his reports created a sensation and made many people at home realise just what the bomber crews were going through.) He also reported the Anzio landings, the Allies' entering into Rome and Montgomery's men crossing the Rhine. He broadcast from the studios in Hamburg which the traitor William Joyce, Lord Haw-Haw, had used only a few days before to send his propaganda messages to Britain, indeed, the Nazi sympathiser's empty gin bottle and script were still on his desk.

The war over, Vaughan Thomas reported on the celebrations on the night that Victory in Japan was declared and became an automatic choice for the big occasion, reporting on the wedding between Prince Charles and Lady Diana in 1981. A member of the Harlech Consortium which took over the Wales and the West television franchise from TWW in 1968, he subsequently became a Director of Programmes for HTV. Other programmes he became associated with were *The Countryside In ...* on Radio 4 which he hosted for many years until his death on February 4th, 1987.

Wynford Vaughan Thomas published his autobiography *Trust to Talk* in 1980. Renowned as a talker and a walker (the *Times* obituarist referred favourably to his silver tongued approach to his chosen profession) he broadcast many series on his journeys round Wales – both on radio and television. His last television production of major importance was *The Dragon Has Two Tongues* in which he shared the limelight with the controversial Welsh historian Professor Gwyn Alf Williams with both men giving their own interpretation of episodes from Welsh history. Awarded an OBE in 1974, he was taken ill in December, 1986 after visiting Buckingham Palace to be presented with his CBE. Taken to Haverfordwest's Withybush Hospital, he underwent a series of tests three days before Christmas but was pronounced fit to go home on January 19th, 1987. He died peacefully at his Fishguard home on Wednesday, February 4th, 1987, and a private funeral service took place at Parc Gwyn crematorium in Narberth attended by about a dozen relatives and friends. He was survived by his wife, Charlotte (whom he had married in 1946) and son, David, (who was born in 1950).

CAROL VORDERMAN

Famed for her ability with numbers Carol Jean Vorderman was born in Denbigh, North Wales (on December 24th, 1960) and raised in Prestatyn. Her Dutch father, shopkeeper Anton Vorderman, left the family home when she was just three weeks old, leaving her mother, Jean (née Davies), to struggle to bring up her three young children alone. Educated at Rhyl's Ysgol Mair Roman Catholic Primary School, she was only ten when she moved a year early to the Blessed Edward Jones School. Her fourteen 'O' Levels (!) and three 'A' Levels helped her win a place at Sidney Sussex College, Cambridge where she read engineering, the first person from her school ever to be accepted at an Oxbridge university. She left Cambridge in 1981 (with a third-class degree in engineering), aged twenty to live with her mother in Leeds and became a management trainee with the frozen food storage firm Christian Salvesen. She then moved on to selling computers for Tandy in Leeds.

Her mother changed her life by submitting her name to Yorkshire Television who were looking for someone with both "brains and beauty" for a programme called *Countdown*. Carol at first demurred but her mother persisted, so that she eventually applied and got the job, beating off the challenge of more than three thousand other female applicants, and thus became the first woman ever to be seen on the new Channel 4 on *Countdown*, the daily conundrum programme. It was Channel 4's first ever TV programme, and the very first *Countdown* was broadcast on November 2nd, 1982. In 1984, her local radio station, Radio Aire, asked her to present her own radio show, *Kiddies' Capers*. In 1987, the BBC invited her to co-present a science programme called *Take Nobody's Word For It* where she met her

Carol Vorderman

husband Paddy (Patrick) King, a management consultant, whom she married on May 19th, 1990, the same year that she joined ITV's science programme for children, *How To...* (Her first marriage to rugby league player Chris Mather when she was twenty-five ended in divorce.)

Some of the many programmes she has appeared on since that first 1982 *Countdown* are *The Vorderman Report, How To, So We Bought A Computer* and *A Way With Numbers*. She has also been seen on *How, Tomorrow's World* and *Mysteries*. She has fronted *The National Lottery Live, Computers Don't Bite, Testing Testing* and also presented *Points of View, Antiques Inspectors* and *Hot Gadgets*. She is still a regular on *Countdown*. Towards the end of 1998, she signed a contract with Channel 4 rumoured to be worth some £5 million. That same year she appeared as the pop singer Cher in a celebrity version of the 'wanna-be' show *Stars In Your Eyes*.

Carol was sacked by the BBC as a *Tomorrow's World* presenter for advertising Ariel soap powder on 'the other side' but this proved to be only a temporary setback. Indeed, Carol's TV career has now blossomed so much that, at the time of writing, she is almost an ever present on our TV channels. She now fronts ITV's *Carol Vorderman's Better Rooms* and BBC1's *Dream House* and she is often to be seen advertising various products on TV. She presented a new five-part programme *Tested to Destruction* on ITV in July, 1999. In October, 1999 she was listed as Wales's highest, and Britain's 28th highest-earning woman. In December, 1999 the *Observer Screen Guide* singled her out for her brains and uncanny ability to be on TV almost all of the time. The paper thought that if there were to be a race to crown the new Millennium's most well-known face, Carol already had a headstart.

Recently, Carol has begun to re-invent herself, shedding some excess weight, wearing trendier clothes and sporting a younger hairstyle. She has been photographed wrapped in nothing but a Union Jack flag to promote the April, 2000 Pride of Britain Awards. She also took part in a special celebrity edition of *Who Wants To Be A Millionaire?* winning a not unsubstantial amount of money for charity, – £125,000 in all, but balking at a question on William Shakespeare, saying afterwards that she found the Bard 'boring'.

Despite her seemingly unstoppable climb to fame, Carol has not lost touch with her North Wales roots. She has re-visited her old school and, on Thursday, May 25th, 2000, she launched the New Community University of Wales at Llandudno's North Wales Theatre. *The Western Mail* quoted her as saying: "I am delighted that North Wales is blazing a trail on this, and other parts of the United Kingdom will follow us from today". In June, 2000, Carol was awarded a CBE in the Queen's Birthday Honour's List. On September 24th, 2000, it was announced that Carol and her husband, Paddy King, had separated.

NAUNTON WAYNE

Naunton Wayne died in a Tolworth, Surrey hospital on Tuesday, November 17th, 1970 at the age of sixty-nine. He took his first steps on the road to acting success in 1920 as a member of a Barry Island concert party rejoicing under the name of 'The Tweenies'. After Barry, Wayne spent ten years entertaining in similar troupes before landing a job as a revue compere in London appearing at such venues as the Victoria Palace, the Palladium, Coliseum and the Holborn Empire. For almost a year he was the front-man for the London Pavilion's non-stop variety show.

Naunton Wayne owes his fame to his quintessential portrayals of a certain type of Englishman, but he was actually born Henry Wayne Davies in Llanwonno, Glamorgan on June 22nd, 1901. A solicitor's son, he spent his school days at Clifton College. (In 1933, Henry Wayne Davies changed his name to Naunton Wayne by deed poll. The 'Naunton' came from his grandfather).

He owed his cinema fame to his portrayal of Charters, one of two cricket-loving Englishmen (the other was Basil Radford) who very nearly stole the show in Alfred Hitchcock's 1938 movie, *The Lady Vanishes* and were to be seen again in the 1940 spy thriller *Night Train to Munich*. Other films the duo appeared in were *Crook's Tour, Dead of Night* and *Passport to Pimlico*. Wayne also featured in the 1953 film *The Titfield Thunderbolt*.

Curiously enough the 1951 film *A Circle of Danger* featured two Welshmen, Naunton Wayne and Ray Milland, in a number of scenes together, the former playing his usual archetypal 'Englishman', the latter an American.

On stage at the Strand, in 1942, Wayne put in some 1,300 performances playing the newspaperman in *Arsenic and Old Lace* who discovers that his two ageing aunts are murdering anyone they can lay their hands on. In the 1960s he again took to the stage playing Mr. Sedley in *Vanity Fair*, the musical version, and both the Earl of Lister and Beecham, the butler, in *The Reluctant Peer* by William Douglas Home.

SIR HUW WHELDON

A Welsh-speaking Welshman, Huw Pyrs Wheldon was born on May 7th, 1916 at Prestatyn, but brought up in Bangor. At the town's Friars School he was bottom of the class and failed his school certificate in 1930, and in 1931, eventually passing it in 1932. In June, 1933, the family moved to London as Huw's father had become Permanent Secretary to the Wales Department of Education. In 1934, Huw spent three months living with a German family in Soest and, in the autumn of 1934, he enrolled at the University College of North Wales, Bangor, but by 1935, he had transferred to the London School of Economics to study sociology. In his first year he was elected Treasurer of the Student's Union. Awarded his degree - an Upper Second - in 1938, he began working for Kent Education Committee in January, 1939. He was first employed as an assistant vocational guidance officer at Beckenham but then moved on to Deal on the south coast. When war came, he was appointed second in command of a company and took part in the invasion of Normandy, winning the Military Cross for his courage under enemy fire. He fought in the Ardennes, crossed the Rhine and achieved the rank of a major commanding a company.

After the war Wheldon was appointed by the Arts Council as their Officer for Wales at a salary of a thousand pounds a year. But his return to Wales was shortlived. Early in 1949, he was appointed to represent the Arts Council on the executive committee that ran the Festival of Britain. He was in London once more and would remain there for the rest of his life. He would visit Wales and holiday there but he was never to work or live in the land of his birth again.

In January 1952, he joined the BBC as its TV publicity officer. More significantly, after October, 1952, Wheldon was also used to present a late afternoon programme featuring children playing instruments, singing and talking about their hobbies. It was called *All Your Own* and Wheldon continued with it until December, 1960 making his name in the process.

In July, 1954, he was appointed a producer in the television talks department. On Sunday, February 2nd, 1958, *Monitor*, a 45-minute Arts programme, was shown for the first time with Wheldon as its presenter. He was quickly to make it 'all his own', doing many of the major interviews himself.

In 1962, Wheldon ceased to formally edit *Monitor*. In the spring of that same year he was promoted to Assistant Head of Talks. In February, 1963, he became Head of Documentary Programmes. *Monitor* came to an end in 1965. In 1968, he tried to become Director-General of the BBC. He failed but was instead made Managing Director. He retired from the BBC in December, 1975. He was knighted in the 1976 New Year's Honours. In August, 1976, he was diagnosed as having bowel cancer, but after being admitted to the private King Edward VII hospital, he appeared to have made a full recovery. His *Royal Heritage* not only received critical acclaim but also sold well all over the world. It also earned him a Silver Medal from The Royal

Television Society in 1978 and he began to earn a good living as a television consultant. But by 1985 the cancer had surfaced again and had now spread to his lung. He died on Friday, March 14th, 1986. His memorial service was held in Westminster Abbey. His gravestone is in Nant Peris, near to those of his father, mother and brother (his father died in 1961 and was buried in the churchyard at Nant Peris. Thomas, Huw's brother, had died earlier that same year) and those of his ancestors dating back to the eighteenth century, whilst his ashes are to be found in Kew Gardens.

Not many people successfully present BBC programmes and climb the ladder to high office within the Corporation - Wheldon was one of the few who did both. David Attenborough who said that he was affectionately known as "Huge Welshman", regarded him as "the best Director-General the BBC never had". A renowned story teller, Wheldon once told of visiting a public toilet in Newport, falling down the steps and breaking his nose in the process.

EMLYN WILLIAMS

Kenneth Griffith called him "the cleverest craftsman of drama" that he had ever read. Richard Huggett thought him the "most sinister actor in English with a special talent for menace and evil". In his private notebooks, Richard Burton wrote that he had "a mind like a cut-throat razor and a tongue to match". Others thought him "saturnine". He was a linguist with an Oxford degree from a desperately poor Welsh speaking background who went on to write and star in his own plays.

He was George Emlyn Williams and he was born in Pen-y-Ffordd, Mostyn, a small village in Flintshire on November 26th, 1905. His father and mother, Richard and Mary Williams, ran their greengrocery business from the front room of the End House. Aged four, the young George (he was only to become Emlyn in 1928, deciding that the change of name would be more suitable to his new professional acting career) went to a convent school run by nuns at nearby Talacre. When he was eight he attended a new council run school in Picton not far from his home. In 1916 he won a scholarship to Holywell County School and landed himself a daily trek of five miles to school and five miles back home again.

From 1906 to 1915, George's father kept the *White Lion* pub at Glanrafon but was too fond of the drink himself to make any profit. Indeed, so bad was his drinking that all the other local pubs banned him. In July, 1915, the *White Lion* was sold on and in the spring of 1916, Richard Williams got himself a job in a munitions factory. In July, 1917 George's father moved the family to anglicised Connah's Quay to be nearer his new job as a steelwork's fireman but George continued to attend his school in Holywell. The move did bring about other changes, however, as before long, his parents had abandoned Welsh as the language of their home and hearth (in reality a slum dwelling not far from the railway line) in favour of English.

At Holywell County School George Emlyn was fortunate enough to make the acquaintanceship of Miss Grace Cooke, a teacher, who, recognising his potential, encouraged him in his studies, lent him books and paid for him to stay in France for three months. He never forgot her kindness towards him and their relationship endured throughout her lifetime. By 1923, George Emlyn, having passed his earlier exams with distinction, had earned an Open Scholarship to Christchurch College Oxford to study French. He would eventually be awarded a Second Class Degree and be entitled to call himself an M.A. (Oxon).

Once at Oxford he discovered the French Club and made his stage debut as the Maître d'Hotel in *La Poudre aux Yeux*, Labiche's comedy. Parts with the Oxford University Dramatic Society followed and he played in *Hamlet, Peer Gynt* and in plays by Pirandello.

After Oxford, he left Connah's Quay to go to London where he secured a walk-on part in a production of *And So To Bed*. On April 4th, 1927, he stepped on stage at The Savoy Theatre and said the six lines he had to say for which he was paid the princely sum of £3-00 a week. The production then moved to New York, Emlyn being promoted to Assistant Stage Manager and his salary going up to twelve pounds.

There was not much work around in 1929 but in the 1930s he appeared in a couple of Edgar Wallace plays in one of which - *The Case of the Frightened Lady* - he played one of his favourite parts, the villainous Lord Lebanon.

He wrote *The Corn is Green* when he was 32 – his first ever play about Wales. It was first performed in London in October, 1938 and, in 1941, adjudged by the New York Drama Critics' Circle to be the best foreign play of that year. Amongst Williams's other plays are *A Murder Has Been Arranged* (1930), *Night Must Fall* (on May 31st, 1935, *Night Must Fall* opened at London's Duchess Theatre, later transferring to the Cambridge, and proved to be one of the box office successes of that year), *Spring 1600* (1934/35), *The Wind of Heaven* (1945) and *Trespass* (1947).

In 1951 he transformed himself into Charles Dickens giving one-man shows and reading from the novelist's works. As Dickens he visited some 30 big cities in the USA, and spent time in Canada, South Africa, New Zealand and Australia. In Europe, he toured Germany, Switzerland, Czechoslovakia, Scandinavia, Russia, Yugoslavia, Bulgaria and Greece. He also played India, Iran, Sri Lanka, Malaysia, Sabah, Vietnam, the Phillipines, Singapore, Japan, Hong Kong and South America as the great novelist. Four years later he became Dylan Thomas in another one-man show based on the poet's output giving his first performance of *Dylan Thomas Growing Up* at Worthing's Connaught Theatre on April 25th, 1955. (He also toured America with this.)

In August, 1977, when he was 72 years old, he inaugurated a new one-man show *The Playboy of the Western World*, taking the part of Saki, subsequently taking the show to America and Canada. He died on Friday, September 25th, 1987 at his London home. He had only recently recovered from a cancer operation. (His wife Molly had died in 1970.) Emlyn Williams's funeral took place on Friday, October 2nd, 1987 at 'the actors' church', St. Paul's, Covent Garden. Amongst the mourners were Sir John Gielgud, Susan Hampshire, Robert Hardy and Richard Burton's widow, Sally. Emlyn Williams's son Brook read Dylan Thomas's poem *And Death Shall Have No Dominion.* The cremation took place at Golders Green.

A Welsh speaking Welshman (he did not speak English until he was eight years old), Emlyn Williams nevertheless left his mark on the English-speaking theatre. *Night Must Fall* and the strongly autobiographical *The Corn is Green* are still regularly performed and both have been filmed twice, the former in 1937 and 1964 and the latter in 1945 and 1978. (And this despite the fact that he had no formal drama training of any kind and picked up the craft of acting by himself.) In fact, he was sixteen before he even saw a play on stage. A talented linguist, (he learnt Latin in school and Modern Greek in later life), he not only performed in English but also spoke Welsh, German, Italian and French on stage

In the 1939 film, *The Stars Look Down* he gave a compelling portrait of Joe Gowlan. He also acted in and directed the 1949 film *The Last Days of Dolwyn,* the only film he would ever direct. His film career prospered from the thirties to the sixties and included *I, Claudius* in 1937, *They Drive By Night* (1938), *Jamaica Inn* (1939), *Major Barbara* (1941), *The Wreck of the Mary Deare* (1959) and the 1962 *L-Shaped Room.* His first Hollywood film was the 1950 *Three Husbands.* As late as 1983, he turned up on the nation's TV screens as Harold Brittling in the first episode of the third series of *Rumpole of the Bailey.*

A bisexual, he married Molly Caris-Wilson (née Molly O'Shann) an Irish actress in 1935 and the couple had two sons, one of whom, Brook, himself went on to act in films, frequently appearing with his father's former protégé, Richard Burton. On stage, Emlyn Williams played Angelo, Shylock, Iago, Sir Thomas More and Patrick Bronte. One of his most famous theatrical roles was as Sir Robert Morton in Terence Rattigan's *The Winslow Boy.* He had what some might call a morbid fascination for murder and murder trials even writing a book about the 1960s Moors Murders.

A member of the Gorsedd, Emlyn Williams was made President of the National Eisteddfod in 1953. He was awarded a CBE in June, 1962. He was a namedropper's dream, having met Marilyn Monroe and Rita Hayworth and rubbed shoulders with Edgar Wallace, Noel Coward, Lillian Gish, Laurence Olivier, and Alec Guinness. He appeared with Yvonne Arnaud, Madeleine Carroll, Celia Johnson, Deborah Kerr, Bette Davis, Elizabeth Taylor, Vivien Leigh, Sybil Thorndike, and Ingrid Bergman. He also shared the same stage with Edmund Gwenn, Charles Laughton, Ralph Richardson, Max Miller, John Gielgud, James Mason, Kenneth More, and Michael Redgrave. He gave Richard Burton his first chance, not only on the professional stage but also in the cinema. He once taught French to Lloyd George's daughter. Noel Coward and John Gielgud were godfathers to his eldest son.

RONNIE WILLIAMS

Born and bred in Cefneithin, Carmarthenshire Ronnie Williams came from a show business background. His father Iori Williams was well known in Welsh language circles as one half of the Sioni and Iori partnership. Ronnie Williams worked for a time on the buses and then as an apprentice newspaperman before going to the Welsh College of Music and Drama in Cardiff to study drama. In 1964 he obtained a post with BBC Wales as an announcer. He played an active part in BBC Wales's satirical programme *Stiwdio B*, the station's answer to *That Was The Week That Was*, but did not act with Ryan Davies until the 1967 Bala National Eisteddfod (although the two had worked together on a TV show *Ryan, Ronnie, Gill and Johnny*, which had not been broadcast by the time of the Eisteddfod). He was then asked to do *Ryan and Ronnie* for television. In the last twenty years of his life, Ronnie tried several businesses - they all failed including his pub in Cerrigydrudion which ended after a seven year partnership - and on one occasion he was declared bankrupt. Despite his many roles on television, Ronnie felt that he had never been allowed to forget Ryan and Ronnie. His last acting job was in the film *Twin Town* after which the offers of work dried up.

They were dubbed the "Welsh Morecambe and Wise", but for one half of the famous Ryan and Ronnie double act - Ronnie Williams - fame brought little lasting fortune and his life ended in tragedy. His father was a miner from the Gwendraeth valley who became an entertainer and earned a bit part in *Pobol y Cwm*. As a young boy Ronnie was said to have "a beautiful singing voice". He began his career entertaining in little halls in and around Cefneithin, Crymych and the Gwendraeth valley. He spent time working as a bus conductor before attending drama school. He also worked as a newspaperman on a West Wales local paper. He worked for the BBC as a continuity announcer before trying his hand at comedy. He became Ryan Davies's straight man, a part of the double act, Ryan and Ronnie. Ronnie provided most of their written material and the duo went from strength to strength. They did four television series in Welsh and one in English, but touring took its toll on Ronnie, and the duo split up in 1975 after a fifteen year partnership. Their last appearance together was at Club Double Diamond in Caerphilly. They performed there for three days and then Ronnie left pleading exhaustion, took three months off and went to North Wales to run The *White Lion* in Cerrigydrudion. His stay in the licensing trade was not to be a long one. After an appearance at the Bankruptcy Court in Wrexham in November, 1976, he joined Theatr Gwynedd, Bangor, writing and directing. He subsequently appeared in a variety of Welsh-language TV productions, carving out a solo career for himself, but he never fully recovered from the break with Ryan and was always being reminded of his glorious past as one half of Wales's own 'Morecambe and Wise'.

In June, 1997, Ronnie was brought to trial at Carmarthen Crown Court accused of misappropriating £1,789 worth of funds from charitable events he had organised. He was acquitted of theft but convicted on lottery regulation offences. After the trial was over, he confessed to having seriously considered throwing himself off Cardigan Bridge. (A further source of worry to him was that, at the time of the trial, he had not worked for over a year).

On December 28th, 1997, at 11.10 in the morning Ronnie Williams's body was recovered from the banks of the Teifi river, at a spot not far from his Cardigan home, by the Cardigan inshore lifeboat. The last time he had been seen alive was on Sunday, December 21st, (his walking stick had been found on Cardigan Bridge on Christmas Eve) and it was soon established that the body had been in the Teifi for some days. A Welsh-language funeral service took place at Narberth's Parc Gwyn crematorium on Tuesday, January 6th, 1998. The inquest at Milford Haven Town Hall on February 26th, 1998 recorded a verdict of suicide.

Ronnie Williams's first and last cinema film was *Twin Town* in which he played a small part. His last appearance on the small screen took place on Boxing Day, 1997 when he played his character, Dan, in a repeated episode of *Licyris Olsorts*, S4C's answer to the BBC's *Last of the Summer Wine*. In his later years Ronnie had begun to drink heavily. He was married three times, but by the end was living alone in a Housing Association flat in Cardigan estranged from his third wife, Lynne. At the time of his death, she was holidaying in New Zealand.

BIBLIOGRAPHY

* Adams, David: Stage Welsh, Gomer, 1996.
* Banham, Martin: The Cambridge Guide to Theatre, Cambridge University Press, 1995.
* Barr, Charles: Ealing Studios, Cameron & Tayleur Limited, 1977.
* Berry, David: Wales and Cinema - The First Hundred Years, University of Wales Press, 1994.
* Blom, Eric; The New Everyman Dictionary of Music, 1988.
* Bloom, Claire: Leaving A Doll's House, Virago Press, 1996.
* Bordman, Gerald: American Musical Theatre, Oxford University Press, 1992.
* Bowyer, Alison: Delia Smith, The Biography, André Deutsch, 1999.
* Bragg, Melvyn: Rich, The Life of Richard Burton, Hodder & Stoughton, 1988.
* Bret, David: Gracie Fields, Robson Books, 1995.
* Bret, David: George Formby, A Troubled Genius, Robson Books, 1999.
* Brinnin, John Malcolm: Dylan Thomas In America, Arlington Books, 1988.
* Brodie, Douglas: The Films of Steven Spielberg, Citadel Press, 1995.
* Burgess, Muriel: Shirley, An Appreciation of the Life of Shirley Bassey, Century, 1998.
* Busby, Roy: British Music Hall, Paul Elek, 1976.
* Callan, Michael Feeney: Anthony Hopkins, The Darkness and Light, Sidgwick and Jackson,1993.
* Carey, Gary: Marlon Brando, The Only Contender, Robson Books Ltd., 1985.
* Carrick, Peter: Thanks for the Memory, A Tribute to Bob Hope, Robert Hale, 1988.
* Cassell Companion to the Theatre, Cassell, 1997.
* Casson, John: Lewis & Sybil, A Memoir, Collins, 1972.
* Caughie, John with Rockett, Kevin: The Companion to British and Irish Cinema, Cassell, 1996.
* Clancy, Joseph P: The Plays of Saunders Lewis, translated from the Welsh, Volumes I to IV, Christopher Davies.
* Clarke, Donald: Editor, The Penguin Encyclopedia of Popular Music, Viking, 1989.
* Collins, Joan: Second Act, Boxtree Limited, 1996.
* Cornell, Paul, Day, Martin and Topping, Keith: The Guinness Book of Classic British TV, Guinness Publishing, 1996.
* Davies, Hazel Walford (Editor): State of Play, Four Playwrights of Wales, Gomer, 1998.
* Davies, John: Broadcasting and the BBC In Wales, University of Wales Press, 1994.
* Davies Russell (Editor): The Kenneth Williams Diaries, Harper Collins, 1994.

* Day, Martin and Topping, Keith: Shut It! A Fan's Guide to Seventies Cops on the Box, Virgin Publishing Ltd., 1999.
* Delfont, Lord: Curtain Up! The Story of the Royal Variety Performance, Robson Books, 1989.
* Dietrich, Marlene: My Life, Weidenfeld and Nicolson, 1989.
* Donovan, Paul: The Radio Companion, Harper Collins, 1991.
* Evans, Sir Geraint and Goodwin, Noel: Sir Geraint Evans, A Knight at the Opera, Michael Joseph, 1984.
* Evans, Jeff: The Guinness Television Encyclopedia, Guinness Publishing Ltd., 1995.
* Falk, Quentin: Anthony Hopkins: Too Good To Waste, Columbus Books, 1989.
* Fawkes, Richard: Welsh National Opera, Julia Macrae, 1986.
* Ferris, Paul: Dylan Thomas, Hodder and Stoughton, 1977.
* Ferris, Paul: Sir Huge - The Life of Huw Wheldon, Michael Joseph, 1990.
* Fields, Gracie: Sing As We Go, The Autobiography of Gracie Fields, Frederick Muller Ltd., 1960.
* Findlater, Richard: Emlyn Williams, Rockliff Publishing Corporation, 1956.
* Foster, Andy & Furst, Steve: Radio Comedy 1938-1968, Virgin Publishing Ltd., 1996.
* French, Yvonne: Mrs. Siddons, Tragic Actress, Derek Verschoyle, 1954 (first edition, 1936).
* Gambaccini, Paul, Rice, Tim, Rice, Jonathan: British Hit Albums, Guinness Publishing, 1983.
* Gambaccini, Paul, Rice, Tim, Rice, Jonathan: British Hit Singles, Guinness Publishing, 1991.
* Gammond, Peter: The Oxford Companion To Popular Music, Oxford University Press, 1991.
* Gielgud, John: An Actor and His Time, Sidgwick & Jackson, 1989.
* Gielgud, John: Shakespeare Hit or Miss, Sidgwick & Jackson, 1991.
* Gielgud, John: Backward Glances, Sceptre, 1993.
* Gifford, Denis: The Illustrated Who's Who in British Films, B.T. Batsford Ltd., 1978.
* Gifford, Denis: The British Film Catalogue, 1895 - 1985, David & Charles, 1986.
* Gilbert, W Stephen: Fight and Kick and Bite, The Life and Work of Dennis Potter, Sceptre, 1996.
* Gittins, Rob: The Last Days of Dylan Thomas, Macdonald, 1986.
* Griffith, Kenneth: The Fool's Pardon: The Autobiography of Kenneth Griffith, Little, Brown & Company, 1994.
* Gwyn, William: Pobol y Cwm, Hughes, 1996.
* Hacker, Jonathan & Price, David: Take Ten Contemporary British Film Directors, Clarendon Press, 1991.
* Hadleigh, Boze: Leading Ladies, Robson Books, 1992.
* Haining, Peter: Bob Hope, Foulsham, 1989.

* Halliwell, Leslie: Halliwell's Film Guide, Granada Publishing, 1979.
* Halliwell, Leslie with Purser, Philip: Halliwell's Television Companion, Grafton Books, 1986.
* Hanson, J. Ivor: Outline of a Welsh Town, Daffodil Productions, 1971.
* Harding, James: Emlyn Williams, A Life, Weidenfeld & Nicholson, 1993.
* Harding, James: Ivor Novello, Welsh Academic Press, 1997.
* Hardy, Phil: The Faber Companion To Twentieth Century Popular Music, Faber & Faber, 1995.
* Harrison, Rex: A Damned Serious Business, Bantam Press, 1990.
* Hartnoll, Phyllis & Found, Peter: The Concise Oxford Companion to the Theatre, Oxford University Press, 1992.
* Hayward, Anthony: Who's Who on Television, Boxtree Limited, 1994.
* Hayward, Anthony: The Guinness Who's Who of Soap Operas, Guinness Publishing, 1995.
* Hayward, Anthony: The Making of Moll Flanders, Headline Book Publishing, 1996.
* Hayward, Anthony: The Emmerdale Companion, Orion Publishing Group, 1998.
* Heatley, Michael: Editor, The Virgin Encyclopedia of Rock, Virgin Books, 1993.
* Hildred, Stafford & Gritten, David: Tom Jones, A Biography, Sidgwick & Jackson Limited, 1990.
* Hildred, Stafford & Ewbank, Tim: David Jason, The Biography, Blake Publishing Limited, 1997.
* Hudd, Roy: Roy Hudd's Book of Music Hall, Variety and Showbiz Anecdotes, Robson Books, 1993.
* Hudd, Roy with Hindin, Philip: Roy Hudd's Cavalcade of Variety Acts, Robson Books, 1997.
* Huggett, Richard: The Curse of Macbeth, Picton Publishing, 1981.
* Huggett, Richard: Binkie Beaumont, Eminence Grise of the West End Theatre 1933-1973, Hodder & Stoughton, 1989.
* International Dictionary of Films & Filmmakers, Actors & Actresses, St. James Press, 1992.
* Jones, Brian: Port Talbot, A Gallery of Past Personalities, Volume 3, 1992.
* Jones, Peter: Tom Jones, Biography of a Great Star, Arthur Barker Limited, 1970.
* Jones, Rhydderch T: Cofiant Ryan, Gwasg y Mynydd Du, 1979.
* Kaplan, Mike: Variety Who's Who In Show Business, Garland Publishing, 1983.
* Katz, Ephraim: The Macmillan International Film Encyclopedia, Pan Macmillan Ltd., 1994.
* Katz, Gary J: Death By Rock And Roll, Robson Books, 1995.
* Kay, Graeme: Coronation Street, Celebrating 30 Years, Boxtree Limited, 1990.
* Kennedy, Michael: The Oxford Dictionary of Music, Oxford University Press, 1985.

* Kilgariff, Michael: Grace, Beauty and Banjos, Oberon Books, 1998.
* Kingsley, Hilary: Soap Box, The Papermac Guide to Soap Opera, Papermac, 1988.
* Kingsley, Hilary and Tibballs, Geoff: Box of Delights, MacMillan, 1989.
* Kingsley, Hilary: Casualty, The Inside Story, BBC Books, 1993.
* Kingsley, Hilary: The Bill, The First Ten Years, Boxtree, 1994.
* Kon, Andrea: This Is My Song, A Biography of Petula Clark, W.H. Allen, 1983.
* Larkin, Colin: The Guinness Who's Who of Fifties Music, Guinness Publishing Ltd., 1993.
* Larkin, Colin: The Guinness Who's Who of Film Musicals and Musical Films, Guinness Publishing Ltd., 1994.
* Larkin, Colin: The Guinness Who's Who of Indie and New Wave, Guinness Publishing Ltd., 1995.
* Larkin, Colin: The Guinness Encyclopedia of Popular Music, Guinness Publishing Ltd., 1995.
* Larkin, Colin: The Virgin Encyclopedia of Seventies Music, Virgin Books, 1997.
* Law, Jonathan (Ed): Brewer's Cinema, Cassell, 1995.
* Levine, Gemma: Faces of British Theatre, Prion, 1990.
* Lewis, Jon E. and Stempel, Penny: Cult TV, Pavilion Books, 1993.
* Little, Daran: The Coronation Street Story, Boxtree, 1995.
* Littlewood, Joan: Joan's Book, Minerva, 1995.
* Lloyd, Ann & Fuller, Graham: Illustrated Who's Who of the Cinema, Ortis Publishing, 1983.
* Luff, Alan: Welsh Hymns and Their Tunes, Steiner & Bell, 1990.
* Macfarlane, Colin: Tom Jones, The Boy From Nowhere, W.H. Allen, 1988.
* McClure, Arthur F., Twomey, Alfred E., Jones, Ken D: More Character People, Citadel Press, New Jersey, 1984.
* Massingberd, Hugh (Ed.): The Daily Telegraph Third Book of Obituaries - Entertainers, Macmillan, 1997.
* Milland, Ray: Wide-Eyed In Babylon, The Companion Book Club, 1976.
* Morley, Sheridan: Spread A Little Happiness, The First Hundred Years of the British Musical, Thames and Hudson, 1987.
* Morley, Sheridan: Our Theatres In The Eighties, Hodder & Stoughton, 1990.
* Morris, John: There's Lovely, J.M. Dent & Sons Ltd., 1989.
* Moules, Joan: Gracie Fields, Summersdale, 1997.
* Nicholson, Mavis: Martha Jane & Me, Chatto & Windus, 1991.
* Novick, Jeremy: Tommy Cooper, Just Like That, Chameleon Books, 1998.
* Osborne, John: A Better Class of Person, An Autobiography 1929-1956, Faber & Faber, 1981.
* Osborne, John: Almost A Gentleman, An Autobiography Volume II, 1955-1966, Faber & Faber, 1991.
* Ogwen, John: Hogyn o Sling, Gwasg Gwynedd, 1996.

* Owen, Bill: Summer Wine and Vintage Years, Robson Books, 1994.
* Palmer, Scott: British Film Actors' Credits, 1895-1987, St. James Press, 1988.
* Parnell, Michael: Laughter From The Dark, A Life of Gwyn Thomas, John Murray, 1988.
* Paton, Maureen: Alan Rickman, The Unauthorised Biography, Virgin Books, 1997.
* Peers, Donald: Pathway, Werner Laurie, 1951.
* Perry, George: The Great British Picture Show, Pavilion Books Limited, 1985.
* Pertwee, Bill: Stars In Battledress, Hodder and Stoughton, 1992.
* Pertwee, Bill: Dad's Army, The Making of a Television Legend, Colour Library, Direct, 1998.
* Pfeiffer, Lee and Philip, Lisa: The Incredible World of 007, Boxtree Limited, 1992.
* Phillips Denver, Editor: Coleshill School, Llanelli, 1891-1977.
* Pickering, David: Dictionary of Theatre, Penguin Books, 1988.
* Price, Cecil: The Professional Theatre in Wales, University College of Swansea, 1984.
* Quinlan, David: Quinlan's Illustrated Directory of Film Character Actors, B.T. Batsford Ltd., 1995.
* Quinlan, David: Quinlan's Illustrated Directory of Film Stars, B.T. Batsford Ltd., 1996.
* Rees, Dafydd & Crampton, Luke: Q Encyclopedia of Rock Stars, Dorling Kindersley, 1996.
* Phil Redmond's Brookside, The Official Companion, Weidenfeld & Nicholson, 1987.
* Reynolds, Aidan & Charlton, William: Arthur Machen, Caermaen Books, 1988.
* Rhys, Dulais: Joseph Parry, University of Wales Press, 1998.
* Rigelsford, Adrian: The Doctors, 30 Years of Time Travel, Boxtree Limited, 1994.
* Ryan, Michelle: Blocking the Channels: T.V. and Film in Wales from Wales the Imagined Nation edited by Tony Curtis, Poetry Wales Press, 1986.
* Ryan, Paul: Marlon Brando A Portrait, Plexus, 1991.
* Sadie, Stanley (Ed.): The New Grove Dictionary of Music and Musicians, Macmillan, 1980.
* Schickel, Richard: Brando, A Life In Our Times, Pavilion Books Ltd., 1991.
* Secombe, Harry: Arias and Raspberries, Robson Books, 1989.
* Sherrin, Ned: Ned Sherrin's Theatrical Anecdotes, Virgin Books, 1993.
* Shipman, David: The Great Movie Stars - 2, The International Years, Macdonald, 1989.
* Siegel, Scott & Siegel, Barbara: The Guinness Encyclopedia of Hollywood, Guinness Publishing Ltd., 1990.
* Stead, Peter: Wales in the Movies from Wales the Imagined Nation edited by Tony Curtis, Poetry Wales Press, 1986.

* Stead, Peter: Richard Burton: So Much, So Little, Seren Books, 1991.
* Stephens, Meic (Ed): The Oxford Companion to the Literature of Wales, Oxford University Press, 1986.
* Storey, Anthony: Stanley Baker, Portrait of an Actor, W.H. Allen, 1977.
* Taylor, Anna-Marie: Staging Wales, Welsh Theatre, 1979 - 1997, University of Wales Press, 1997.
* Taylor, John Russell: Anger and After, A Guide to the New British Drama, Methuen & Company, 1971.
* Taylor, John Russell: The Penguin Dictionary of The Theatre, Penguin Books, 1993.
* Thomas, Gwyn: The Keep, A Play in Two Acts, Elek Books, 1962.
* Thomas, Nicholas (Ed): International Dictionary of Films and Filmmakers - 3, Actors and Actresses, St. James Press, 1992.
* Thomson, David: A Biographical Dictionary of Film, André Deutsch, 1995.
* Tibballs, Geoff: The Golden Age of Children's TV, Titan Books, 1991.
* Tibballs, Geoff: The Boxtree Encyclopedia of TV Detectives, Boxtree Limited, 1992.
* Tibballs, Geoff: Total Brookside, The Ultimate Guide to the Ultimate Soap, Ebury Press, 1998.
* Tighe, Carl: Theatre (or Not) in Wales from Wales the Imagined Nation edited by Tony Curtis, Poetry Wales Press, 1986.
* Tracy, Sheila: Who's Who On Radio, World's Work Ltd., 1983.
* Trenberth, Siân: Welsh Greats of Today, Alan Sutton Publishing, 1993.
* Truitt, Evelyn Mack: Who Was Who On Screen, R.R. Bowker Company, 1984.
* Vahimagi, Tise: British Television, Oxford University Press, 1996.
* The Virgin Film Guide, 1997.
* Walker, Alexander (Editor): No Bells On Sunday, The Journals of Rachel Roberts, Pavilion Books Limited, 1984.
* Walker, John: Halliwell's Who's Who In The Movies, Harper Collins, 1999.
* Warren, Patricia: British Film Studios, An Illustrated History, B.T. Batsford, 1995.
* Webber, Richard: Dad's Army, A Celebration, Virgin Books, 1997.
* Who's Who 2000, A. and C. Black, 2000.
* Williams, Alun: Alun Williams, Gwasg Gwynedd, 1982.

ACKNOWLEDGEMENTS:

I would like to, most of all, thank my wife, Bovena, for her patience and forbearing, especially during the months when I was desperately putting the finishing touches to the book and it began to border upon an obsession. Thanks also to my publisher, Terry Breverton, for all his help and advice.

Thanks also go to: The British Film Institute. Dalzell and Beresford Ltd., Theatrical Agents. Cardiff Local Studies Library. Cardiff Reference Library. Deborah Owen Literary Agency. Geoff Cripps. Ken Dodd. Mike Evans of Black Mountain Records. Efa Gruffudd, Literature Officer, Arts Council of Wales. David Jones. Marilyn Jones, Local Studies Librarian, Swansea Central Library. Llanelli Area Library. Newport Reference Library. Richard Hughes, Community Arts Officer, Blaenau Gwent. Alun Prescott, Reference & Local History Librarian, Treorchy Library. Hannah Shepherd and her scrapbooks on the new generation of Welsh bands. Brett Hayes. Mark Vernon of Firebrand Management Ltd. Stow Hill Library, Newport for ordering many of the books I needed. Swansea Library.

PICTURE ACKNOWLEDGEMENTS

I would like to thank the following for supplying me with photographs and allowing me to use them:
Petula Clark Fan Club for the photograph of Petula Clark. Annabel Rademacher and The Vue for the photograph of Peter Greenaway. Godfrey Brangham for the photograph of Arthur Machen. Bethan Davies for the photograph of her late father, Ryan Davies. Julian Belfrage Associates for the photograph of Jonathan Pryce. Deborah Owen Literary Agency for the photograph of Delia Smith. Dalzell and Beresford Ltd. for the photograph of Gwen Ffrangcon-Davies. Sylvia Firth of the Tom Jones Appreciation Society for the photograph of Tom Jones. The Glenn Ford Library & Archives for the photograph of Glenn Ford. Glyn Houston for the photograph of himself. Alwyne Jenkins and Swansea Reference Library for the photograph of The Iveys. Terry Kenny for the photograph of Charlotte Church. Firebrand Management Ltd. for the photograph of John Cale. Lady Brenda Evans for the photograph of Geraint Evans. The Ivor Novello Appreciation Bureau for the photograph of Ivor Novello. Cyfarthfa Castle Museum and Art Gallery for the photograph of Joseph Parry. The South Wales Argus for the photograph of Desmond Llewelyn. Lady Ellen Baker for the photograph of Stanley Baker. Elin Jenkins and S4C for the photographs of John Ogwen, Wynford Vaughan Thomas, Philip Madoc, Dylan Thomas, Saunders Lewis, Richard Burton, Meredith Edwards, Ioan Gruffudd, Rhys Ifans and Rachel Thomas. Karl Jenkins for the photograph of himself. Griff Rhys Jones for the photograph of himself. Gwyneth Jones for the photograph of herself. Terry Jones for the photograph of himself. John Lloyd of the Dorothy Squires Fan Club for the photograph of Dorothy Squires. Newport Reference Library for the

photograph of Lyn Harding. Siân Phillips for the photograph of herself. Sioned Jones and Harlequin Agency Limited for the photograph of Bryn Terfel. Victor Spinetti for the photograph of himself. Rolf Harris Fan Club for the photograph of Rolf Harris. Carol Vorderman for the photograph of herself.

I also wish to thank BBC Cymru Wales for allowing me to quote from some of their television and radio programmes. S4C for allowing me to quote from their television programmes. *The South Wales Argus* for allowing me to quote from various articles in *The Argus*. *The Western Mail* for allowing me to quote from various articles in the *Western Mail*. Summersdale Publishers Ltd. for allowing me to quote from Gracie Fields by Joan Moules. *Buzz* Magazine for allowing me to quote from articles in *Buzz* magazine. Steven Wells and *The New Musical Express* for allowing me to quote from *The New Musical Express*. Lady Brenda Evans for allowing me to quote from her husband Sir Geraint Evans' book, A Knight At The Opera. University of Wales Press for allowing me to quote from several of their publications.

The extract from *Fight, Bite and Kick: The Life and Work of Dennis Potter* by W.S. Gilbert is reproduced by permission of Hodder and Stoughton Limited. The extract from *Tommy Cooper - Just Like That* is reproduced by permission of Essential Books. The extracts from *Shirley, An Appreciation of the Life of Shirley Bassey* by Muriel Burgess are reproduced by permission of The Random House Group. The extracts from *Gracie Fields* by David Bret and *George Formby* by David Bret are reproduced by permission of Robson Books.

The author and publisher have made all reasonable efforts to contact copyright holders for permission, and apologise for any omissions or errors in the form of credit given. Corrections may be made in future printings.

Other titles from Wales Books

see www.walesbooks.com *for details on:*

THE BOOK OF WELSH SAINTS (610 pp Hardback)
T. O. Breverton

THE SECRET VALE OF GLAMORGAN
T. O. Breverton

Forthcoming titles include:

100 GREAT WELSHMEN

and

100 GREAT WELSH WOMEN